Lecture Notes in Computer Science 1429

Edited by G. Goos, J. Hartmanis and J. van Leeuwen

Lecture Notes in Computer Science 1420
Edited by G. Goos, J. Hartmanis and J. van Leeuwen

Springer-Verlag Berlin Heidelberg GmbH

Frank van der Linden (Ed.)

Development and Evolution of Software Architectures for Product Families

Second International ESPRIT ARES Workshop
Las Palmas de Gran Canaria, Spain
February 26-27, 1998
Proceedings

 Springer

Series Editors

Gerhard Goos, Karlsruhe University, Germany
Juris Hartmanis, Cornell University, NY, USA
Jan van Leeuwen, Utrecht University, The Netherlands

Volume Editor

Frank van der Linden
Philips Research Laboratories
Prof. Holstlaan 4, 5656 AA Eindhoven, The Netherlands
E-mail: flinden@natlab.research.philips.com

Cataloging-in-Publication data applied for

Die Deutsche Bibliothek - CIP-Einheitsaufnahme

**Development and evolution of software architecture for product
families** : Las Palmas de Gran Canaria, Spain, February 26 - 27,
1998 ; proceedings / Frank van der Linden (ed.).

(... International ESPRIT ARES workshop ; 2) (Lecture notes in
computer science ; Vol. 1429)
ISBN 978-3-540-64916-8

CR Subject Classification (1991): D.2.11, D.2

ISBN 978-3-540-64916-8   ISBN 978-3-540-68383-4 (eBook)
DOI 10.1007/978-3-540-68383-4

Typesetting: Camera-ready by author
SPIN 10637590   06/3142 – 5 4 3 2 1 0   Printed on acid-free paper

Preface

This book originates from a workshop organised by ESPRIT project 20 477, ARES in Las Palmas de Gran Canaria, Spain, February 1998. ARES is an acronym for Architectural Reasoning for Embedded Systems. Within this project we investigate techniques to deal with problems of software architecture of families of embedded systems. It is the second workshop organised by this project. Its predecessor was held in Las Navas de Marques, Spain, November 1996. The proceedings of the first workshop are only available in electronic format at "http://www.dit.upm.es/~ares/". The second workshop succeeded, even more than the first one, in gathering many of the most prominent people working in the area of software architecture for product families or product lines.

This second workshop consisted of six sessions. The first session was meant to report the ARES results, according to the topics of the next five sessions. The remaining sessions dealt with different aspects of software architecture, focussed on applications for product families or product lines. Because there will be a separate book covering all ARES results, the first session is not included in this book.

The workshop was chaired by Henk Obbink from Philips Research and Paul Clements from the Software Engineering Institute at Carnegie Mellon University. They prepared and presented an overall conclusion at the end of the workshop. This conclusion was used in the introduction to this book.

The programme committee consisted of people from all ARES partners:

Wolfgang Eixelsberger	ABB Research
Mehdi Jazayeri	Technische Universität Vienna
Jeff Kramer	Imperial College
Juha Kuusela	Nokia Research
Frank van der Linden	Philips Research
Jeff Magee	Imperial College
Henk Obbink	Philips Research
Juan Antonio de la Puente	Universidad Politécnica de Madrid
Alex Ran	Nokia Research

The workshop was held at a great place, with a good climate, due to the good work of the local organisers: Juan Carlos Dueñas and Alejandro Alonso from Universidad Politécnica de Madrid and Javier Miranda and Francisco J. Guerra from the Universidad de Las Palmas de Gran Canaria.

Sessions were chaired by people from outside the ARES project: William Scherlis, Dewayne Perry, Jean Marc DeBaud, Paul Clements, and David Weiss. They had a facilitator's role in guiding the discussion. Because of the structure of the workshop there was a large amount of discussion. Reports of the sessions were prepared by people from the programme committee and reviewed by the session chairs. These reports are presented as the introductions to the sessions in this book.

Eindhoven, June 1998   Frank van der Linden

Table of Contents

Introduction 1
H. Obbink, P.C. Clements, F.J. van der Linden

Example Architectures

Session 1: Example Architectures 4
W. Scherlis, J. Kuusela

Reusable Framework for Telecontrol Protocols 6
G. Cysewski, T. Gromadzki, H. Lyskawa, M. Piechowka, S. Szejko,
W.E. Kozlowski, O. Vahamaki,

A Software Bus as a Platform for a Family of Distibuted Embedded System
Products 14
E. Niemelä, H. Perunka, T. Korpipää

A Three-Tier Design Approach for a Family of Large AC Drive Control
Systems 24
P. Kolb, B. Huber

Modular Turbine Control Software: A Software Architecture for the ABB Gas
Turbine Family Control System 32
C. Ganz, M. Layes

Experiences with the Evolution of an Application Family Architecture 39
A. Rösel

Architectural Description

Session 2: Architectural Description 49
D.E. Perry, J. Kramer

Generic Architecture Descriptions for Product lines 51
D.E. Perry

A Model of Interaction in Concurrent and Distributed Systems 57
N. Pryce, S. Crane

An Integral Hierarchy and Diversity Model for Describing Product Family
Architecture 66
P. van de Hamer, F.J. van der Linden, A. Saunders, H. te Sligte

Koala, a Component Model for Consumer Electronics Product Software 76
R. van Ommering

Architecture Recovery

Session 3: Architecture Recovery 87
J.-M.DeBaud, M. Jazayeri

Recovery of Architectural Structure: A Case Study 89
W. Eixelsberger, M. Kalan, M. Ogris, H. Beckman, B. Bellay, H. Gall

Reengineering C/C++ Source Code by Transforming State Machines 97
R. Knor, G. Trausmuth, J. Weidl

An Experiment in Distributed Software Architecture Recovery 106
N.C. Mendonça, J. Kramer

Reverse Engineering to Recover and Describe a System's Architecture 115
B. Bellay, H. Gall

Can Legacy Systems Beget Product Lines? 123
N. Weiderman, J. Bergey, D. Smith, S. Tilley

The Relation Between the Product Line Development Entry Points and
Reengineering 132
J.-M. DeBaud, J.-F. Girard

Analysis of Software Architectures

Session 4: Analysis of Software Architectures... 140
P.C. Clements, J. de la Puente

Diagnostic Software Architectures 143
R.T. Bechtold

A Software Architecture Evaluation Model 148
J.C. Dueñas, W.L. de Oliveira, J.A. de la Puente

An Architectural Infrastructure for Product Families 158
R. Balzer

Assessment of Timing Properties of Family Products 161
A. Alonso, M. García-Valls, J. de la Puente

Development Process

Session 5: Development Process.. 170
D.M. Weiss, F.J. van der Linden

Stakeholders in Software-system Family Architectures 172
T. Dolan, R. Weterings, J.C. Wortmann

Handling Variant Requirements in Software Architectures for Product Families... 188
C.C. Yu, A.L. Ananda, S. Jarzabek

Architecture-Centric Software Development Based on Extended Design Spaces . 197
L. Baum, L. Geyer, G. Molter, S. Rothkugel, P. Sturm

Architecting for Domain Variability 205
J. Meekel, T.B. Horton, C. Mellone

Commonality Analysis: A Systematic Process for Defining Families 214
D.M. Weiss

Structuring Design Decissions for Evolution 223
A. Karhinen, J. Kuusela

Structural Views, Structural Evolution, and Product Families 235
W.L. Scherlis

Product Family and Reuse in Separate Market Driven Profit Centers 241
J. Brouwer, A. Jurriens, H. van Kessel, A. Schippers

ERW'97 Session Report: Reuse Adoption Experiences Across a Large
Corporation.. 249
S. Bandinelli

Author Index 257

Introduction

Henk Obbink[1], Paul C. Clements[2], Frank van der Linden[1]

[1]Philips Research Laboratories, Prof Holstlaan 4
5656 AA Eindhoven, The Netherlands
{obbink,flinden}@natlab.research.philips.com
[2]Software Engineering Institute, Carnegie Mellon University
Pittsburgh, PA 15213 USA
clements@sei.cmu.edu

Many companies are looking for ways to minimise the costs of developing new products and to maximise sharing and reuse of software structure and components used in a product family. The ESPRIT IV project 20.477, ARES (Architectural Reasoning for Embedded Software), focuses on methods, techniques and tools to manage the diversity of products in a family at the level of software architecture. The charter of ARES is to find ways to help design reliable systems with embedded software that satisfy important quality requirements, evolve gracefully and may be built in-time and on-budget. ARES also addresses the problem of relating the features which differentiate the members of a product family to an architecture for that family. ARES aims to address the variance required by a product family at the architectural level and to map a feature selection to an instance of an architecture. Topics of interest also include specification of software architecture, architecture recovery, assessment of software architecture, and other subjects related to development and evolution of software architecture for product families. This project is a joint project between Nokia (prime contractor), Philips, ABB, Imperial College London, Technical University of Madrid and the Technical University of Vienna.

In order to share and compare the results of the ARES project with the results of external efforts the ARES project has organised two *workshops on the Development and Evolution of Software Architectures for Product Families*. These proceedings are the result of the second of these workshops[1]. An explicit goal of the second workshop was to gain insight in the state of the art (academia) and the state of practice (industries) in the development of software architectures of product families/product lines. Moreover we wanted to know what are the most promising paths to be taken for both industries and academia. Finally insight should be obtained for the usefulness of the work of the academia for the industries.

There were 45 participants:

- 36 from Europe
- 8 from the United States
- 1 from Singapore
- 17 from the ARES project
- 20 from Universities
- 25 from Industries.

1. Sessions

Based upon the topics of interest for ARES, and the expected participants, we separated the workshop into the following sessions:

1.   ARES session
2.   examples of architectures for product lines
3.   architecture description
4.   architecture analysis
5.   architecture recovery
6.   process issues

---

[1] The proceedings of the first workshop were not published. The accepted position papers can be consulted at the ARES web-site at UPM: http://www.dit.upm.es/~ares/

Frank v. d. Linden (Ed.): ARES '98, LNCS 1429, pp. 1-3, 1998.
© Springer-Verlag Berlin Heidelberg 1998

During the ARES session an ARES representative spoke about current ARES work in each of these areas. ARES work revolves around running case studies with tractable but real systems:

- Automatic train protection (ABB)
- Cellular Phone (Nokia)
- Network element (Nokia)
- TV-set (Philips).

Most case studies are winding down, since the ARES project itself is coming to a close this year. The result will be a book detailing the case studies and their results, with a publication target of late 1998.

The majority of the workshop time was spent in technical discussion sessions. Each session was represented by 4-9 papers submitted by attendees (and assigned sessions in advance). Each session was assigned a facilitator/chairman from outside the ARES consortium and an ARES representative who acted as a scribe and who produced a summary of his session.

2. Results of the Workshop

The emphasis was on discussion, not presentation, and so authors were permitted only a couple of a slides and a few minutes at most to present their ideas. Each session lasted 90 minutes.

As most sessions are preceded in this book with an introduction presenting the main results. We will only give a global view of the results of the workshop. The following themes permeate all of the sessions:

Towards Engineering Practice

Recognition of specific goals at each step, and orienting the work (creation, description, analysis, recovery, process) towards the fulfilment of those goals. We are not interested in architecture manipulation for its own sake, but only for the furthering of enterprise aims.

Recognition of business and organisational concerns. This is an instantiation of the first two points. What are the arguments for and against a separate organisational structure for core asset creation and maintenance? The major non-academic organisations present were asked, to explain their organisations' approach to architecture evaluation. Experiences with SAAM, ATAM and SARB process. The ARES industrial representatives (ABB, Nokia, Philips) had initial experiences with the use of architecture reviews.

The Architecture examples were very much welcomed, but there was a feeling that little insight given as to how these architectures were created. Interesting were the economic issues that were raised here.

A mature product family development process includes architecture recovery. Messy though it is, architecture recovery was thought to be an essential part of product line development: The assertion was made, and not challenged, that the great majority of product lines are built from existing assets. There are three sources of information for architecture recovery:, all are even important

1.   Source code, which is authoritative and dependable but contains by no means all of the information;
2.   Documentation, which is undependable, incomplete, and informal; and,
3.   Human experts, who are dependable, but biased.

A short (and potentially incendiary) discussion ensued about the role of academia in investigating product line issues: Are they fulfilling their mission by providing only technology with little concern for the organisational and enterprise issues we know to predominate in product line production? Can the technologists not team with business schools in their institutions to better serve the practicing community? As one might expect, this issue was not settled.

Stakeholders

Recognition of the importance of stakeholders. Similar to the first point, this makes it clear that architects answer to stakeholders, and a beautiful but unprofitable architecture is in demand by no one. The highest risk, it was felt, was being able to meet all the different clients' needs with systems that were versions of each other produced from a single common asset base. Examples of stakeholders, unique to a product line development, were mentioned: product line architect, builder of generic (core) assets, builder of product from generic assets, product line maintainer, marketer / funder

People

Emphasis of people over technology. At this workshop, at least, people issues tended to dominate the presentation of exotic new technologies. (During the response session, technology was roundly defended as essential. But for whatever reason, it was not the main focus of this gathering.)

Economic models, it was felt, were talked about quite a bit but not used as justification to launch a product line effort. Rather, convincing appeals in intuitive and intellectual grounds suffice to convince management to proceed. Note the absence of 'lower cost' as main economic issue, which is dominated the non-availability of skilled people for hire at any price.

Relation to Other Fields

More than one speaker pointed out that other engineering disciplines have been building product families for generations. Is it not possible that we can learn from them? At this point, the workshop adjourned.

Variability

At precisely the same minute that the session on architecture description began, a near-total solar eclipse engulfed the locale. This may have distracted the focus of the discussion, which was about a common purpose, goals, or the audiences for whom ADLs are intended to serve. Less emphasis was upon the specific ways variability can be described, using indifferently whichever ADL is appropriate. There were several contributions dealing with this issue. In many circles these days mentioning 'architecture description' conjures up ADLs automatically. So it was here.

Fulfilment of the Goals

Not all goals of the workshop were fulfilled. We got insight in the state of the art (academia) and the state of practice (industries) of the development of software architecture of product families. Some insight is obtained about the relationship between them. We may conclude that we are just starting to investigate the field and not many successes can be claimed. The academia need to learn about the problems that occur during large scale developments. The industries use any techniques that seems useful. The best way to proceed is in co-operation where academia are involved in industrial development. There still are too many open issues and no clear paths about the way to proceed in the future, both for academia and industries. Each of the activities presented here may grow to be an important issue in future product-line development.

This was the second such workshop, sponsored by ARES. Since ARES is concluding, there will no third workshop, at least sponsored by ARES. The general chair asked for a show of interest of continuing the workshop under some other auspices. As interest in product line production is clearly on the rise, and we have but scratched the surface of interesting and compelling technical and organisational issues. Most participants expressed interest. We are presently investigating new sponsors to step in and take the leadership in this important community.

Session 1: Example Architectures

William Scherlis[1], Juha Kuusela[2]

[1]School of Computer Science, Carnegie Mellon University
Pittsburgh, PA 15213, USA
scherlis@cs.cmu.edu
[2]Nokia Research Center, P.O. Box 45
FIN-00211, Helsinki Finland
Juha.kuusela@research.nokia.com

This session was presented on a number of examples on architecting product families. Based on these examples the panellist discussed:
- Economic issues
- Management and risk
- Measures
- Personnel

related to product families.

The examples were
- Reusable Framework for Telecontrol Protocols presented by W.E.Kozlowski, ABB Transmit.
- Software bus - a generic framework to achieve system extendibility, location independence, configuration support and hardware independence presented by E. Niemelä, VTT.
- Three-Tier Design Approach for a Family of Large AC Drive Control Systems presented by P. Kolb, ABB Corporate Research.
- A Control Software Architecture for the ABB Gas Turbine Family presented by C. Ganz, ABB Power Generation.

1. Economic Issues

Based on these examples it seemed that development of product family is incremental and also the costs are incremental and large up front investment is not needed.

In ABB AC Drive control the profit centers came together saying they need a new control model - together with a bunch of ideas that should be included. Obviously they expected the development based on the new and common control model be cheaper than the approach they were using at the time.

In ABB Turbine case originally there was an attempt to develop product family based on extra effort within a single product development project. It turned out to be impossible and a separate organisation was needed to build the basis for product family.

Reliable economical justification is hard to get and often high management is required to support development of a product family based on belief.

ABB Telecontrol case shows that sometimes there are clear business reasons - to enable the development work to be shorter in time and to move it outside to external subcontractors.

Paul Clements pointed out that in a SEI workshop devoted to product families no one claimed that it would be cheaper - faster and with less people (plus subcontracting) is the need.

Dewayne Perry reminded that product line requires reorganisation in the development unit. In ABB Turbine case the development is now running in the unchanged organisation but it is a problem.

To estimate the gains produced by product line architecture we need estimates on how effort is distributed between generic and specific parts. In ABB turbine case the generic platform 5 py- common parts 6 py - application months.

Bob Balzer noted that in estimating the economics we should remember that very few novel product lines are developed. The question is how to capitalise on previous system development to create the framework. If this is successful up front investment is actually pre-existing system development.

We also noted that evolution is a problem. Actually product line is also evolving like products this creates problems in evolving each product based on separate versions of product line.

Frank v. d. Linden (Ed.): ARES '98, LNCS 1429, pp. 4-5, 1998.
© Springer-Verlag Berlin Heidelberg 1998

Where is assessment applied - on the final product it is mandatory. Is product line assessed like an extension to the model - part of the model has to be replaced and thus triggers all Vs related to target platforms.

2. Making Commitments

Discipline is required to keep product family together. Several alternative to build in control like practices, processes, frameworks, patterns, and language features exists. What kind of discipline to use?

ABB AC used language based restrictions - application engineers are familiar in programming in function block - not in a programming language like C - States already defined in the common layer - but activities can be assigned to them on higher layers.

William Scherlis - With this scheme risk is in the blocks themselves - not in the mechanism to use them since for development you can use what ever you want but users get only the function block tool to create products.

3. Styles

These examples were based on Layers, Bus+agents, Components.

4. Techniques

Compose components, select components, configure/Intermediate components, Tailor/Customise, Rework/Replace

5. Maturity in Organisations

What maturity level you need to run a product line. Pane concluded that it is necessary to structure organisation according to roles determined by the architecture the organisation does not necessary be on higher maturity level in terms of CMM.

Reusable Framework for Telecontrol Protocols

G. Cysewski[1], T. Gromadzki[1], H. Lyskawa[1], M. Piechowka[1], S.Szejko[1],
W. E. Kozlowski[2], O. Vahamaki[2]

[1]Department of Applied Informatics, Technical University of Gdansk, Poland
macpi@pg.gda.pl
[2]ABB Transmit Oy, Relays and Network Control, Finland
wojciech.kozlowski@fimit.mail.abb.com

Abstract. The paper presents a so-called COMSOFT framework of communication software development model based on object oriented architecture and design patterns. The library of reusable components supports reuse in all phases of the development process; it is intended to be generic with respect to the family of telecontrol protocols. The framework is supplemented with customisation guideline to help in refining the reused library so that deriving a working application becomes easier and more systematic. The elaborated solution is based on experience obtained during the development of the IEC-870-5-101 protocol interface for ABB monitoring and control devices.

1. Introduction

ABB Transmit Oy is currently developing a range of control and monitoring units with different number of process I/Os and scaleable hardware and software functionality. The product series REC 500 can be used for remote and local control and monitoring of pole mounted switches, ring main units, secondary substations and other equipment of medium voltage network. REC 500 units have to support serial communication with Network Control Centres (SCADA systems) and with the protection equipment installed in the substations. A variety of remote control protocols has to be implemented to enable REC 500 units to communicate with different types of SCADA systems according to international and national standards or due to specific customer requirements. These protocols include ANSI X3.28, RP570, IEC870-5-101, DNP, MODBUS and others, using such media as fixed cables, public and leased telephone lines, radio telephones, packet radio, cellular telephones, DLC. A suitable practical approach to develop portable and reusable communication software has become necessary to enable fast adaptation of REC 500 units to different market requirements.

Frank v. d. Linden (Ed.): ARES '98, LNCS 1429, pp. 6-13, 1998.

The main objective of COMSOFT project was a *communication software development model* of telecontrol protocols [2,6] aiming at the following improvements:

- to make new protocol developments more effective by application of reusable components and design patterns (hence, the project focused on generic and applicable model of the telecontrol protocol class);
- to shorten the time of protocol software portability to new environments (operating system, device application, functional profile);
- to assure the product quality by reuse of reliable components and design patterns and by following documented development procedures.

The proposed solution is based on:

- placing the protocol software among well defined *generic interfaces* to the environment,
- elaborated *generic object oriented model of the protocol software*,
- *reuse-based* development process .

In this paper we describe the framework derived from design and implementation of the IEC-870-5-101 protocol interface on REC 501 unit. We show what architecture, design patterns and components can be reused, how the library of these components is organised, and provide the set of rules of framework customisation.

2. COMSOFT Reusable Object Oriented Design Framework

A framework is a reusable, "semi-complete" application that can be specialised to produce custom applications. It is described by a set of abstract classes and the way how instances of those classes collaborate. Frameworks focus on reuse of existing designs, algorithms, and implementations in a particular programming language [4]. Components in a framework work together to provide a generic architectural skeleton for a family of related applications. A complete application can be composed by inheriting from or by instantiating framework components. Design pattern describes how to solve a particular kind of the design problem.

A framework is documented in terms of its architecture and design patterns. To facilitate the development of a specific protocol software in a target environment a set of adaptation patterns may be used. Each of them contains a set of steps that the protocol developer is suggested to perform during framework customisation to include new protocol services and features (e.g. to apply to a new platform, profile or device).

A model component is seen as any artefact through the development cycle. A reusable component may be a code module, but bigger benefits of reuse come from a broader and higher-level view of what can be reused. In the COMSOFT framework we decided to refer to the reusable design artefacts as follows:

- software architecture, which describes the structure of a system on the level of its organisation and control; it describes the main components and objects, their functional responsibilities, the division of control, and the protocol (interface) for communication, synchronisation and data access,

- design patterns, which are solutions to specific design issues,
- class libraries, which are collections of classes,
- reusable skeletons that can support creation of project documentation.

2.1   Software Architecture

We assumed a layered system architecture as the basis for protocol software development [6]. It is organised as a hierarchy of layers, with each layer providing services to the layer above it and each layer being a client for the services provided by the layer below it. The architecture of a layer is object oriented. The main architectural decisions have been as follows (see Figure 1):
- assumption that the development of the communication protocol interface is embedded into the identified generic interfaces: to the operating system (GEOPSY), to the device application based on Application Communication Interface concept (GACI), and to the communication link handler (GLHI);

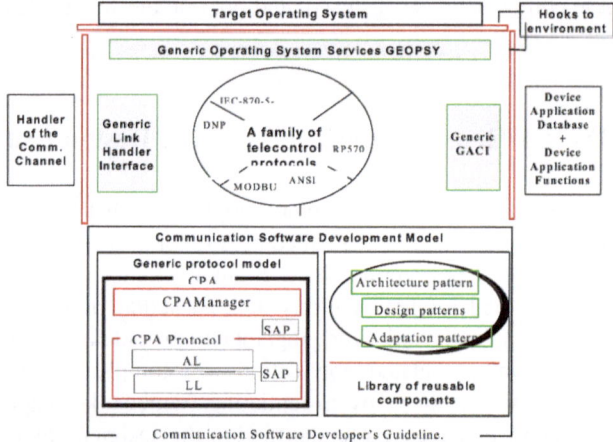

Figure 1 COMSOFT protocol framework context and protocol model boundaries.

- decomposition of the protocol software (the so-called CPA - Communication Protocol Adapter) into two parts: *CPAProtocol* responsible for protocol transmission procedures and *CPAManager* responsible for handling complex transactions with the application software of the device. Services offered by these components are characterised by a set of use cases (corresponding to the services typical in the family of telecontrol protocols) [1];
- introducing service access point (SAP) subsystems to transport messages between layers;
- introducing scheduler objects for scheduling operations of active objects (realisation of concurrency);

- separating components used to build a protocol into the following categories: environment dependent (interfaces), protocol dependent, application-independent.

Abstract classes used in the CPA architecture make the design flexible. They are designed to be used as templates for specifying subclasses rather than objects. The main generic components of the CPA software architecture are given in figure 2.

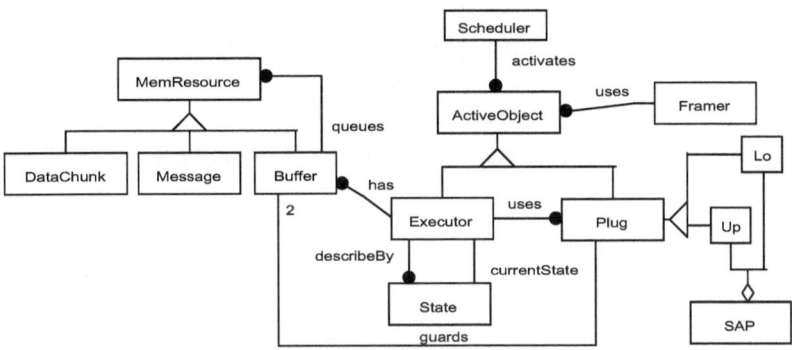

Figure 2 The overall object model of the CPA generic components.

Generic components of the CPA are assigned the following responsibilities:

MemResource - abstract class for all objects used to store and keep information for some period of time;

Scheduler - decides which objects need to be activated;

Executor - abstract class, specialisation of ActiveObject, used to run state machines of its inheriting subclasses, responsible for accepting messages, delegating them to its currentState;

State - abstract class for objects representing states of *Executor* (owner of the state). Provides the following services:

   apply - this method tries to identify an event passed by the message and undertakes an appropriate action,

   activate - performs entry action defined for the state,

   perform - performs an action defined for a given state;

Plug - abstract class, specialisation of ActiveObject, for object organised message transfer;

SAP - abstract class, introduces an architecture to guard message buffers located between layers; it is used to transfer messages between the adjacent layers;

Framer - abstract superclass which defines all operations required to manipulate the contents of frames. It is a protocol dependent object and should be specialised for all protocols and their layers. Each layer of the protocol stack has only one framer that supports operations on frame structures.

Based on these generic classes the architectures of CPAManager and CPAProtocol are built. The architecture of the CPAManager is given in figure 3. The subclasses of Executor class correspond to protocol application functions (e.g. clock synchronisation, interrogation). Protocol Object Dictionary describes the mapping between protocol objects and device application objects.

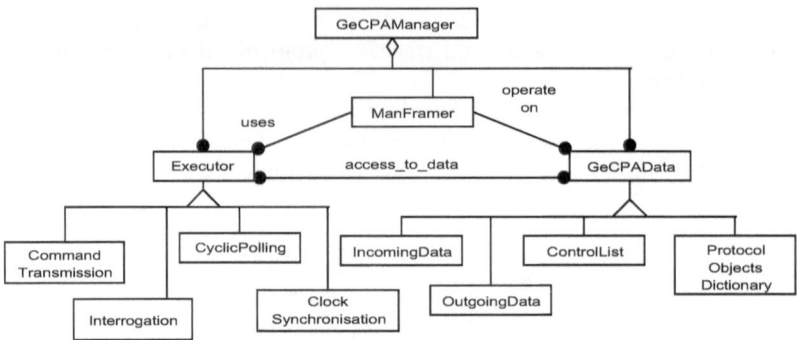

Figure 3. Generic object model of CPAManager

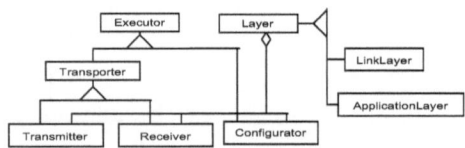

Figure 4. Generic protocol layer model.

The protocol layer architec-ture is given in figure 4. The transmitter class is responsible for outgoing transactions and the receiver class for incoming ones. The configurator manages layer configuration and exception handling.

The CPA object model resulted from the protocol use case specifications and their related interaction diagrams. The latter allowed to represent behaviour of active objects using state transition diagrams [3].

2.2   Communication Protocol Adapter (CPA) Design Patterns

A design pattern represents a solution to a design problem that might arise in a given context. The design pattern format used in COMSOFT framework explains the problem and its context, constraints, the solution, and a discussion of consequences of adopting the solution. The solution describes objects and classes that participate in the design, their responsibilities and collaborations (with examples). The main design patterns of COMSOFT framework are: *Mapping between protocol and application objects, Composition pattern, Communication pattern, Scheduling pattern, Performance pattern, State pattern, Object testing, Protocol testing, Mapping object model to C language.* As an example, the *Scheduling pattern* skeleton is presented below.

Problem: Object oriented concurrency model making the composition of scheduling operating system tasks and of scheduling active objects within the operating system task.

Constraints: The protocol software is embedded in the defined environment. For the IEC-870-5-101 implementation it is assumed that the CPA Protocol and CPA Manager are mapped to a single task each, and there is no pre-emption while an object is processing a request.

Solution: Realisation of concurrency relies on scheduling operations of objects. All active objects have been generalised into ActiveObject class that can be registered by the CPAProtocol (CPAManager respectively) scheduler and invoked by it (activated) if required. The scheduler object's method runCPAProtocol (runCPAManager) must be registered in system tasks scheduler to make CPA Protocol (CPA Manager) alive. Every object of ActiveObject class must have its implemented abstract operation activate. This operation is invoked by the CPAProtocol (CPAManager) scheduler when it decides that the object needs to be activated.

The scheduler has two queues: normal and urgent. The normal queue is filled up during initialisation phase of the CPA Protocol (CPA Manager). This queue contains references to objects needed to be run periodically.

The urgent queue is filled up during normal activity of CPA Protocol (CPA Manager) objects. This queue allows to resume all operations that have been stopped or invoked. Since the processor must be returned to the operating system in limited time, some operations need to be divided into steps. The urgent queue ensures that divided operations will be continued.

The indicated patterns originate from project experience. They create basis for solutions of new problems, required modifications or extensions. Design patterns provide a common vocabulary for designers to communicate, document and explore design alternatives. They help to reduce the required learning time for a library user.

3. COMSOFT Repository Organisation

How the repository is structured can have a significant impact on its usability and maintainability. The COMSOFT repository is subdivided into a series of libraries referring to different software products (depending on a protocol variant, device, operating system, scope of applicability) [2]. Each library is organised into a hierarchy starting with components of general use; components in lower tiers have increasing specialisation resulting in narrower applicability. Two views of the library organisation can be distinguished: catalogue-based and methodological. The first one is based on creation of the structure of component catalogue according to software design concepts. This helps the designer to decide what components belong to the library and helps the user of the library in searching for needed components.

The methodological view of the COMSOFT library organisation is determined by the assumed object oriented approach and Prosa/om CASE tool [5] capabilities corresponding to the defined COMSOFT development procedure. Prosa/om supports creating and managing the hierarchy of components needed in the protocol development. Its hyperlink facilities permit traversing between hierarchical components in conformity with applied communication software development model.

4. Usage of Patterns and Library in Protocol Development

Adaptation patterns are semiformal recipes that describe how a documented framework in the library form is used to develop an application in a new situation resulting from changes in the requirements corresponding to protocol profiles, devices, HW/SW environments.

The main architecture of the proposed COMSOFT framework can remain a stable kernel in the future protocol software evolution/adaptation responding to requirements changes. In the reuse process the main objective is to find similarities between an existing protocol framework and the new project. Classification is the primary mean for the library user to search for suitable components. Our classification dimensions are the protocol type, protocol profile, environment requirements (device, operating system, channel). The designation of the change points is supported with design and adaptation patterns. It is worth to notice that adaptation patterns say what to do in order to make a change, while the design patterns instruct how to implement the change. The set of produced adaptation patterns is reflecting characteristics of the IEC-870-5-101 protocol and its implementation in REC 501: *Initial change analysis (similarity), New protocol, Changes in the frame format, Link transmission procedure change: unbalanced vs. balanced mode, Extension of basic application functions, Changes in the number and types of application objects, changes in the contents of objects lists for cyclic acquisition or group interrogation, Communication with application database, Mapping a layered protocol structure into operating system tasks.*

Our suggested framework top-down customisation assumes the creation of a new library for the new project.

The first step is finding a library project which is similar to the current one. The choice is based on results of using *Initial change analysis* adaptation pattern. The output of this step is a copy of the selected project and a list of changes demanded by the new project to fulfil its requirements. Next, in each phase of the protocol development adaptation patterns corresponding to the introduced changes can be applied. In case of the protocol framework we can identify most of the reusable components immediately. Adaptation involves removal of inappropriate parts or their replacement. For each particular situation we can use the related design patterns.

This solution allows different projects not to interfere. However, having knowledge of the framework enables to start a new project not from scratch but by transferring elements of the previous project to the new one (figure 5). The main problem is to assess what changes are required by the new project.

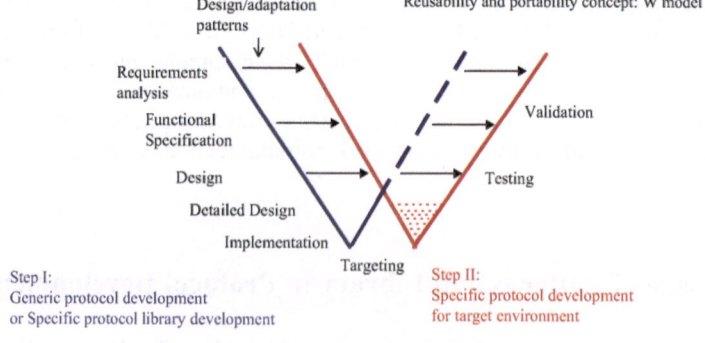

Figure 5. Reusability and portability concept - W model.

5. Conclusion

The project was considered successful and the framework is intended to be used for subsequent protocol development. This paper has focused on an architectural model of telecontrol protocols and how identified design and adaptation patterns improve the framework flexibility and reusability. We have argued that understanding the architecture is the key issue in reusing the framework.

The generic model of a class of telecontrol protocols has been defined in a way covering the system life cycle from requirements to its detailed design. Use case specifications were used for protocol application functions, interaction diagrams described the required protocol behaviour, high-level object structure conformed to protocol layer decomposition. It is, of course, difficult to draw any decisive conclusions from one project but the assumed concepts proved their value and usability. Moreover, it has shown effective to combine them in a sequence of steps leading from user requirements elicitation to detailed design and implementation. The main goal of the protocol framework was to serve as a logical scheme for development of the protocol software. The components are placed in a library allowing their storing, retrieval, referencing and manipulation, thus leading to shortening the time of producing communication software and assuring its quality.

6. References

[1] Cysewski G., Gromadzki T., Lyskawa H., Piechowka M., Szejko S.: COMSOFT Protocol Framework and Library Organisation, Report for ABB Transmit Oy, TUG Gdansk, 1997

[2] Bobkowska A., Cysewski G., Gromadzki T., Lyskawa H.: Object oriented design of telecontrol protocols, 22nd IFAC/IFIP Workshop on Real Time Programming WRTP'97 Lyon, 1997

[3] Booch G., Jacobson I., Rumbaugh J.: The Unified Modelling Language for Object-Oriented Development., Ver. 1.1, Jan. 1997.

[4] Gamma E., Helm R., Johnson R., Vlissides J.: Design Patterns: Elements of Object-Oriented Software Architecture. Addison-Wesley 1995.

[5] Prosa/om documentation, Insoft Oy, Finland, 1997

[6] Piechowka M., Szejko S., Kozlowski W.E., Vahamaki O.: Communication Software Development Model, EUROMICRO'97 Budapest, Sept. 1997.

A Software Bus as a Platform for a Family of Distributed Embedded System Products

Eila Niemelä, Harri Perunka, Tomi Korpipää
VTT Electronics P.O.Box 1100
FIN-90571 Oulu, Finland
{Eila.Niemela, Harri.Perunka, Tomi.Korpipaa}@vtt.fi

Abstract. Flexible distributed embedded systems require a different kind of software development. Domain and product analysis defines the software features, dividing the architecture of the application software into stable platform services and customisable software components. The software platform supports transparent communication between reactive sub-systems, and a software bus acts as an intelligent agent utilizing the knowledge of the application and configuration domain to provide system-level services through a generic service interface.

Each sub-system has a federative software architecture and co-operative application components. Communication is controlled by one component, which manages local connections between reactive application agents and networked connections through the configurable software bus. Application components with new product features can easily be added to the software bus by using the communication control component and the generic service interface.

1. Introduction

Distributed embedded systems need to be adjusted according to various customer requirements and commercial and customer specific technologies. The increasing number of product features and the diversity of customer requirements have resulted in a need to alter development and production processes to support evolution. A product family concept with well-defined software adaptability strategy is needed for expanding and scaling systems effectively during the evolution steps.

Flexible distributed systems require a software development approach that takes into account the common requirements of the application domain but also focuses on the forecasted future needs. The software architecture designed

Frank v. d. Linden (Ed.): ARES '98, LNCS 1429, pp. 14-23, 1998.

according to the given application domain requirements and constraints forms a basis for configurable and extendible embedded systems [1, 2].

We describe in this paper an application domain-specific distributed software platform for co-operative and distributed embedded applications. The applications act as reactive agents with responsibilities and capabilities for making low-level decisions, and co-operate with each other via a software bus, which acts as a network agent making decisions on the basis of the system-level application information incorporated in it.

Although the application domain-specific distributed software platform is demonstrated in a distributed control system, the design approach is suitable for other kinds of distributed embedded real-time systems which use the services of a commercial real-time operating system and a field bus, e.g. LON or CAN, as a communication medium.

2. Flexible Distributed Embedded Systems

Distributed real-time systems are often heterogeneous embedded systems, the response time requirements, use of memory, operation environments, etc. of which vary between the different parts. Software flexibility, scalability and robustness can be achieved in such environments by constructing an application domain-specific distributed software platform and heterogeneous application components that are suitable for it. Certain criteria have been laid down for the distributed software platform and its architectural components.

- *Customisation.* The platform must contain generic services such as configuration and system-level control, which need a knowledge of product features and the application domain for decision-making purposes. Since the network configuration and connections between components are based on these product features, the platform has to have built-in intelligence regarding the application domain in order to make system-level decisions.
- *Software independence and extendibility.* Application components must be able to be allocated freely to any node in the system, and the platform should provide transparent communication mechanisms. Application components should be as autonomous as possible, providing the system with its flexibility.
- *Heterogeneous implementation environment.* The memory and timing requirements of a typical embedded real-time application should be guaranteed in heterogeneous environments.

2.1 Control System Application Characteristics

Modern control systems are decentralised, typically involving a number of embedded real-time controllers and possibly embedded PCs. For demonstration purposes we will refer here to an automatic repayment system for handling returnable bottles and cans. The system is responsible for different functions such as identification and acceptance of the bottles and cans, their transfer to a store and repayment (Figure 1). Optional features of the repayment system product family include different types of identification method, different repayment modes, user interfaces and conformity to particular national regulations.

The demonstration system consists of two neuron chip based nodes for process control, and an embedded PC with QNX operating system for the user interfaces, identification and control. Interfaces to external systems are also needed. Identification is based on measured data from a video camera or an EAN code. The sum repaid is stored directly on a deposit card.

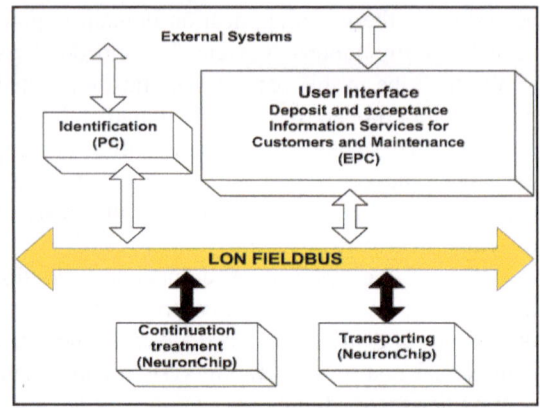

Figure 1. Sub-systems of a distributed depositing system

Neuron chips are used as embedded real-time controllers at the process level. An example of a process-level system is the transportation sub-system, which takes the form of a reactive agent able to carry out transportation jobs according to given orders. As the sub-systems have only a few configurable features, they are allocated to neuron chips with special size, performance, reliability, and safety requirements.

2.2   Component-Based Software for the Product Family

Software architecture has a significant influence on its flexibility, decomposition and adaptability. The application domain requirements establish the main characteristics of the architecture, and the software variations to be included in the product family define the necessary configuration methods.

Domain Analysis

The objective of domain analysis is to identify a set of autonomous software components, each of which fulfils a well-defined function in the system. This means that the basic function of the component should be clear, its optional features known, and its interfaces with other components adequately defined.

The components identified in the domain analysis also define constraints on the software architecture. The viewpoint adopted in architecture modelling is purely functional rather than object oriented, and therefore methods such as ROOM and RT/SA which emphasise functional decomposition and state-based behavioural modelling are used for designing the mode and event-based operability of the system at the architectural level [3, 4]. Thus the framework provides a set of generic services and a software platform where the application components can be installed. One of the generic services could be a software bus allowing component interactions.

Configuration

When software adaptability is required a configuring viewpoint has to be added to the software analysis, design and implementation. Feature-based software configuration can be based on component selection and/or component configuration. In the first case the system is constructed of components selected according to the product features, and in the second the configuration of the generic software components is fixed by setting the values of instantiation parameters. It is also possible to mix these component selection and parametrisation approaches.

2.3   Systems Extendible by an Application-Specific Software Bus

The increasing need for flexible systems brought about by changes in customers' needs and general evolution means that distributed embedded systems have to be designed as autonomous software packages that can be added to the system afterwards or can replace an existing package.

Despite the recognition of the importance of software components in reuse-oriented embedded programming, not very much attention has been paid to the connections between components. CORBA and DCOM specifications are used in information systems to achieve interoperability between distributed applications [5, 6]. The interface definition language (IDL) in CORBA describes interfaces as parts of components, by contrast with module interface languages and configuration programming languages [7]. Due to restrictions on CPU performance and the amount of memory in embedded systems, commercial CORBA implementations cannot be used in embedded real-time systems. To meet the needs of a particular application domain and product family, we have integrated these requirements as a set of features in an application-specific software bus. The following requirements are laid down:
- It should be possible to add a new application to the system with a minimum of work.
- Applications should be location-independent.
- Hardware changes should not affect the applications.
- Applications have to be loosely coupled.
- The same software platform should be used for all product variants.

The properties of the software bus and software architecture are based on these requirements. Firstly, a new application can be added to the system when applications are designed as agents that perform their own duties without any system-level decision, so that the system-level decisions can be made in the software platform.

Secondly, applications are location-independent if they use a broker to achieve interoperability and have standard interface descriptions for their connections to the platform. Interface descriptions have been replaced by interface components and a software bus service interface.

Thirdly, the services of the software bus attend to software interoperability. Contrary to the CORBA specification we describe the software bus as an application-specific broker which offers the basic services for component interconnections, but application-specific services are also needed for message routing and synchronising the interoperation of application components. A facilitator which connects application agents to the software bus and to each other assists in loosening coupling between applications [8].

Lastly, we decided to use layered software architecture to meet the needs of a product family. Layered agent architectures can be based on data abstraction levels, functional decomposition or responsibilities. Hybrid agent architectures, as customarily employed with control systems, use the first two of these, i.e. hierarchical layers deal with data at different levels of abstraction and are named according to their functions, e.g. a modelling layer, a planning layer and a reactive layer [9]. The responsibility-driven approach is nevertheless more suitable for applying object-oriented or object-based technology to control systems, as the system is decomposed into autonomous sub-systems, or reactive agents, which take care of the defined functional responsibilities and provide state information and services for other sub-systems. Messages of two kinds are needed between sub-systems: service requests for the software bus, and events for updating the state of the reactive agent. State information is distributed to other agents by the routing rules of the software bus.

3. Mechanisms for Flexible Control Systems

Stable architecture with a configurable software bus is an application-specific solution designed to increase the productivity of software development. The model is flexible in terms of the extendibility and scalability of the system, but it has strict rules for interfaces and communication.

3.1 An Application Framework

The software architecture can be divided into three abstract layers according to the scope of the control and the responsibilities discharged (Figure 2). The component layer controls the behaviour of reactive agents making low-level decisions, e.g. identifying an object using a predefined manner of identification and comparing the measurements with the reference object stored in the database, and the group layer consists of a communication component which is configured according to the needs of a group. If the group consists of numerous application agents, the communication component sorts out local and network messages.

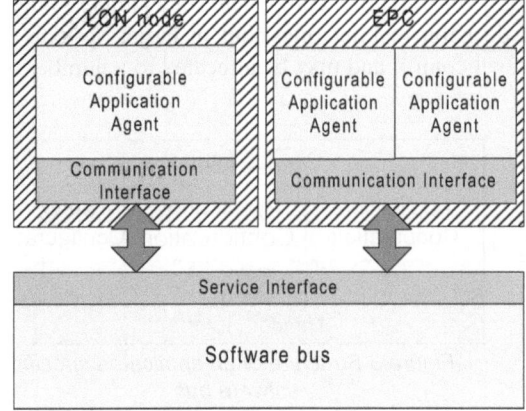

Figure 2. A federation of software agents.

The software bus has global knowledge of the representation of the system layer in the software architecture. Because of the differences between product variants and the physical extensions needed, configuration management is integrated into the software bus, which is an intelligent agent that includes configuration and co-ordination mechanisms in addition to different manners of communication. Communication with external systems is also supported by the software bus, e.g. that in the example application includes network interfaces for LON and RS-232. Messages between communication media are forked on the base of the network configuration. The services of the software bus are used through a simple interface which provides the functions for receiving and sending asynchronous messages.

3.2   A Lightweight Communication Interface for Application Agents

The communication interface in sub-systems handles all communication between the sub-system and the software-bus. In LON nodes the interface is simply the LON network image, which consists of information about the network variables and knowledge of their bindings. In sub-systems other than the LON nodes, the communication interface is a bit more complicated, and directs all messages between the sub-systems to the software-bus, which routes the messages into the correct sub-system. Thus, there are two different communication interfaces, the type of which is judged by the sub-system they reside in.

Communication inside the sub-systems is based on service-on-request principle. Each sub-system consists of the communication interface and one or more application agents. If one application agent needs information from another, a request is placed and the information is supplied when available. The communication component is placed in the blocked state while waiting for an answer.

3.3   A Configurable Software Bus as an Intelligent Router

The software bus is divided into interfaces and components, with their own responsibilities as presented in Figure 3. The network includes its own component for managing network configurations and interfaces with both networks and application components. Applications are configured by the application configuration management service. The application domain platform is built into the application co-ordination component. In a simple system this component needs restricted decision making rules, but in larger systems it comprehends the whole system-level control and may be allocated to a number of nodes.

The software architecture and communication rules form the stable part of the system, and configuration is only allowed by the software bus in accordance with the communication rules. Thus the system can be extended by adding new sub-systems which communicate in the same manner, i.e. according to same

Service Interface		
Application Cooperation	Application Configuration	Network Configuration
Routing		
Network Interface		

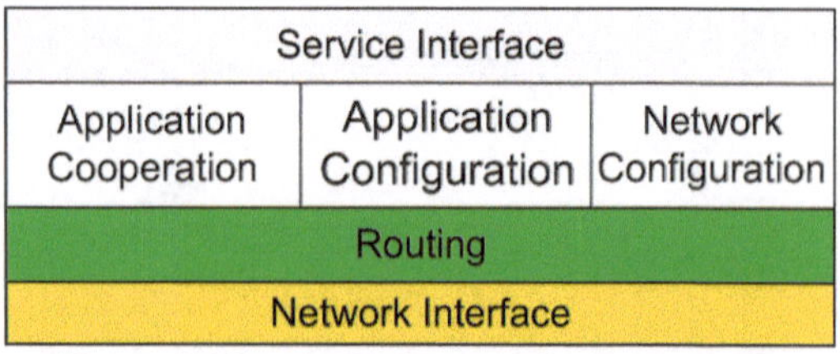

Figure 3 Structure of an applicaton specific sofware bus.

rules. Adaptability in the system is achieved by configuration mechanisms integrated into the software platform. Different features of the product variants could be implemented by adjusting the functions of the sub-systems, i.e. by increasing or configuring their internal components.

The software bus has been implemented for a control application which uses a LON network and a serial communication connection as its communication medium and it currently includes the following services:

- asynchronous message passing,
- memory management,
- network interface,
- intelligent routing mechanisms, and
- configuration management for application agents and the network interface.

The passing of asynchronous messages and memory management are primary level services. The network interface is a necessary set of two-level interfaces, in which a LON network is used a basic distribution medium in the example application, although external equipment, e.g. a card reader, may be connected via a serial communication channel. The software bus offers a transparent communication in both networks. The connections between the network interface layer and other components of the software bus are illustrated in Figure 4. The network configuration consists of the configuration component for the connections of the LON network variables and the message frames for the card reader. In the application example, LON configuration is performed manually with a LonBuilder tool and exported to the neuron chips of the application nodes.

Co-ordination of application agents and message routing are managed by means of intelligent routing mechanisms and the primary services, asynchronous message passing and memory management services. The message types that the software bus can handle are defined in data structures inside the software bus itself.

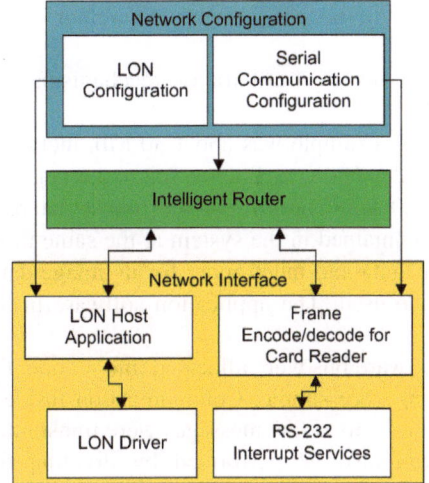

Figure 4. Components of the configurable network interface layer.

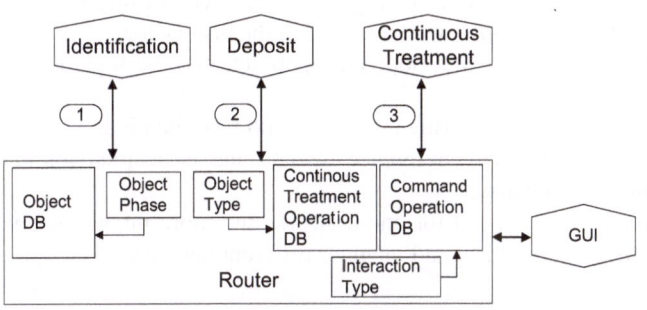

Figure 5. The intelligent routing mechanism.

The intelligence of routing is based on the contents of the message being handled (Figure 5). The status of the phase attribute in objects defines the message to be sent and the recipient application. Information on objects is stored in an object database and updated from the results of the application agents. Continuos treatment operations of different kinds are classified in a separate database according to the types of objects. The router co-operates with the user interface on the basis of interactions between the user and a command operation database, which consists of interactions and the corresponding information to be routed to the graphical user interface. Since transportation is handled through the message passing services, it does not affect to the object data.

Management of the configuration of application agents is very simple and is based on data configuration. Data for all possible configurations at the product family level are stored in the software bus and active parts of a configuration are defined when initializing the system.

4. Lessons Learned

The application-specific software bus yields the following advantages for software development in a product family context:

- Existing systems can easily be extended by means of new applications.
- Applications are location-independent, on account of the transparent communication mechanisms.
- The centralized communication component in a node simplifies connections with other application agents.
- The lightweight communication interface is suitable for demanding real-time applications with limited memory.

- Implementation-specific parts are hidden in the software bus and are not visible to the application agents.
- Customization is easy due to the gathering of configuration mechanisms into one place, the software bus.

The size of the software in our application example was about 30 Mb, including the following commercial components: the QNX, a Photon micro kernel, and drivers. The software bus takes about 80 Kb. The size of the object database depends on the number of objects to be contained in the system at the same time. Each object needs 52 bytes for its status data and much more for its image data, depending on the identification technique used. The application software in the neuron chips amounted to 2 Kb.

In the example, the services of the software bus were allocated into a node, the embedded PC, and the other nodes were very simple. Communication inside a node was frequent and fast in this case, and only a few messages were transmitted between nodes. Software allocation can also be performed by dividing the software bus into nodes in order to balance the work load inside them. On the other hand, this allocation procedure can cause network capacity problems, because the load in the network tends to increase. Exceptions are dealt with an exception handler, which logs them in error logs and tries several times to solve the resulting problems. These attempts are also stored in the history log.

The following restrictions on the development approach may be regarded as weaknesses:

- The maturity of the software engineering process should be quite high.
- The configuration is performed by reference to data and is decided for the product variants known in advance.
- The routing intelligence is designed for one network, and more intelligence is needed if the network is hierarchical and includes different networks.

5. Conclusion

Flexible distributed control systems need support to achieve customisation, extendibility, and scalability. This is possible by developing a configurable software bus and generic interface technique for applications. The software bus supports distribution by the transparent communication and a feature-based configuration. A standard service interface is provided for application agents which are connected to the software bus by a lightweight interface and a generic communication component. The software bus provides intelligent message routing and configuration support for the changes in application software components and the communication media. The requirements of the application domain are fulfilled without any additional features which are not useful for the product family. For this reason, the code size and execution time can be optimized according to the real-time requirements.

The next phase of our work will focus on enhancing the intelligence of the software bus by developing a form of configuration support which is able to configure itself for a hierarchical network with heterogeneous sub-nets.

6. References

[1]   van der Linden, F.J., Muller, J. K. *Creating Architectures with Building Blocks*, IEEE Software, **12** (6), pp. 51-60 (1995)

[2]   Kalaoja, J, Niemelä, E., Perunka, H. *Feature Modelling of Component-Based Embedded Software*. Proceedins of the 8th IEEE International Workshop on Software Technology and Engineering Practice, Los Alamitos, CA: IEEE Comp. Soc. pp. 444-451 (1997)

[3]   Shlaer, S., Mellor, S. *Object Lifecycles, Modelling the World in States*, Prentice Hall Inc, Englewood Cliffs, New Jersey (1992)

[4]   Selic, B., Gullekson, G., Ward, P. *Real-time object-oriented modeling*, John Wiley & Sons, New York (1994):

[5]   Siegel, J. *CORBA Fundamentals and Programming*. John Wiley & Sons, Inc. New York (1996)

[6]   Grimes, R., *Professional DCOM Programming*, Wrox Press Ltd., Canada, (1997)

[7]   Bishop, J., Faria, R. *Connectors in Configuration Programming Languages: are They Necessary?*. The 3rd International Conference on Configurable Distributed Systems. IEEE Comp. Soc., Los Alamitos. pp. 11-18 (1996)

[8]   Genesereth, M., Ketchel, S. *Software Agents*. Comms. of the ACM. **37** (7) pp. 48-53 (1994)

[9]   Wooldridge, M., Jennings, N. *Intelligent Agents: Agent Theories, Architectures, and Languages: A Survey*. Lecture Notes in Artificial Intelligence, Vol. 890. Springer-Verlag Berlin Heidelberg New York (1995)

A Three-Tier Design Approach for a Family of Large AC Drive Control Systems

Peter Kolb[1], Beat Huber[2]

[1] Computer Engineering Dept., ABB Corporate Research LTD
CH-5405 Baden-Dättwil, Switzerland
peter.kolb@chcrc.abb.ch
[2] R&D Drives and Power Electronics
ABB Industrie AG
CH-5300 Turgi, Switzerland
beat.huber@chind.mail.abb.com

Abstract. Software for large embedded systems (e.g. control systems for locomotives or large industrial drives) consumes a steadily increasing proportion of the engineering costs for development and maintenance. For this reason our goal is to share the effort by developing software that fits for several related products or product families. Not only the implementation, but also the software architecture and design shall be reused in similar applications. Replacing a hardware component or adding a customer desired feature in an application shall result in very limited changes in the control system software. As a solution for this common situation this paper defines a layered software architecture, which is designed for maximum reuse on different levels. The paper illustrates the internals of the common software layer, describes how it is used to build variants for different drive topologies, and how the lower layers were designed for fast application building.

1. Motivation for Reuse

The last two decades have shown that computing power grows much faster than innovation emerges for power hardware of large industrial drives (i.e. motors, power converters, transformers, etc.). Therefore an increase in efficiency of an industrial drive can be reached more easily by utilising the computer power of modern control systems instead of exchanging power hardware parts of the machine, which are five times more expensive.

With the traditional life-cycle of a large industrial drive of 20 to 30 years, the current situation arises, where the drive control system will be updated or replaced up to three times before decommissioning - assuming that computer technology continues to progress at its current rate.

Frank v. d. Linden (Ed.): ARES '98, LNCS 1429, pp. 24-31, 1998.

Exchange of a control system in an existing industrial drive by a more powerful one offers many new opportunities, like improving control algorithms or adding more and more features and realising them in software instead of electronic hardware. This is the reason why control systems rapidly grow in complexity. Inherently with the complexity comes increased effort for the engineering of the control system software according to customer demands.

The only way to reduce engineering costs and to cope with increasing complexity is the well-proven concept:

1. Proper structuring of the control software.
2. Reuse of components and, as far as possible, also of software design and architecture.

This means we need to look for a hardware independent software description which allows the reuse of general solutions in the problem domain, software architectures, and software components when the control system hardware is replaced. This paper shows how control software can be structured to improve reusability on several levels and to support easy portability between platforms.

Apart from life-cycle considerations there is another motivation for reuse of control system software: Industrial drives are not only needed in a wide spectrum of applications, ranging from rolling mills over chemistry to marine applications, but also vary greatly in their structure (see Figure 1). At ABB Industrie these various power hardware topologies are classified in a few main families, e.g.

- The *Cyclo* Converter Family (consisting of a transformer, several line converters and an excitation) with excellent behaviour at very slow revolutions.
- The Load Commutated Converter (*LCI*) Family, which consists of an intermediate circuit that de-couples the line from the effects of the motor.

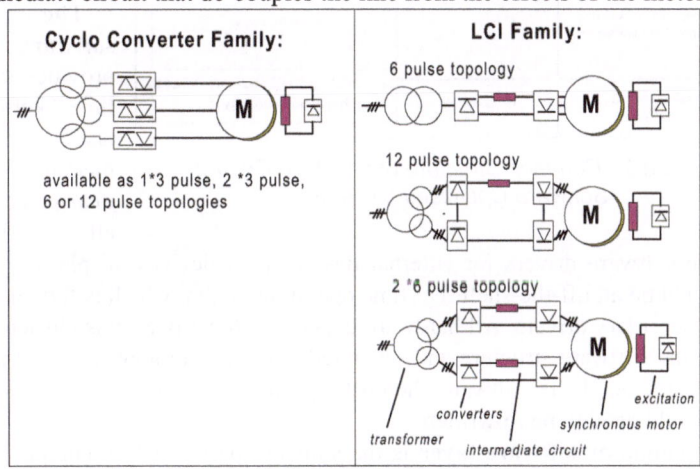

Figure 1: Classification of Drive Topologies at ABB Industrie

These large variations in topology combined with a small number of drives sold per year are the main reasons for high average engineering costs for the drive control software.

Effective means to reduce the engineering effort for drive control applications are the reuse concept and the subsequent software architecture, both covered by the three-tier design approach which has been recently developed at ABB Industrie supported by ABB Corporate Research in Switzerland.

2. Overall Software Structure

2.1   Software Levels for a Product Family

Structuring of the software for the broad family of drives has been done under manifold objectives:

- Maximising the portion of reused software in spite of distinct topologies and a priori unknown individual customer demands.
- Separating hardware specific parts to ease porting of the software and to improve software reuse when the control system hardware is replaced.
- Providing optimal programming tools and languages for software engineers working on different abstraction levels.

The result is the layered software architecture consisting of four layers (see Figure 2).

Engineering:	Programming Language:	Software Layers:
customer specific add-ons	Function Block Language	Application Layer
one solution for each drive topology	C	Topology Layer
framework considering all predicted variations	C	Common Layer
hardware specific functionality	C, Assembly	Basic Software Layer

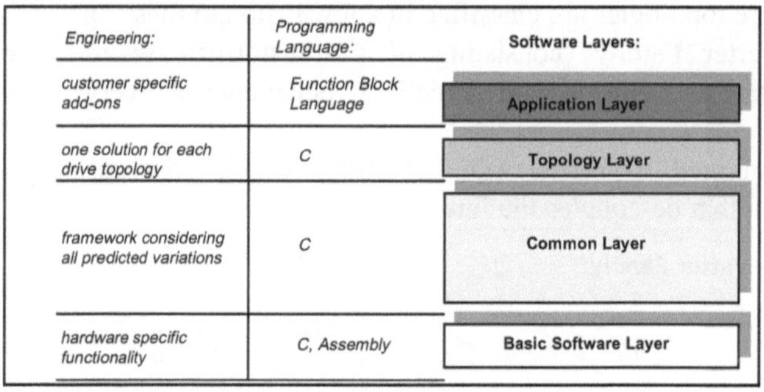

Figure 2: Common Structure of the Drive Control
Software Optimised for Reuse

In summary, these layers describe a bottom-up abstraction hierarchy:

The basic software layer provides the real-time kernel with task scheduling, memory management, and all hardware specific software drivers for external devices (I/O devices, displays, etc.). This part might be an off-the-shelf real-time operating system which is further enriched by the necessary drivers. All hardware dependent functionality is clustered in this part of the software structure and separated from the commonly reused part by a clear interface. If the software should be ported to another control system, this layer would need to be re-written.

The common software layer is the software part which is comprised of the components for creating all the variants in topology that have been foreseen. With these components the control software for a specific drive topology can be designed, and may then be used to realise all species of this drive family. The application building interface of this layer is a set of function blocks. For the internals of this layer the programming language C was chosen to retain utmost flexibility in developing the real-time functionality needed in every motor control application that has been predicted. This layer is the software with the highest reuse potential and therefore the longest life-cycle. Its future evolution must be thoroughly controlled and its internal structure must be designed to enable the addition of topologies that have not been considered at moment.

The topology layer gives the opportunity to design the control software for a new power hardware topology, which can then be used for a set of slightly varying applications. This means that on the topology layer the model diversity is narrowed to one specific topology. The life-cycle of topology layer software is determined by the market demands for this specific drive topology. The topology layer is written in C by experts who know the function blocks of the common software layer.

In the application layer, remaining customer specific features are added to the software for a certain drive topology. As application development is done by engineers in a profit centre with no deep programming experience, we proposed for this layer a graphical function block language, for instance IEC 1131-3. Thereby, an application engineer can program customer desired functionality on a high level of abstraction by simply selecting and combining appropriate function blocks provided by the topology layer.

3. Details of the Software Layers

3.1   Common Layer Framework Architecture

In order to provide a set of function blocks for creating drive topologies, which are used for application development, the common software layer must be structured into entities that are required in all topologies (see Figure 1). This is called domain engineering ([5]). Preferably the division of operational functionality among software architectural types should lead to software entities which coincide with the boundaries of the smallest power hardware entities of the drive. Thereby we achieve that a replacement of a power hardware component has only local effects on the software. The result is a set of functional units, each of which solves a limited functionality.

Once a rough decomposition of the common part is established, it is necessary to design means for creating a specific topology with the common part components. In [1] this aspect is called the "coordination model used among the architectural types". Next there must be a clear interface defined for application building with the topology specific software. Guidelines must be established which describe how the software shall be extended by customer demanded features.

To establish a basis for reuse of the common software layer we clearly defined which program behaviour is to be pre-defined and fixed for every topology, and which shall be left unspecified for individual customer design. In this respect the common software part can be seen as a framework ([6]) which is "a set of classes or modules that embodies an abstract design for solutions to a family of related problems" (from [7]). Unlike a library the framework not only provides a set of functions, but also pre-defines how these functions are already partly connected and shall be completed by a topology and application builder using this framework.

The building blocks of our framework are the functional units which provide one or more solutions for commonly identified software components, i.e. *Current Control, Firing Logic*, or *Synchronisation* which are common to all applications. Further, the common software layer offers alternatives for only partly specified components, or components that are mainly assembled by an application engineer.

With this concept of supplying not only completed functional units, but also sub-components to build new functional units on application level, we define different levels of modularization between system functions in the context of variation (modular design, [8]). However, the variation is restricted to lie within the predicted topologies, otherwise a re-design of the framework would be necessary.

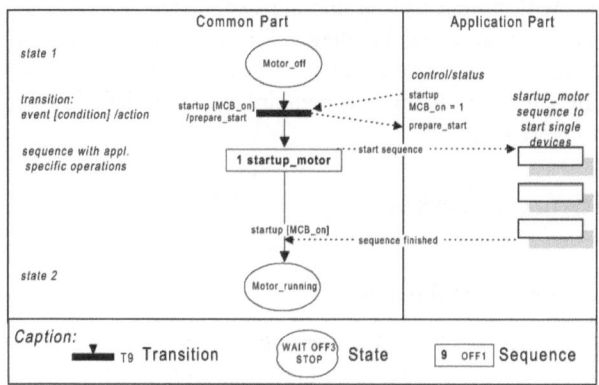

Figure 3: State Diagram Behaviour

Further, in the common layer we realised a general concept of a pre-defined system behaviour (i.e. start-up the controlled drive, behaviour in normal operation or in case of an error). The system behaviour description consists of a special state diagram, which is mainly defined in the common software layer (see Figure 3), but whose execution is controlled from the application layer (firing a transition by events, executing a application specific sequence as a state activity).

3.2   Topology Layer Concepts

At the topology layer, instances of functional units are connected with each other. A functional unit is a component with limited functionality realised by several internal calculation routines and a standardised interface (Figure 4):

Internal calculations in a functional unit are either called repetitively with a specified task cycle-time, or are triggered by events which are passed from the outside to the functional unit via its control inputs.

The control outputs are binary values which indicate the current calculation status of the functional unit. A change of status can be interpreted as an event which is passed through the control output and might trigger other functional units.

For internal calculations in a functional unit, e.g. a PID control algorithm, several sampled continuous time signals (process variables in real value format)

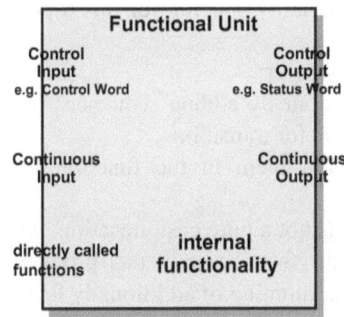

Figure 4: Typified Interface of a Functional Unit

are required. They are provided by the continuous input. The quasi-continuous time results of a functional unit calculation are passed on to its continuous output.

Further, a functional unit might provide additional functions that can be called directly by an application builder (and not via an control input event).

Interconnection of continuous time signals of functional units is done on the topology layer. It does not require further explanation. The connection of control and status words between different functional units is more sophisticated. We have to distinguish two types of communication: loose coupling without synchronisation and tight coupling with synchronisation between functional units (for an exact definition see [4]). For most of the control events exchanged in the drive control systems product family, the communication types can already be defined at the common software layer. Thus, the communication details can be hidden within the functional units. At the topology layer an engineer then only has to connect the right events to the control input of the functional unit and need not worry about the communication type or the internal realisation of the functional unit.

Similarly, it is possible to provide task cycle-times for quasi-continuous time calculations of functional units (as far as the computing power of the target system is already determined) to a great extent in the topology or even common layer. For instance the process signal sampling rates for fast control algorithms, are most often not a subject of customer demand, but a characteristic of the algorithm chosen. Nevertheless, there must be sufficient computing power reserved for the less time-critical features added on the application layer.

4. Three-Tier Reuse Approach

4.1 Steps to Go

Now that the software architecture for the family of drive control systems has been well established, we show how it shall be used to develop software for a certain topology, and to build upon this layer customer specific applications.

This three-tier design approach requires the following steps (Figure 5):

Step 1: Learn to understand the framework of the common layer.

Step 2: Apply the framework to a single topology and thereby narrow the scope to a small set of similar applications:

a) Create a specific program instance by selecting building blocks for the topology from the functional units of the common software layer.

b) Interconnect the building blocks (control signals and continuous time signals) according to the topology.

c) At this stage, it is still possible to add functionality specific for this topology in the programming language C.

Step 3: Build applications on top of the topology layer:

a) Define the customer specific program behaviour by adding sequences to the main state machine and providing firing events for transitions.

b) Add customer specific features and program them in the function block language.

In our case application development (Step 3) is not a pure customisation, which is done by selecting an active set of components from an universal product by customisation procedures [8]. We allow free programming of additionally features if a customer pays for it.

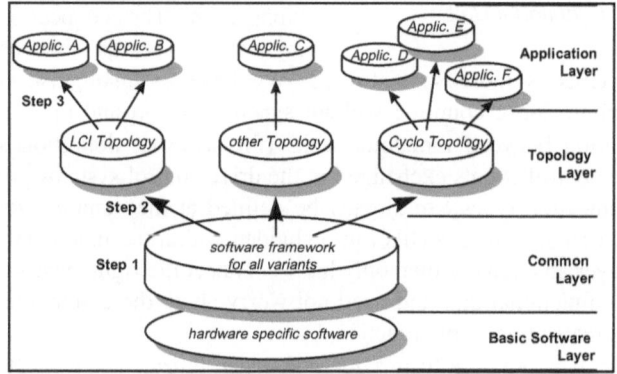

Figure 5: Three-Tier Design Approach for Application Building

4.2   Gained Reuse Potential

The estimated ratio of software size for common software layer : topology layer : application layer is 7 : 1 : 2. The small proportion for application layer software contributes much to reducing engineering costs for a customer specific product.

Corresponding to the three steps in the design approach proposed above, there are three levels of reuse:

Highest level of reuse: If a new customer specific product with a foreseen topology has to be developed, an engineer at the profit center only has to run through Step 3. He or she starts with the software created for the desired topology and thereby reuses all code up to this layer (80 %).

Medium level of reuse: If a remarkable step in drive technology innovation is reached, a new topology has to be designed on which applications can be built again. Step 2 and Step 3 must be run through. All software on the common layer can be reused (70 %).

Low level of reuse: If the control system hardware is replaced by a more powerful one, modules of the common software layer might be ported to run efficiently on the new processors. But the overall structure and framework of this layer remains, as it was designed to be hardware independent. The effective reuse is the framework (about 40 %).

5. Conclusion

The development of the three software layers (basic, common, and topology for two topologies) including the framework for application building of drive control systems took several person-years. From this project at ABB Industrie we gained not only a profound understanding of the diversity of our drive applications, but also much experience in developing a software framework covering a wide spectrum of variations. Our experience widely corresponds to the statements given in [2] about object-oriented frameworks, which was recently published.

With this approach of considering different types of product variations, namely specific end customer demands, families of drive topologies, and portability on new computer platforms, we were able to improve our reuse potential for this control software substantially. Now, reuse is no longer limited to code, but includes the software architecture and even domain knowledge.

6. References

[1]   L. Bass, S. Cohen, L. Northrop. Product Line Architectures. International Workshop on Development and Evolution of Software Architectures for Product Families, Ávila, Spain, 1996.

[2]   M. E. Fayad, D. C. Schmidt. Object-Oriented Application Frameworks. Communication of the ACM, Vol. 40, No. 10, October 1997.

[3]   E. Gamma et al. Design Patterns - Elements of Reusable Object-Oriented Software. Addison-Wesley, 1995.

[4]   H. Gomaa: Software Design Methods for Concurrent and Real-Time Systems. Addison-Wesley, 1993.

[5]   H. Gomaa. Feature-Based Reusable Architectures for Families of Systems. International Workshop on Development and Evolution of Software Architectures for Product Families, Ávila, Spain, 1996

[6]   R. E. Johnson, B. Foote. Designing Reusable Classes. Journal of Object-Oriented Programming. University of Illinois, Urbana-Champaign, 1991.

[7]   R. E. Johnson, V. F. Russo. Reusing Object-Oriented Design. Technical Report UIUCDS 91-1696, University of Illinois, Urbana-Champaign, 1991.

[8]   A. Karhinen, A. Ran, T. Tallgren. Configurable Designs. International Workshop on Development and Evolution of Software Architectures for Product Families, Ávila, Spain, 1996.

Modular Turbine Control Software: A Control Software Architecture for the ABB Gas Turbine Family

Dr. Christopher Ganz, Michael Layes

ABB Power Generation Ltd.
CH-5401 Baden, Switzerland
christopher.ganz@chkra.mail.abb.com

Abstract. ABB Power Generation's family of gas turbines covers the power range of 35 to 270 MW with five basic turbine types, which vary in size, combustion technology and equipment. Each type comes in several variatons, which in turn can be customized by adding or removing options or by following customer requirements not covered by standard options. This situation imposes high flexibility requirements on the turbine control system software. The scheme presented in this paper was developed to meet these requirements and ease turbine control engineering. It is based on the ideas of object oriented programming, which has been known to be very well suited for this kind of problems in conventional software engineering for quite some time. The architecture which results from this approach not only eases reuse of standard solutions throughout the whole turbine family, the design guidelines based on the object oriented principles also improve stability of the designed code. The concepts presented are currently being implemented for the ABB reference plant product family control system.

1. Introduction

1.1 Turbine Control

A turbine control system has three basic tasks:
- Closed loop control: Controlling typical values like speed or temperatures, mostly by PI-control
- Open loop control: binary control, concerned with sequence control of startup or shutdown procedures. Although called open loop, the binary loop is usually closed.

Frank v. d. Linden (Ed.): ARES '98, LNCS 1429, pp. 32-38, 1998.
© Springer-Verlag Berlin Heidelberg 1998

- Protection: The turbine state is continuously monitored and the turbine is deloaded or shut down (tripped) if any dangerous state is reached.

The protection system is usually structured as a list of trip signals, which are continuously analyzed to be in the allowed ranges or states, whereas the control structures are more complicated. The closed loop controls comprises a hierarchy of control loops with various objectives and varying tasks, depending on the current state of the turbine (connected to grid, starting, stopping, etc.). The open loop controller mainly manages the startup and shutdown sequences by governing a number of sub-systems with their individual startup and shutdown sequences.

1.2   Family Variation

The gas turbine family is designed to cover the desired power range in both 50 and 60 Hz. Each family member comes with a number of options, e.g. fuel selection or cooling system. In addition, customer requirements may result in further adaptations of the standard solution. Each of these variations and modifications has to be covered in the corresponding control software. However, developing a customized control system for each turbine is clearly no longer possible in the current market situation in the power business.

The family variation therefore had to be analyzed for typical variations, for subsystems which are stable throughout the whole family, within one family type, or which are supplied in a limited set of well definied options. For each of these system variations, the optimal software solution has been available in previous projects. What kept the software from being easily implemented and adapted to other turbine configurations was the lack of an architecture which not only supported a modular structure of the software, but also eased the exchange of typical options and allowed the application of a consistent version management.

2.   Reuse

The similarity of the turbine hardware (or hardware of sub-systems) over parts or the whole family is well suited for the idea of software reuse. This idea has been circulating in software developing companies for some time, but the non-technical problems (organisatorial or psychological) of this approach have left the concept in many companies in a rather obscure state (see [1]). When asked, many people do answer 'we have it', but a closer look mostly reveals that the concept is not widely supported in the organization.

2.1   Current Control Structures

If we look at the control structures which have been established over the years in a power plant, we already find a basically well structured design in the open loop controller (e.g. binary or sequence controller). The main sequencer is responsible of switching on and off various sub-systems, commonly referred to as function groups. Each function group then controls its associated devices. Function groups are usually the representation of a physical sub-system in the process.

A brief look at the variations in the turbine family makes the development of a strict reuse scheme quite obvious. In many cases, the process hardware of auxiliary systems are equal or only differ in device redundancy. However, a closer look at the multiplicity of current implementations confirms, that simple copy-paste type of reuse is not easily possible, and that sub-systems have to be designed for reuse and can not simply be extracted from a previously implemented solution. However, the current engineering process is based on a 'cloning' technique (as described in [2]), which selects a previous project closest to the new plant, copies it, and adds the modifications.

2.2   Requirements

The analysis of the family structure and of common project requirements reveal the following levels of possible reuse:

Function block level: Library of generic solutions (controllers, drive control, sequencer, etc.). Independent of their application.

Drive group level: Simple automation solutions comprising a small number of redundant devices, including voting.

System-level: Systems or subsystems which exist as stable implementations, i.e. are not changed per project, but which may be exchanged as standard options

Family-level: Systems or subsystems which can be shared among part or the whole product family.

The analysis showed quite clearly, that with increasing automation level, a common standard structure is more difficult to find. Although a gas turbine startup sequence always performs the same actions, such details as number of measurements to use as state transition conditions or details of device control differ greatly.

If we analyze these possible levels of reuse, we can derive the following general requirements for our reuse supporting architecture:

- It shall be possible to exchange predefined options.
- It shall be possible to share a module among several (all) turbine types.
- Project specific parts shall possibly be isolated from standard code.
- The reuse scheme shall not only speed up project engineering, it shall also improve code quality.

3.   Object Orientation

Despite the absence of object oriented design techniques in control system programming, the analysis of the requirements for software modules showed some parallels to requirements set up for object oriented systems. Since tool support for object oriented implementations is still rare, the focus was not put on object oriented coding, but on using an object based methodology for the design. Special features of the programming tool currently in use were then used to relate this methodology to implementation guidelines.

3.1   Object Hierarchy Design

The first task in any object oriented design, the identification of objects, is straight forward when designing a turbine control system: The objects can be distinguished on the plant floor: the pumps and valves have traditionally been regarded as functional sub-systems in power plant control (cf. function block level in Section 3.2). Object hierarchy does not need to stop at the drive level. In general, a whole plant can be regarded as one object, with its sub-systems and functions being interpreted as objects on the lover level. The current open loop control structure shows this quite clearly. If we regard the main sequencer as the control structure of the top level object (turbine), each of the function groups or sub-systems it controls can be modelled as objects as well. We will see below, that they can even be related in functionality to a common abstract class of controllable object. A closer look at function groups then shows the possibility of once again identifying functionality on a lover level which can again be packed into an object structure, which even relates to the same common object class.

This hierarchical structure is achieved when only functionality and sub-systems which can clearly identified in corresponding process hardware are structured in terms of plant hierarchy. A very similar organization results, if options and variants are identified and grouped for easy, modular replacement. To benefit from the ease of engineering as well as from the functional clarity, functional decomposition was applied with special regard on optional or varying functions.

3.2   Data Encapsulation

One of the main properties in object oriented design is data encapsulation. If we compare conventional, object oriented programming languages to the way control systems are usually programmed in function chart, we have difficulties to distinguish data from functionality, since in a data flow representation data is not collected in variables, but can be regarded as flowing through a graph. The area where we do have a compareable situation where data can be retrieved and stored back are the I/O devices. Extending the idea, data encapsulation can be regarded as defining an object's interface, e.g. a number of signals leaving an object. We will denote these objects as 'services' in the sections to come.

These services can be classified in several different categories:

State Modifying Services:

Conventionally denoted as commands or orders, these services perform some action on the object's internal state. By the object's state we do not only mean some software internal structure, but also the state of the field devices controlled by the object (e.g. valve open or closed).

Information Services:

To consistently organize all information provided by an object, all data used by any entity outside the object is to be included as an information service. As we will see later, the definition of information services is an essential step towards data abstraction.

In addition to these services commonly used by other objects on the controller level, additional services are defined which ease the appication of an object:

Administration Services:

Commissioning and maintenance procedures are included in an object definition. These services are not available for automation structures, since they assume in-depth knowledge of the plant when being operated, since commissioning procedures may require disabling or testing some safety equipment.

Parameters:

Plant specific data is defined as an object parameter. Valve characteristics or controller settings are parameter attributes of an object, which can also not be modified by process control.

3.3   Inheritance

One key feature of object oriented programming, and also the most difficult to implement in a non-object oriented environment is inheritance. However, the inheritance concept – to define an abstract superclass with a constant interface and subclasses whose function implementation varies – is very well suited for the implementation of exchangeable standard options. The approach taken is to define a common interface for all variants, which can then be regarded as the definition of the abstract superclass of these options. It can so be guaranteed, that all other modules subscribing to services of that module only rely on data provided by all variants through the common interface, therefore reducing the influence of a modification in one module on other, unrelated modules.

A subclass can then fulfill the requirements of the interface according to the needs of the process option it represents. Please note, that in order to keep object interchangeability, a subclass instantiating the abstract interface definition is required to provide the services of the class. If it does require additional information for its internal operations, this information does not need to be wired through the interface, since it can not be regarded as one of the object's services. Subscribing to services exported by other objects does not limit interchangeability. We did also limit the object's possibility to access other object's services to information services. Using any other services would not limit interchangeability, but it would increase the functional interdependence of the objects. State modification services should only be accessed by the superordinate automation structure, or superordinate object only.

3.4   Abstraction

Current implementation of control software is still very much focussed on single signals. Whenever some information is required by a functional entity, it is calculated from field measurements or state signals. This greatly reduces readability of the code and minimizes interchangeability.

Consider the situation, where one option is providing pressure by one pump, the other option is to install two redundant pumps. If another object wants to check, whether the pressure is indeed provided (assuming there is no pressure measurement available), it has to check the status of one pump in the first case, or the status of pump 1 OR the status of pump 2 in the second case. If the pressure building sub-system provides a service which returns the information 'sub-system pressurized' and does the signal voting itself, an object which requires the pressure information does not need to know how many pumps are available.

Informatin condensation at this stage reduces the number of signals exchanged between two objects, but not the amount of information, since the information proviced by the signals is more meaningful.

3.5   Use Cases

The individual object's services are found by defining use cases. Following a top-down approach, the use cases for a plant level object (e.g. a turbine) are its interfaces for manual operation (i.e. the machine states which can be selected by an operator). Recursively, the use cases for all sub-objects are then defined by the requirements of the superordinate automation structure. Most sub-systems have to be started or activated in the sequence of the start of their 'owning' object, or they can be commanded to switch to another state by that same automation authority.

The information services of an object are defined by collecting all requests for data from that object by any other object. That number of requests may be arbitrarily large. Since the number of required services of an object renders its reuse increasingly difficult, a reduction of services it to be attempted. As we have seen before, requests of conventionally designed modules will mostly directly access some internal state of the object to decide themselves on the required information. Not all service clients do this in the same way. It is therefore mostly possible to detect the information all these subscribers are interested in, to then gather that information within the object, and defining a service which provides the desired condensed information.

3.6   Implementation and Design Rules

As mentioned before, these object definitions finaly need to be implemented using conventional function block programming languages without any object support. Although some implementation rules, naming and programming conventions were introduced to enforce the object properties on the control system level, additional rules and guidelines are introduced to keep the object oriented paradigm during the design phase. Handling of object internal states, strict use of object services for information retrieval, and data abstraction guidelines are required to fully benefit from the advantages of the approach.

Furthermore, some properties of the conventional tools in use are beneficial for an object approach. The capability of assembling independent source files just before downloading onto the controllers is used to implement what can in a broad sense be regarded as 'late binding'. Some of the mechanisms implemented rely on the tool's ability to automatically connect signals on a name reference basis.

Additional tool support to ease the application of object orientation is currently being investigated. However, we consider the availability of object oriented features in future control systems programming languages to be highly probable and intend to rely on commercial tools in the foreseeable future.

4.   Conclusion

Designing for reuse, and therefore providing a level of standardization requires extra discipline from all participants. The concepts presented in this paper are currently being implemented designing software for ABB Power Generation's reference plant family.

Designed to improve reuse and option interchangeability, the object oriented principles defined to achieve that have the appreciated side effect, that they do not only speed up engineering, but also improve code quality. This result is generally expected when applying reuse, but object methodology also improves the quality of the automation concepts by more clearly identifying data owners and responsibles, i.c. by setting up a well structured object hierarchy.

In addition, the side effects when exchanging modules were reduced to a great extent when compared with modules not designed for reuse. It was these effects which made error tracking very difficult and time consuming, especially when they occurred on site.

5.   References

[1]Jacobson, I, Griss, M, and Jonsson, P: *Making the Reuse Business Work*, IEEE Computer, October 1997, pp. 36
[2]Dikel, D, et. al: Applying Software Product-Line Architecture, IEEE Computer, August 1997, pp.49

Experiences with the Evolution of an Application Family Architecture

Andreas Rösel

ABB Informatics, Advanced Software Center
Mannheim, Germany
roesel@decrc.abb.de

Abstract: The evolution of the Semantic Graphics Framework from prototype to a base framework for more than ten industrial applications is reflected upon. The framework approach is regarded as a success, over a period of several years, solutions for various business units could be implemented and significant commercial impact has been achieved. The evolution of the framework is considered from the perspectives architecture, documentation and organizational issues. We summarize our experience with controlling the evolution of an object oriented framework in form of propositions.

Keywords: object oriented frameworks, software architecture, domain frameworks, framework evolution, evolutionary software development

1. Introduction

In this paper we present some experiences gained in arriving at a framework architecture and evolving it through its application in various projects over a period of years.

The paper is organized as follows: Chapter 1 outlines the history of the ABB Semantic Graphics Framework (SGF). Chapter 2 is concerned with the architecture and trade-off made in its evolution. In chapter 3 we focus on the documentation aspects. Chapter 4 briefly looks at organizational issues. Chapter 5 and 6 summarize our conclusions.

1.1 Semantic Graphics at ABB

The SGF framework is based on a portable commercial class library (providing graphical user interface basics etc.) and supports the development of graphical engineering applications. The major components of the SGF are a configurable graphical editor and a set of classes designed to be refined with specific application know-how. The need for a framework in this domain arose from the painful realization that standard offerings of graphical tools did not (in 1992) and still do not (in 1997) cover all the requirements for specialized engineering. The

Frank v. d. Linden (Ed.): ARES '98, LNCS 1429, pp. 39-48, 1998.
© Springer-Verlag Berlin Heidelberg 1998

choice was either to make significant efforts for adapting standard tools or developing once-off solutions. There had been negative experiences with both. Adaptation often took longer than expected and was not able to meet all initial and especially later emerging requirements. Once-off solutions took a long time to develop, were of high risk and had a high price.

1.2   History

The SGF emerged as the common core of two engineering tool prototypes that were completed at the ABB Corporate Research Center at Heidelberg, Germany, in late 1992 using Smalltalk. In 1993 the first C++ version of the SGF was completed in conjunction with two projects.

The first SGF applications were engineering tools, Geta/View and Kreisl/Graph, providing graphical shells around existing FORTRAN programs. Geta/View, used at ABB Kraftwerke, Baden, Switzerland requires a complex input data file that contains the topology, as well as engineering data of components modeling the air flow through a gas turbine. It allows for drawing schematics, checking consistency and then generates the input file. Kreisl/Graph is used by ABB Turbinen Nürnberg for calculating steam cycle processes. Again, a specific graphical editor allows for drawing steam cycles.

The largest application built on the SGF is the Integrated Data Engineering System (IDES). IDES allows to configure complex power distribution networks with transmission lines, stations, substations and their internals. While the network is entered with the graphical editor, the topology information is derived, verified and together with data from configuration dialogues it is entered into a database.

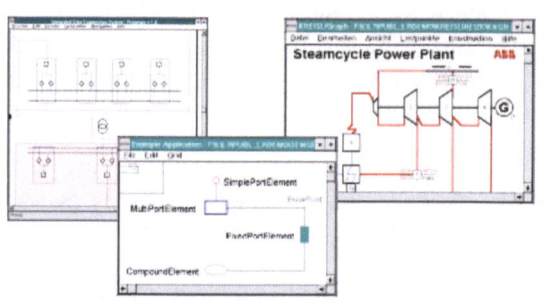

Figure 1: SGF application examples

2. Concepts and Architecture

When the SGF was designed many of the applications which were later built using this framework could not be envisaged. The fact that two different applications provided guidance in the development was most helpful.

Architectural choices were considered in terms of how they help to implement increased reuse and if they satisfy basic needs for graphical engineering. That is, the architecture would suffice to cover the essential needs of the applications being built at this time. For flexibility the approach was to provide hooks for customization as they were foreseeable. Extensions due to possibly emerging future requirements were not built in. Rather the approach was to trust that

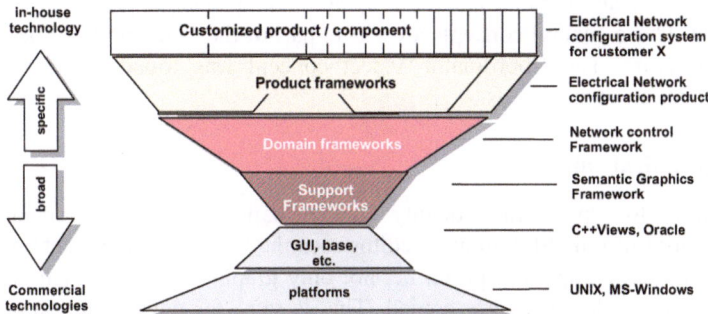

Figure 2 : Layered architecture of the SGF

essential objects and services, containing as little specifics as possible, will be useful (and customizable) for other applications in the same domain.

The general approach taken was to build a light-weight framework that is customizable in a layered fashion. The above figure illustrates how the SGF is focusing on its domain. The shading of the SGF layer indicates that with increasing maturity of commercial offerings a major part of this layers functionality will be able to be bought in. The specific domain of a company provides most interesting opportunities for framework benefits. In Figure 2 this is shown by a separate layer for the domain of network control.

2.1   General Concepts

One of the general concepts is support for graphical hierarchies. For example: detail levels may be represented as sub-drawings in separate editors. Connectivity between components of higher and lower levels of the graphical hierarchy is kept consistent. Another general concept is the Coordinator-Aspect-View triple. The concept of coordinated aspects (a variation of the Model View Controller paradigm) supports systematically partitioning application complexity. Each application object can be represented in the framework by a coordinator which is responsible for consistency between the graphical representation (graphic aspect), the engineering data (data aspect), textual information and other aspects, such as interface representations. This is illustrated in the following figure.

Application Layer - here: SteamCycle Engineering

customisation of editor beaviour	SteamCycleLists		Pump	
	SubAggregateList	PumpDisplay		PumpData

GraphicalEditor	DisplayLists		Coordinator	
	SubDisplayList	DisplayElement - Aspect 1-		DataSet - Aspect 2-

SGF - Framework Layer

Figure 3: Excerpt from the instanciation of the SGF for a particular application

A (customizable) mechanism for updating and change propagation is also provided. These general concepts are a core part of the SGF and have been stable over the years. The Coordinator-Aspect concept was found to be useful for several later emerging needs.

2.2   Graphical editor

In addition to typical functionality (rubber banding, zooming, standard and reduced printing) the SGF graphic editor uses the Coordinator-Aspect concept to provide semantic copy and paste, i.e. not only graphics but also their semantics (e.g. associated data etc.) are copied. This is vital for engineering applications where hierarchies of components with various associated information aspects need to be manipulated. The graphical editor also allows for customizing object behavior. For example, the type of connections accepted, consistency checks, restrictions on selection and moving can be defined for individual and groups of components. - The graphical editor is also an essential concept of the SGF. For each application one or more graphical editors are customized.

2.3   Synchronized graphical views

Several graphical views (editors or read-only views) can be open at the same time (typically with different zoom factors or scrolling offsets). All views are kept up to date. - One instantiation of this concept which became popular in applications of the SGF is a small sub-view showing an overview of the complete world picture of the respective editor.

2.4   Object persistence

Entire systems (i.e. graphics and their semantics) can be written to disk. This mechanism takes a version number to facilitate coping with changes of object definitions over time. - The need for a version number was soon realized. This allows application builders (and SGF maintainers) to read in objects stored by a previous version of the application (using *getFrom*) and check (if version < currentVersion) whether update activities need to be initiated.

2.5   Customizability

We use the terms configuration and tailoring to distinguish between activities of black-box customization and white-box customization. The differences in effort and competence require-ments are illustrated in the figure below.

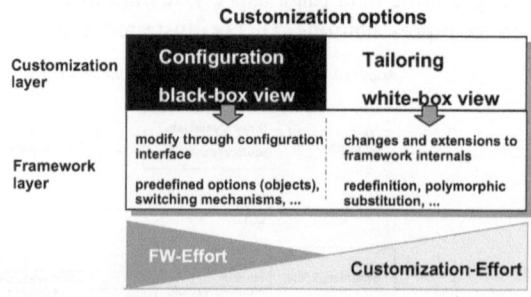

Figure 4: Customization options

The customizability of the SGF is based on the mechanisms of object technology (sub-classing, etc.). Specific extensions are designed for by providing hooks (redefinable base methods) and containers for specialized functionality (custom classes, clusters). These are white-box customization mechanisms in the framework. Such tailoring can only be done by people with a good understanding of the internals of the framework. Initially tailoring was the only way to customize the SGF.

The symbol editor coming with the SGF is an example of black-box customization (i.e. the user does not have to know about the internals to be able to define customized behavior). It also exemplifies the balance between efforts at the framework layer versus effort at the application layer.

3. Documentation

A framework encapsulates knowledge about a specific area of application and makes available components and templates with which complete applications can be implemented predominantly through combination, generation and specialization. The benefits of frameworks can only be realized on a larger scale when people other then the original designers can understand how to use and adapt the framework. In our experience the documentation of a framework will very much determine its usability and spread of use.

Documentation of the SGF was to address several audiences: *Potential customers:* communicate the features and capabilities of the framework and build up confidence for end customers. *Application builders:* communicate the concepts of the framework and the recipes of how to instantiate relevant aspects for an application to new developers. *Framework designers / maintainers:* communicate the concepts and implementation of the framework to enable extensions and improvements. Overall it was realized that it was necessary to move towards a product quality of documentation.

3.1 Source code based documentation

The initial documentation at the source code level was supported by a tool to extract comments and produce a class level document [4]. The approach has several advantages: it is simple, it is based on a single source of comments and the documentation is at a place where it can be modified even if small changes are. We recognized several disadvantages including the fact that incremental update of framework documentation was not supported and that the document structure does not reflect the relationships between classes.

A next step was to investigate tool support for design and design level documentation. Several tools like ParadigmPlus were tried and evaluated. Together/C++ [5] was adopted since it was in 1995 the only tool evaluated which was able to effectively support full cycle documentation.

3.2   Evolution of the SGF Concept book

Initially core concepts of the SGF were described on a few pages. As the size of the framework and the number of readers grew this was found to be insufficient. We decided that it would be valuable to not only improve the concept documentation, but to try and identify a suitable template structure for concept documentation of frameworks in general.

To identify an appropriate structure the requirements of readers and writers of the documentation were collated and categorized. The following documentation techniques for meeting the requirements were applied: uniform structuring, referencing of standard terminology, such as design patterns and utilization of tools at various levels of documentation.

In the following we describe the generic structure for documentation of framework concepts. A concept chapter is subdivided into the following paragraphs:

- NAME OF THE CONCEPT (= title of the concept chapter)
- INTENT. Short description of the purpose of the concept and the problems to be tackled.
- INTERFACE. A listing of the essential methods / classes made available by the interface (and the implementation) of the presented concept.
- DESIGN. How does the framework support the concept? Which classes and/or objects play a role in this concept? What are their responsibilities and how do they work together? Which behavior is made available through this framework as a standard procedure?
- RELATED DESIGN PATTERNS and CONCEPTS. Design Patterns and other concepts which are related to the concept at hand.
- RELATED CLASSES and METHOD. Listing of the related classes and methods which implement/ utilize/ or are utilized by this concept.
- SUNDRY. The following sub-chapters discuss continuing topics and are optional; i.e.: they provide a place for capturing open points and documenting potential for improvements.
- DISCUSSION (optional). Detailed discussion of specific aspects of the presented concept, in particular the documentation of the design decisions.
- REORGANIZATION (optional) How can the current design and the implementation of this concept be better organized with respect to improved reusability. In the area of design, these aspects could be considered: adaptability, flexibility, black- box vs. white-box framework. Aspects such as: readability, consistency, simplicity are relevant to the area of implementation.

The idea for the presented structure for the description of concepts has been borrowed from the uniform description of design patterns in [2]. In accordance with our requirements however, a different structure emerged.

4. Organizational Issues

Developing the SGF and developing applications with this framework has brought up several organizational issues. Since the SGF was the first framework being developed in the organization there was no previous experience or culture for this type of approach

The organization of the SGF was started in an Ad Hoc Model for Reuse and has evolved into an Expert Services Model as described in [3]. We have recognized that the SGF should be treated more like a product, but several questions have to be addressed before the organizational setting has reached the level of a Product Center Model.

4.1 Ownership issues

Who owns a framework used across domains? What about maintenance and warrantees? How are financial investments shared and benefits distributed?

The SGF can be applied in the broad domain of Graphical Engineering and is therefor of interest to a number of business units within ABB. Neither of these businesses has a primary focus on building or maintaining software of this generic nature. The internal information technology unit did not have appropriate resources and the transfer to a (small) external software house was regarded as too risky. Thus, the responsibility stayed with Corporate Research. There is a possibility that several of this type of software activities will lead to a spin-off organization in the near future.

4.2 People issues

How to built up appropriate expertise? Use external ones, acquire, re-train, use a combination? What to do with staff who can not make the step change?

If good designers are a precious commodity - good framework designers are even more so. That a number of good people were available to evolve the SGF was more by chance than organization. The transfer to others was done within the context of projects in small teams.

From the SGF and other framework projects it became apparent that the quality of the people involved is particularly critical, since the effects of design decisions are multiplied to all projects building on the framework. Therefore training is regarded as extremely important.

4.3 Process responsibilities

How to synchronize framework upgrades with application development? How to recognize and include additions of application developers which have generic value?

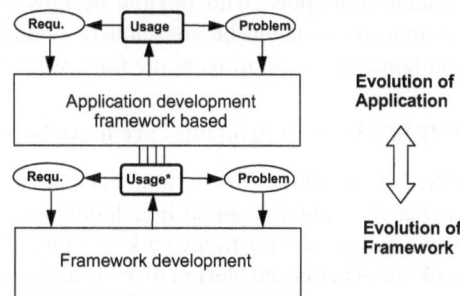

Figure 5: Framework processes

The two distinct processes associated with frameworks are illustrated below. The framework development process is executed at first very much in iteration with application development. Organizational responsibilities and the interactions have to be assigned for the two type of processes to work effectively.

One key for succeeding in this is identified by the box 'usage' above. The organization must be ready to use the frequent baselines of the development and provide early feedback. One important aspect is the decision which additional features are to be included in the framework. For the SGF the pragmatic approach was to leave as much responsibility as possible with the application developer and provide advice from the framework developer side.

5. Lessons Learned

In this chapter we summarize our experience in terms of several propositions. They express findings that are likely to be also applicable to other organizations evolving frameworks.

THESIS 1:   No framework success without application success.

What distinguishes a *successful* object oriented Framework from others? In our experience the primary distinguisher is the number of applications that have been successfully realized using the framework. Therefor the driving force must be the applications. The first two or three applications provide the essential requirements. While the framework architect will keep openness and extendibility for future applications in mind we found it vital to accept the reality that there will be no future applications unless these first few are 'out there' within the window of opportunity. Some chances for better design decisions, better documentation and so on have been sacrificed in this pragmatic view.

THESIS 2:   No framework without a customizable architecture.

A customizable architecture is the key to fulfilling the demands of the variants required by applications in the framework domain. Designer know-how and modeling techniques are vital, but in our experience they must be consciously focused on identifying key concepts which are general and 'simple' enough to survive many years of framework usage. Design patterns can help to address the variable 'hot spots' with flexible designs that are maintainable. Effort spent for customization should be consciously evaluated to determine if it is best spent in configuration or tailoring, at the framework layer or at the application layer.

THESIS 3:   OO principles are more important than language choices.

Whether the framework is implemented in Java, Smalltalk, C++ or some other language - without a sound foundation on object oriented principles it will not be worth being called a framework. As two adoptions which provided a good pay-back we experienced 'design by contract' and use of design patterns.

THESIS 4:   The law of increasing entropy applies to Framework evolution.

This law of the universe tells us that a framework will deteriorate as it is developed and maintained unless conscious efforts are expended to counteract this. Metrics support for the framework designer as described in [1] are a way to provide objective checks where such efforts are most needed.

THESIS 5:   No framework acceptance without documentation.

The influence of the documentation of a framework on its success should not be underestimated. The benefits of systematic documentation techniques will already be felt during the design of the framework. Framework developers will benefit as much as application developers. Tool support for reducing the effort for tedious update tasks are available.

THESIS 6:   No framework without organizational changes

It is our experience that developing and utilizing an object oriented framework successfully - requires organizational changes. While here too an iterative approach with small changes may be useful it is our recommendation to not leave such developments to chance. Definition of the organizational responsibilities and interaction processes are a prerequisite for creating a 'win-win' situation for framework suppliers and framework users. The goal should be to implement a Product Center Model [3] for utilizing the potential of good framework developments.

THESIS 7:   No framework benefit without commitment and investment.

We found a framework
- takes longer to built than traditional libraries as it contains additional design information
- takes longer to learn than traditional libraries as more complex interfaces must be understood
- requires more careful design than individual programs
- requires better documentation and support than individual programs
- changes the software life cycle as efforts are shifted for example from designing individual systems to deriving systems from or integrating systems with the framework design.
- changes to a framework may require rework in existing derivations

In our experience the cost of a framework may be 50% of the total cost of the first three applications. Once three or more applications are implemented and being used the framework will most likely have paid for itself. To reach this pay-off level significant commitment and investment are required.

6. Summary and Conclusions

The Semantic Graphics Framework evolved over a period of years from a prototype to a framework for more than ten industrial applications. The approach resulted in tangible benefits and is regarded as a success. The lessons learned in the process are to a large extend old lessons in a new form.

It is common knowledge that aspects like architecture, documentation, and organization are important for producing successful software. One challenge is to apply the principles of these areas to the framework approach and refine appropriate actions in accordance with the emerging needs. On the one hand, frameworks are the same (a complex software system, a product, etc.), on the other hand, they are different. New ways of abstracting complexity are available, new skills are required, faster development cycles are possible and new types of metrics are necessary.

The experiences gathered during evolution of the SGF were found particularly valuable because of the mix of activities possible through our role of being responsible for technology transfer rather than pure product development. This helped us to stick with a more systematic approach not dominated by deadlines alone, yet directly driven by practical applications in various industrial domains. Of course, many aspects of the development could be improved in hindsight and reporting the experiences is helping to pinpoint places for improvements.

7. References

[1] Erni K., Lewerentz C., "Applying design-metrics to object-oriented frameworks", Proceedings of Metric Symposium 1996, Berlin

[2] Gamma E., Helm R. , Johnson R. and Vlissides J. *Design Patterns: Elements of Reusable Object-Oriented Software*. Addison-Wesley, 1995

[3] Goldberg A. and Rubin K.S., *Succeeding with Objects* - Decision Frameworks for Project Management, Addison-Wesley, 1995.

[4] Intersolv, C++Views Manuals, Intersolv Inc, 1996

[5] Together/C++ Manuals, Object International, Stuttgart, 1995.

Session 2: Architectural Description

Dewayne Perry[1], Jeff Kramer[2]

[1]Bell Laboratories, 600 Mountain Avenue
Murray Hill, NJ 07974, USA
dep@research.bell-labs.com
[2]Dept. of Computing, Imperial College of Science, Technology and Medicine
180 Queens Gate, London SW7 2BZ, UK
jk@doc.ic.ac.uk

1. Main Issues

The main issues identified in the area and which were selected for discussion are listed below:

- Basic models for product line descriptions (PLDs)
  - what are the first class description components?
  - how is `form' described?
  - how is the rationale for the architectural elements/decisions described?
  - is the architectural instance description (AID) language different from PLD language?
- Generic Descriptions
  - when and how do you move from the business domain to the solution domain?
  - what are the language structures to describe
    - shared architectural elements
    - product specific architectural elements
  - how are the architectural instance descriptions (AIDs) instantiated or derived from the PLDs
- Use of PLDs
  - what forms of analysis are supported
    - behavioural
    - non-functional
  - how well does the PLD support project planing for architecture based software development
    - at the PLD level
    - at the AID level
- Evolution of PLDs/AIDs
  - how is the relationship between the PLD and AIDs managed?
  - how do you maintain consistency between
    - the evolved PLD and the derived AIDs
    - the PLD and the evolved AIDs
    - evolved PLD and evolved AIDs

Frank v. d. Linden (Ed.): ARES '98, LNCS 1429, pp. 49-50, 1998.
© Springer-Verlag Berlin Heidelberg 1998

- how are the dependencies between architectural drivers and PLD managed (ie, how is the rationale evolved and maintained)

2. Discussion

Each of the papers in this session contributes to this area and addresses some of the above issues.

The paper by Peter van de Hamer et al at Philips describes their model which addresses complexity and product families through hierarchy and a means for describing diversity. The need to ensure compatibility between variants of the architecture could be addressed through the use of architectural constraints.

The Koala component model by Rob van Ommering of Philips provides insight into the use of components and modules for multi-system decomposition. One of the particularly interesting features of the model is the use of diversity interfaces as the means of controlling the specialisation of PLDs to AIDs. These exploit the binding mechanisms to decide where and when diversity parameters are set.

In the work of Nat Pryce and Steve Crane, support is provided for selectable, diverse interaction protocols. This is an integration of the Darwin ADL, Midas language for interaction definition and Regent platform for distributed computing. Bindings are elaborated into abstract interfaces and interaction protocols.

Jan Bosch raised issues related to problems of composing architectures - essentially the transfer of an architecture from use in one domain to another.

As a result of discussion, it was generally agreed that there was no need for different languages for the PLD and AID, and that the same architectural description should support both. However, there was some indication that an architecture description language (ADL) might be appropriate for only a particular application domain, and that different domains might require different languages. Finally, there was some discussion as to how ADLs, PLDs and AIDs should integrate with design notations such as the Unified Modelling Languges (UML). This was left as an open question

Generic Architecture Descriptions for Product Lines

Dewayne E. Perry

Bell Laboratories, 600 Mountain Avenue, Murray Hill, NJ 07974 USA
dep@research.bell-labs.com, www.bell-labs/com/usr/dep/

1 Introduction

Two of the fundamental needs in defining an architecture for a product line are

- to be able to generalize or abstract from the individual products to capture the important aspects of the product line and
- to be able to instantiate an individual product architecture from the product line architecture.

In other words, having a product line implies having a generic architecture from which the individual product architectures can be derived in some manner.

There are a number of different ways in which one might go about defining the product line architecture so that this desired level of genericity can be achieved. Five possible ways of doing this are

- use a software architecture style,
- use an under–constrained architecture description,
- define a variance–free architecture,
- use parametric descriptions with varying binding times, and
- use a service oriented description for selective provisioning.

In the end, I think you will need all of these for a systematic and complete generic product line architecture. I will discuss each of these in turn and delineate their strengths and weaknesses.

2 A Style as a Generic Architecture

There is a certain intuitive appeal in using a product line specific architectural style as the generic architecture for a product line. It would capture the essential characteristics of the product line while ignoring the variations and leave them to be supplied as needed in the actual product architecture. These essential characteristics would encompass the necessary components that each instance must have, the basic minimum interactions that each instance must have and the basic constraints on these components and interactions.

The utility of a style description is that it represents the minimalist approach to software architecture in general and product line architecture in specific. Only the critical aspects of the product line need to be considered in the architectural

Frank v. d. Linden (Ed.): ARES '98, LNCS 1429, pp. 51-56, 1998.

specification. One primary advantage is that new products can be added to the line with ease as long as they conform to the basic product line stylistic constraints. This provides a wide degree of latitude in the the various products and what they provide relative to the core essence of the product line.

One of the negative side effects of this approach is the amount of work needed to refine the product line style into a particular product architecture. With the intent of a style as capturing only the essential architectural aspects of the product line, those aspects must be extended and added to in order to create in individual product architecture. As such the product architecture must be analyzed for conformity to the product line architecture.

As a result of this lack of completeness other aspects of architectural based development suffer as well. For example, analysis of the product line architecture will, of necessity, be less comprehensive. Project planning will be similarly less comprehensive at the product line level and the majority of planning work will be delayed until after a complete product architecture has been extended from the core style.

Further care must be taken in evolving the product line's architectural style so as not to invalidate existing product architectures. With each change to the product line style, the individually derived product architectures will have to be re–analyzed to ensure that the product architectures remain conforming to the style.

On the whole there are better uses of styles for product line architectures than defining the generic product line architecture itself. For example, one could define a set of styles defining such things as initialization, fault recovery, etc that all the various components in the architecture must adhere to.

3   An Under–Constrained Architecture as a Generic Architecture

The difference between an architectural style and an under–constrained architecture is a subtle one. The difference is fundamentally the difference in the completeness of the architectural description. A style is meant to focus on certainly critical features and isolate them from non–essential and non–stylistic features. There is no requirement for completeness of an architectural description in any way.

With an under–constrained architecture the idea is to capture the product line as completely as possible but in such a way that the variations are not ruled out by overly constraining the architecture. The variance is within the confines of the architectural constraints, not within the aspects that have not been defined.

This approach goes a long way towards solving the weaknesses of the stylistic approach in terms of analysis and planning at the product line level. Further it is much easier to create a product architecture from the product line architecture. However, it is still not a simple matter to produce the product architecture from the product line architecture (it is still primarily a creative process as with styles but one which has marrower bounds) and one will have to analyze the product architecture to ensure its conformance to the product line constraints.

This approach seems to be an appropriate one to use if the primary difference among the products is something like performance and in which the functionality is primarily the same. On the negative side, extending the product line is a significantly more constraining task. Unless you evolve the product line architecture, the new products must be definable within the current constraints. In evolving the under–constrained product line architecture, care must be taken in its expansion not to inadvertently nullify current products as constituents of the line through the addition of further components or constraints. Constraint relaxation, of course, does not cause such a problem.

4   A Variance–Free Architecture as a Generic Architecture

Again the differences between this and the preceding ones are subtle. Here the architecture is not under–constrained. It is instead a fully described architecture but one in which the variances among the products are not considered to architecturally important – that is, the product differences are an issue of design and implementation, not an issue of architecture.

This approach is useful when your product line spans a significant range of options with respect to a particular aspect. One such example is that of whether the system is centralized or distributed. If the products range from simple centralized systems through to complex multi–processor and distributed processor systems, then this characteristic of the system might well be one that you want to bury in the infrastructure and not have as an important architectural issue. In this case, you might want to have a distribution independent architecture. Distribution then becomes an implementation or even a administrative issue, but not an architectural issue.

What is interesting in this case is that there is a significant implication for the implementation to support this kind of variance independence. To make the architecture independent of issues of distribution implies a class of architectural components which will support that independence.

Another example might be platform independence. Here again, there is an implication about what the structure of part of the architecture must be in order to bury the actual platform specific aspects in the design and implementation rather than have them visible at the architectural level.

There is a significant appeal in this approach. Analysis and planning can be done at the product line architecture level. If the right product characteristics are made independent of the architecture, then new products can be derived from the product line architecture with relative ease merely by providing the appropriate implementation specific components in the design and coding phase in such a way that they conform to the product line architecture. The individual product architecture is the product line architecture; there is no derivation involved. Evolution of the product line architecture implies evolution of the product architectures.

Because of the identity of the product and product lines architectures, issues of analysis and planning at the product line level apply to the product level.

The downside of this approach is that it may not be possible to isolate all the variations in this way. Certain properties such as distribution, fault–tolerance, etc may be amenable to this, but differing functionality may not be.

Another negative aspect is the standard specification problem of talking about what is not there.

5   A Parametric Architecture as a Generic Architecture

A standard approach for generalizing is that of parametric abstraction. The parameterized component is then applicable across a wide range of arguments (in programming languages defined typically by types). The limits of applicability depend on the constraints that are checked on those arguments. That partly depends on the type system and what is allowed as a first class parameter types. For example, in Ada generics, the range of types usable as parameters is larger than for functions and procedures. In macro languages there are typically no constraints at all. But then there is no guaranteed substitution safety either.

The utility of this approach is the same as for packages and operations: the architecture specification defines a family of possible instantiations and for which the properties of the product line can be ensured for the various instantiations. The variations required for each possible product in the line are well–defined and known. Moreover, the instantiation of a specific product architecture is a well–understood technology and the instance can be derived automatically from the argumented product line description.

Here again, analysis and planning are doable at the product line rather than the product level.

Evolution of the parameters may seriously affect individual product architectures. If the evolution is limited to broading the types of the parameters, or perhaps upward–compatibly extending the parameters, then the individual product architectures should remain valid.

There are two limiting factors. First the kinds of the parameters allowed may seriously affect how well the generic architecture serves to cover the necessary products. If the kinds of first class objects are too limited, then one may not have sufficient descriptive power to satisfactorily describe the product line. Second is the question of whether parameterization covers all the kinds of variation that one might need to have among the products in a product line. We have seen examples above that suggest that parametric approaches are not sufficient in and of themselves.

6   A Service Oriented Architecture as a Generic Architecture

One of the typical kinds of problems found in developing such large and complex systems such as telephone switches is the need to provision the various products with different features. Provisioning these systems is not the kind of thing that can be done with parametric or variation independent approaches. One can always of course do it with either styles or under–constrained descriptions, but that does not help much if one wants these provisioned features to be architectural features.

Thus an approach to describing a product line architecture is one in which the various architectural services that may be provisioned are defined as part of the architecture and are then selected in an instantiation process to define a particular product. One advantage of this approach is that the possibilities are explicit in a more tangible way than in a parametric approach. Moreover, if done properly, the architectural dependencies of these services are also made explicit and the implications of choices are thus more explicit.

As with the parametric approach, instantiation is accomplished with well–understood technology. Analysis and planning both can be done relative to the product line description with the added advantage that the planning of a specific product can be derived from the product line planning itself via the selection mechanism of provisioning.

As long as the evolution of the product line architecture is done via the addition of new services, existing product architectures will remain valid instances of the new product line architecture.

While this goes a long way towards a useful approach for provisioned products, it is likely to be insufficient in itself for a complete product line specification.

7   Putting The Pieces Together

I think it is clear at this point that a comprehensive approach to defining a generic architecture for a product line requires all of these different ways of addressing various product line issues.

Styles are certainly needed for aspects of the product line that are orthogonal to the specific component structure. For example, one may want to define a style for initialization or fault handling that must be satisfied by all the components in a product line to ensure appropriate cross–product use.

Under–constrained descriptions always provide a wider degree of flexibility than over–constrained ones. Clearly some aspects of a product line will be best served by this approach where large degrees of design and implementation freedom are useful to respond to such things as changes in technology.

The variation–independent architecture is certainly needed where you want to delay such considerations as platform or distribution until build time or even execution time.

Parametric and provisioning approaches are again obviously useful for various kinds of generic descriptions and provide the most direct means of deriving their product architecture from the product line architectures.

8 Summary

I have considered a variety of useful ways of 'genericizing' architectural descriptions (or prescriptions). I claim that a generic architecture is a fundamental requirement for a product line and that each of these approaches is needed as a means of defining some important elements in such a generic architecture.

A Model of Interaction in Concurrent and Distributed Systems[1]

Nat Pryce[1] and Steve Crane[2]

[1]Department of Computing, Imperial College
np2@doc.ic.ac.uk
[2]Systems Architecture Research Centre, City University
jsc@cs.city.ac.uk

Abstract. Distributed programming environments commonly restrict programmers to one form of intercomponent interaction. This forces programmers to emulate other interaction styles in terms of the dominant paradigm, obscuring their intent and resulting in a loss of clarity. Starting from a clear model of interaction between program components, this paper attempts to restore this missing clarity of intent. It achieves this by proposing a language tailored to the description of new and existing interaction styles that separates the specification of intercomponent interaction from the programming interface visible internally to the component.

1 Introduction

Distributed programming environments usually restrict programmers to a single form of interaction between system components. Remote Procedure Call [BN84] and its object-oriented descendents [OMG95,Rog97] are popular because they generalise the familiar centralised intercomponent interaction, provided by the programming language, into one between address spaces. However, distributed programs are quite unlike centralised programs. In this paper, we concentrate on one difference: concurrency. Since it is constrained to a single address space, a centralised program typically possesses a single thread of control. When concurrent, its threads communicate using shared data and use monitors or semaphores for synchronisation and mutual exclusion.

A distributed program, on the other hand, is always multi-threaded. When the motivation for distribution is the exploitation of parallelism, RPC imposes "too much policy by enforcing an explicit two-way synchronisation on every communication" [FKT94]. Middleware designed for the development of efficient parallel programs declines RPC in favour of asynchronous message passing [MPIF93].

---

[1] This research funded by British Telecom as part of the Management of Multiservice Networks project.

Frank v. d. Linden (Ed.): ARES '98, LNCS 1429, pp. 57-65, 1998.
© Springer-Verlag Berlin Heidelberg 1998

If the middleware does not support more than one interaction style, programmers are forced to implement the required styles in terms of the dominant paradigm. While this is possible [LN79], it is often error-prone and obscures the programmer's intent, impeding clarity.

2 Component Interaction

Before an interaction between two components can occur, their interfaces must be bound together. This binding action is often specified in an architecture-description language[2]. This section briefly describes our model of component and binding semantics.   Salient features are illustrated with examples using the Darwin architecture-description language [MDEK95]. Although Darwin lends a brevity and clarity to architectural description, the core ideas are applicable in general, even to implicitly-configured systems.

2.1   The Component Model

A component is a unit of distributed program structure that encapsulates its implementation behind a strict interface comprised of services *provided* by the component to other components in the system and services *required* by the component and implemented by other components. The explicit declaration of a component's requirements increases component reuse by decoupling components from their operating environment.

A program is constructed through composition: components are instantiated and services required by each component are *bound* to those provided by other components in the system. Once two components are bound, they can interact through the communication endpoints at each end of the binding. In addition to directionality, a service provision or requirement also specifies a *type* defining the semantics of the interaction and increasing clarity by expressing the component programmer's intent.

Structural complexity is managed through hierarchical composition: *composite* components are defined in terms of other components. While algorithmic components are always found at the leaves of the composition tree, composites may partially or completely expose the interfaces of their contained instances, thereby providing *structural transparency*: whether a component is primitive or composite is encapsulated within the component. Compositions can be specified using an architecture description language, such as Darwin. Architecture definition languages enforce a strict separation between the algorithmic and structural concerns of the system and aid programmers by generating the code to instantiate configurations.

A feature of Darwin is the correspondence between its graphical and textual notations. While the textual notation is richer, supporting conditionals and

---

[2]   Also known as a configuration language, coordination language or module interconnection language.

iterations, the graphical form is a convenient shorthand for a program's *instance structure* for a particular parameterisation.

Example: Mobile Telephony

A GSM telephone network [GSM92] is composed of a number of *mobile switching centres* (msc) each responsible for providing connectivity and billing services in a particular domain. The structure of an msc is described by the following *Darwin* code and depicted in Figure 1. When a mobile phone is created, it announces itself on the *mobile* interface, the switch creates a "home location record" for it and instantiates a pop, the phone's point-of-presence in the network. Then switch connects the mobile into the network by binding its interfaces to its pop. Additionally, switch provides an interface, *roam*, over which existing phones are "handed over" to it. While it also creates a pop in response to a *roam* stimulus, it does not create a home location record, instead it requests the mobile's home switch to update it.

```
component msc (int ns) {
    require n[ns];
    inst switch s;
    bind mobile -- s.mobile;
    bind net -- s.net;
    bind roam -- s.roam;
    bind s.create -- dyn pop;
    forall i=0 to (ns-1) {
        bind dyn pop.nets[i] -- n[i];
    }
}
```

Figure 1. The internal structure of a mobile switching centre

In this example, a GSM network is comprised of a fully-connected set of switches; the network component is parameterised by the number of mscs to instantiate; a configuration of three mscs is shown in Figure 2. The network exposes each msc's *mobile, roam* and *phone* interfaces to the top level component, the gsm *system*, also depicted in Figure 2.

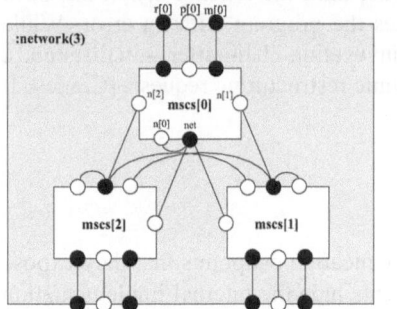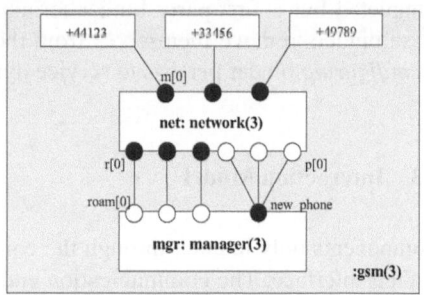

Figure 2. A network of switching centres (left) and the entire gsm system (right)

When the program represented by this configuration is run, an anonymous instance of the root component, gsm, is created. This creates network and manager instances and exports each of network's mobile interfaces into a global namespace so that external programs (i.e., the mobile phones themselves) may bind to them. The function of manager is to maintain a window on behalf of each msc showing the mobile phones currently active in each domain. It also permits roaming to be simulated by dragging a mobile from one window and dropping it into another, hence its bindings to the network's *roam* interfaces. When a new mobile announces itself to its home network, manager is notified on its *new_phone* interface and creates a new icon for it in its home window.

2.2   Binding Actions

In our model, the establishment of a binding between endpoints can be classified by one of two idioms named for the originator of the binding action [CDFK95]. A *first-party* binding is initiated by the component in the client role of the ensuing interaction. A *third-party* binding is established by an entity which is neither client nor server.

Third-party binding arises most often in the elaboration of a configuration description; it serves to create an initial 'binding harness' out of components' public interfaces. The first-party idiom exploits this binding harness to permit evolution of dynamic binding patterns between components' private interfaces. Modern distributed programming environments [OMG95,Rog97] often only recognise the need for first-party binding, with third-party binding relegated to support for reconfiguration [Fried87].

Irrespective of its originator, a valid binding action must conform to two rules which support the intuitive notion of a requirement as a placeholder for the service to which it is bound: the bound interfaces must be of the same type and compatible roles and a required interface may only be bound to one peer, although many required interfaces may have the same peer.

The semantics of accessing an unbound requirement are determined by its *binder*. A third-party binder blocks its invoker until the binding action has been completed but a first-party binder terminates the program with an error. While these binders remove themselves from the invocation chain after initialisation, a *reconfiguring* binder persists to service dynamic restructuring requests [Crane97].

2.3   Interaction Model

Components only interact through the communication endpoints that they expose at their interface. The communication endpoints hide the internal implementation of the component from outside, and provide *distribution transparency* to the component implementation.

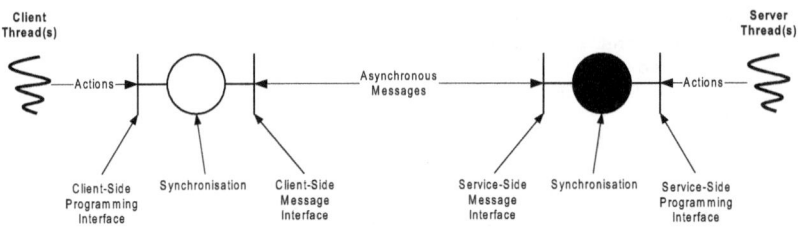

Figure 3. Model of Interaction

An interaction between two communication endpoints, a service endpoint and a client endpoint, can be defined in terms of the messages accepted by the service (the server-side message interface), the messages that the service requires the client to accept (the client-side message interface), the synchronisation of threads at those endpoints and the programming abstractions through which those threads view the interaction (termed the client- and -server-side programming interfaces)

The messages define an application-layer protocol by which components communicate over a binding; a pair of message interfaces constitutes a contract [Meyer88] between two endpoints. That is, a service guarantees to react meaningfully to messages received from a client as long as those messages are within the service's accepted message set and as long as the client reacts meaningfully when the service sends it messages that are within the service's required message set. Further constraints upon the interaction can be specified using state machines, specified separately for each endpoint of the interaction.

3 A Language for the Definition of Interactions

We have defined a language, Midas, for the definition of interactions in terms of message interfaces and state machines. Midas specifications are compiled into implementation language constructs that define message interfaces and provide distribution transparency. Midas is based upon CORBA IDL [OMG95] in that it uses IDL syntax for constant and type definitions. It is straightforward to translate IDL definitions into Midas interaction specifications.

The example code below shows how Rendezvous is specified in Midas and illustrates the main features of the language.

```
interaction Rendezvous <type T> {
    messages ServiceMsgs { data( T value ); }
    messages ClientMsgs  { wake(); }

    endpoint Client : in ClientMsgs, out ServiceMsgs {
        actions { send }
        spec {
            CLIENT = READY,
                READY = (send -> out.data -> BLOCKED),
                BLOCKED = (in.wake -> READY | send -> ERROR). }
    }
```

```
endpoint Service : in ServiceMsgs, out ClientMsgs {
    actions { read }
    spec {
        SERVICE = (in.data -> read -> out.wake -> SERVICE).  }
}

Client provide;
Service require;
spec { ||RENDEZVOUS = (CLIENT || CHANNEL || SERVICE). }
}
```

The interaction statement introduces a new interaction type, Rendezvous, parameterised by the type of data passed from client to service. The body of the interaction statement contains nested definitions. The messages statements define the message interfaces as sets of named, parameterised messages, similar to IDL interfaces except that messages are always one-way: they do not return a value and only take input parameters. The endpoint statement defines an endpoint in terms of the messages received and transmitted it, the actions that can be performed upon it via it's API and a state machine that defining its behaviour, specified in FSP notation [Magee97].

4 Implementation of Midas Endpoints

A specification defines the externally visible attributes of an interaction but does not define how those interactions are implemented within a component. Those details are encapsulated by the component and depend on the details of the component's implementation: the synchronisation of threads within a component and the programming abstractions visible to the component's threads are outside the scope of Midas.

A Midas specification is compiled into code which defines the abstract message interfaces for each end of the interaction in the implementation language, e.g. a C++ abstract class. The generated message interfaces contain one operation for each of the messages accepted at the interface, operations to support binding client-side endpoints and operations for memory management and garbage collection.

A developer provides reusable endpoint abstractions to component programmers, by defining classes that implement the abstract interfaces, provide a programming interface to the interaction and perform thread synchronisation.

In addition to the abstract message interfaces, the Midas compiler generates proxies supporting distribution transparency. These proxies are independent of any particular implementation of the message interfaces and perform marshalling and unmarshalling of message data.

4.1 Interactions between Concurrent Components

Midas can describe and implement interactions between concurrent components in the same address space. The generated abstract message interfaces are used by the developer to implement the programming abstractions visible within components. The threading model used within the component is independent of the type of interaction used: the same role of an interaction can be implemented in many different ways each substitutable for any other.

A client endpoint is bound to a service endpoint using a pointer to the message interface of the service endpoint. Because endpoints implement the abstract message interface, any implementation of a client-side message interface can be bound to any implementation of a service-side message interface as long as they are opposite roles of the same interaction type. Developers may implement the operations of the message interfaces in any way they like as long as their implementation supports message passing asynchrony. This constrains the implementation of an endpoint: it must not cause threads that call the operations of its message interface to block within the endpoint object. Synchronisation between threads can only be implemented in terms of asynchronous messages passed across the binding. An endpoint object that synchronises the calling thread with threads at the other end of its binding must use encapsulated synchronisation objects, such as semaphores. The calling thread must invoke an operation on the bound message interface and then wait on a semaphore that it owns. When another thread delivers a message to the endpoint, it can wake the blocked thread by signaling the semaphore, as shown in Figure 4.

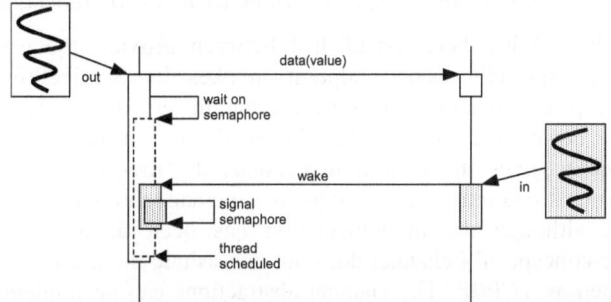

Figure 4. Thread Synchronisation for the Rendezvous Interaction

4.2   Interactions between Distributed Components

The model of binding and interaction in a single address space extends between address spaces, providing distribution transparency through the use of proxy objects [GHJV94]. Because messages can be sent in either direction at any time, depending on the current state of the sending endpoint, a proxy is required at each end of a binding: a ServiceProxy provides the illusion that the service endpoint is within the same address space as the client endpoint and a ClientProxy providing a similar illusion. Proxies are connected by a communication channel.

When components in different address spaces need to interact, the client endpoint is bound to a ServiceProxy, created in the client's address space and connected by some transport channel to a remote service endpoint. The ServiceProxy implements the service-side message interface of the interaction and, to the client, is indistinguishable from a true service endpoint.

For a service endpoint to be able to interact with remote clients, it must make use of some uniquely identified transport-level service access point (TSAP) through which it can accept connections. This TSAP is managed by an interaction-specific Acceptor object [Schmidt97] that accepts transport-level connection requests from remote clients and creates a ClientProxy to manage each connection. Acceptor classes for each interaction type are generated automatically by the Midas compiler.

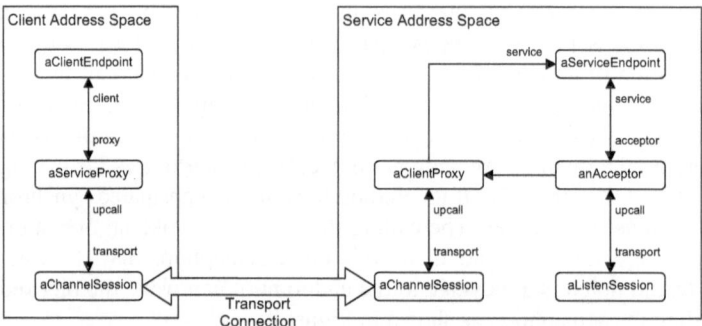

Figure 5. Proxies and Acceptors Provide Distribution Transparency

Once a channel has been established between proxies, the endpoints can interact. When the client-side endpoint invokes its ServiceProxy message interface, the proxy marshals the message parameters into a data buffer and transmits the buffer over the channel. When the ClientProxy in the service's address space receives the data it unmarshals the message and invokes the appropriate operation on the service endpoint's message interface.

Note that although the implementation has been described in terms of channels, the concept of a channel does not necessitate the use of channel-based protocols, such as TCP/IP. The channel abstractions can be implemented using light-weight adaptor objects layered above packet-based protocols, such as UDP/IP, or implemented using shared memory within the same host.

5 Related Work

The *Open Distributed Processing Reference Model* [ODP95] specifies three kinds of interaction: asynchronous *signals, flows* or streams, and *operations* or remote procedure call. The model describes two kinds of binding action, *primitive* which links the endpoints directly and *compound* which interposes a *binding object*. A primitive binding action requires the endpoints to be compatible: of the same interaction type and opposite polarity. In a compound binding action, a series of primitive binding actions links each of the endpoints to the mediating binding object which, for example, may adapt incompatible interactions, or allow management operations or quality-of-service control to be performed on the end-to-end binding. The model enforces no correspondence between the initiator of a binding action and the objects which communicate over the resulting binding, somewhat obliquely recognising the utility of third-party binding.

References

BN84   A. Birrell and B. Nelson. *Implementing Remote Procedure Calls*. ACM
            Transactions on Computer Systems, 2(1): 39-59, February 1984.

CDFK95   S. Crane, N. Dulay, H. Fosså, J. Kramer, J. Magee, M. Sloman and K. Twidle.
            Configuration Management for Distributed Software Services. In Y. Raynaud,
            A. Sethi and F. Faure-Vincent, editors, Integrated Network Management IV,
            pps 29-42. Chapman and Hall, 1995.

Crane97   S. Crane. *Dynamic Binding for Distributed Systems*. PhD Thesis, Imperial
            College, University of London, March 1997.

FKT94   I. Foster, C. Kesselman and S. Tuecke. *Nexus: Runtime Support for Task-
            Parallel Programming Languages*. Technical Report, Mathematics and
            Computer Science Division, Argonne National Laboratory, Argonne Il.
            60439, August 1994.

Fried87   S. Friedberg. *Transparent Reconfiguration requires a Third-Party Connect*.
            Technical Report 220, Department of Computer Science, University of
            Rochester, November 1987.

GHJV94   E. Gamma, R. Helm, R. Johnson and J. Vlissides. *Design Patterns: Elements
            of Reusable Object-Oriented Software*. Addison-Wesley. 1994.

GSM92   M. Mouly and M.-B. Pautet. *The GSM System for Mobile Communications*.
            ISBN 2-9507190-0-7. 1992.

LN79   H. Lauer and R. Needham. *On the Duality of Operating System Structures*.
            Operating Systems Review, 13(2): 3-19, April 1979.

Magee97   J. Magee. *FSP Notation*. Electronic document available on the World Wide
            Web at the URL http://www-dse.doc.ic.ac.uk/~jnm/LTSdocumention/FSP-
            notation.html

MDEK95   J. Magee, N. Dulay, S. Eisenbach and J. Kramer. *Specifying Distributed
            Software Architectures*. In Proceedings of the Fifth European Software
            Engineering Conference, Barcelona, September 1995.

Meyer88   B. Meyer. *Object-Oriented Software Construction*. Prentice-Hall
            International Series in Computer Science, 1988.

MGK96   K. Moazami-Goudarzi and Jeff Kramer. *Maintaining Node Consistency in the
            Face of Dynamic Change*. In Proc. of the 3rd International Conference on
            Configurable Distributed Systems, pp. 62-69, IEEE Computer Society Press,
            Annapolis Maryland, U.S.A, May 1996.

MPIF93   Message Passing Interface Forum, University of Tennessee, Knoxville,
            Tennessee. *Document for a Standard Message-Passing Interface*, 1993.

ODP95   Secretariat: ISO/IEC JTC1/SC21/WG7. *Reference Model of Open Distributed
            Processing, part 3: Architecture*. Document ITU-T X.903 (ISO/IEC 10746-3),
            Standards Association of Australia, PO Box 1055, Strathfield, NSW, Australia
            2135, May 1995.

OMG95   The Object Management Group, *The Common Object Request Broker:
            Architecture and Specification, Version 2.0*. The Object Management Group,
            OMG Headquarters, 492 Old Connecticut Path, Framington, MA 01701,
            USA. July 1995.

Rog97   D. Rogerson. *Inside COM – Microsoft's Component Object Model*. Microsoft
            Press, 1997.

Schmidt97   D.C. Schmidt, *Acceptor and Connector: Design Patterns for Actively and
            Passively Initializing Network Services*. In *Pattern Languages of Program
            Design*, Reading, MA, Addison-Wesley, 1997.

SV97   D. C. Schmidt and S. Vinoski. *Object Adapters: Concepts and Terminology*.
            Object Interconnections #11, SIGS C++ Report, October 1997.

An Integral Hierarchy and Diversity Model for Describing Product Family Architectures[†]

Peter van den Hamer[1], Frank van der Linden[1], Alison Saunders[2]
and Henk te Sligte[1]

[1]Philips Research Laboratories, Prof Holstlaan 4
5656 AA Eindhoven, Netherlands
{vdhamer, flinden, tesligte}@natlab.research.philips.com
[2]Philips Medical Systems, Veenpluis 6
5684 PC Best, The Netherlands
alison.saunders@best.ms.philips.com

Abstract. Formal and informal methods for describing software architectures traditionally focus on a system's components and the interfaces between these components. They assume a design process in which the architect basically defines the architecture of a *single* product. If *variants* of this product are required, they are either handled implicitly or are defined at a later stage. Since industrial development processes which result in families of products are becoming increasingly common, there is a need for architectural models and notations in which diversity is modelled as *an explicit and integral part of the architecture definition process*. We believe that the use of such models can promote the overall optimisation of product families and can facilitate validation of architectural decisions. This paper presents a model which can be used to describe and manage architectures in a number of product family-oriented design processes

1. Introduction

1.1 Product families

Industrial organisations increasingly need to develop software or software embedded in hardware systems in multiple variants. This product diversity can be necessary to accommodate different levels of functionality, regional requirements or differences in preference between market segments. A major challenge for the

---

[†] Parts of this work have been performed within the ESPRIT project 20477, ARES: Architectural Reasoning for Embedded Systems

Frank v. d. Linden (Ed.): ARES '98, LNCS 1429, pp. 66-75, 1998.
© Springer-Verlag Berlin Heidelberg 1998

architect of such a product family is thus to satisfy the required commercial diversity while limiting the number of software components which need to be specified, implemented and tested.

The potential business benefits of family-oriented product development are significant: decreased development effort due to component reuse and the opportunity to optimise the overall family (global optimisation). In addition, product family development tends to go hand in hand with the validation of whether an architecture is future-proof: if one has explicitly considered the impact of various optional features, this tends to increase the likelihood that the architecture can accommodate unanticipated requirements.

1.2 Diversity-aware architecture models

Unfortunately, although many organisations employ (often implicit) forms of family-oriented product development, this does have its price. It requires the software architect to take yet another factor into account during the design of the architecture. In addition it requires the organisation to make its planned commercial diversity explicit in an early stage of the product development process.

Family-oriented product development poses thus considerable demands on the ability of an organisation to internally communicate. We therefore believe that the methods and tools used by architects to describe software architectures should explicitly accommodate the diversity or variant dimension [7] of architecture design. This supports the architect when dealing with this complex web of information. It also gives the other stakeholders the opportunity to validate the architect's plans from the perspective of their field of expertise.

1.3 Goals of model

In this paper we describe a model for representing the architecture of a family of technically related products. To visualise examples of such architectures, we use a simple graphical notation. We want to focus on the underlying model, rather than on the various somewhat arbitrary graphical or syntactical elements of a particular notation.

With this model we attempt to satisfy the following main goals:
1. The model should cover system *hierarchy* or system composition as well as component *diversity*.
2. The model should be *unambiguous* because it serves as a means of communication about strategic information between persons with a wide variety of backgrounds.
3. The model should cover a broad range of family-oriented software *development styles and processes*.
4. *Minimal training* should be required to learn how to interpret the model's concepts and notation.
5. The model should be compatible with *mainstream methods* for designing hardware and software systems.

6. The model should be sufficiently general in the sense that it can be applied for software systems, hardware systems and mixed *hardware/software* systems.

With respect to the last goal, it is worth pointing out this model is the result of a larger project within Philips in which the impact of product families and diversity was analysed in software development, Printed Circuit Board design, and system design.

2. Hierarchy and Diversity Model

2.1   Hierarchy-only models

Architectures of software systems are complex to describe and involve multiple aspects of the design. By most definitions, e.g. [5][6][10][12], an architectural model describes how a system is decomposed

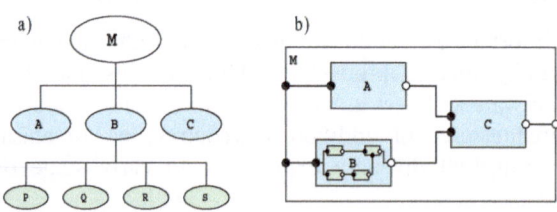

Figure 1 Representing Hierarchy of an Architecture

into smaller subsystems. Such decomposition is typically displayed as a tree or as nested boxes. Figure 1a shows the hierarchical decomposition of system M into three subsystems A, B and C. Subsystem B is further decomposed into elements P, Q, R and S.

Figure 1b shows the same decomposition, but also shows how the various subsystems relate or interface to each other. Such a graphical diagram is typically augmented with extra textual information about this relationship e.g. the name or type of the interface or which functions are part of it. The interface notation in this diagram is inspired by the interfaces representations in Darwin [9]. The hollow and solid circles represent interfaces with "opposite polarity" (e.g. interfaces which provide a service and interfaces which require a service).

Note that both representations in Figure 1 denote a hierarchy-only model of the architecture e.g. system M always contains the same B which always contains the same Q. The model thus describes the structure of a single product. In the following sections we will explain via stepwise refinement our model for describing the architecture of families of products or software systems.

2.2   Modelling Hierarchy and Diversity

In our model we combine two major aspects of product family architectures, namely the product's hierarchical decomposition and the variations that are supported by the product family. This is shown in Figure 2, using a schematic example. We will use every day examples from the automotive world to ease overall understanding of our model.

As in Figure 1, a system named M.1 (Figure 2a) is hierarchically decomposed into components named A, B and C. For example a family of economy cars is stated to have a chassis A, a transmission B and an engine C. Unlike the model shown in Figure 1, our model in Figure 2 explicitly distinguishes between *abstract* components (shown in dark) and component *variants* (shown in white). An abstract component is essentially a partially defined component (e.g. the concept "engine"). Figure 2a thus states that any member of this car family has an engine. It does not state exactly what type of engine is used because the design is assumed to support multiple types of engines.

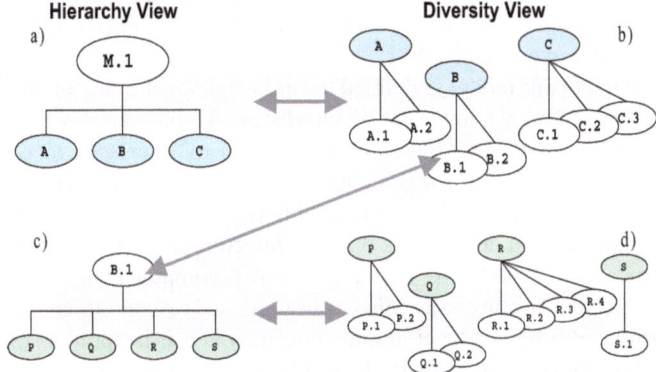

Figure 2 Hierarchy and Diversity

Figure 2b shows that the abstract component transmission (B) can be one of 2 components (e.g. manual and automatic transmission). Compared to an abstract component, a component variant is more fully specified. Another way of looking at this is that an abstract component is a place-holder for one or more implementations ("component variants") of the same basic idea or design. As shown in Figure 2b, the car family supports 2 different chassis, 2 different transmissions and 3 different engines.

A particular component variant (e.g. manual transmission B.1) can have a known internal structure. Here B.1 consists of (abstract) components P, Q, R and S. Note that component variant B.2 will generally have a different structure (not shown) which may or may not share (abstract) components used in B.1.

Our model is fully recursive in the sense that B.1 may itself be a family of manual transmissions. This family has a fixed structure in terms of abstract components (Figure 2c), but achieves its diversity by supporting alternative variants for the lower level components. Note that on the one hand Figure 2b states that there are 2 variants (B.1 and B.2) of the abstract component B. On the other hand Figure 2d indicates that B.1 is actually a collection of (more precisely defined) variants because it contains 3 selectable components (P, Q and R) and 1 fixed component (S).

The recursion in our model is characterised by a Z-pattern as shown in Figure 2. The example shows only 2 levels in the hierarchy, but our model supports any number of levels. However, in practice it is very well possible that the diversity view at some levels may get somewhat degraded, because each abstract component has only one variant.

2.3   Adding interfaces

Another ingredient of our model is that we use *interfaces* to link the components of a hierarchical decomposition. Figure 3 shows the same sample product family, but in a more elaborate/detailed notation. The small circles on the border of the component rectangles represent component interfaces. The lines connecting these interfaces show how the (abstract) components are interrelated in the family architecture. Example: the chassis (A) and the transmission (B) directly interface to the engine (C) in car family M.1

An interface in our model is defined as an independent item, and thus reusable. Each component has a known set of interfaces. A component which is used in multiple contexts will have the same collections of interfaces in each context. Interfaces are typed and components can only be linked via "compatible" interfaces. The advantage of having typed interfaces is that rules can be defined to verify a certain level of correctness of an architecture. By regarding interfaces as a property of a component it is easier to reuse a component in another context. Interfaces treated in this way also allow us to reason about a component independently of a higher level architecture in which it is applied. Example: the engine and/or transmission can also be used in other car families.

2.4   Constraining Combinations

In the previous sections we introduced abstract components as place-holders for component variants. In some ideal case, it may be possible to combine each component variant with every variant of the other abstract components in an architecture, resulting in maximum flexibility. Figure 3b shows that combining component variants without any restriction will result in a total of 12 (=2x2x3)

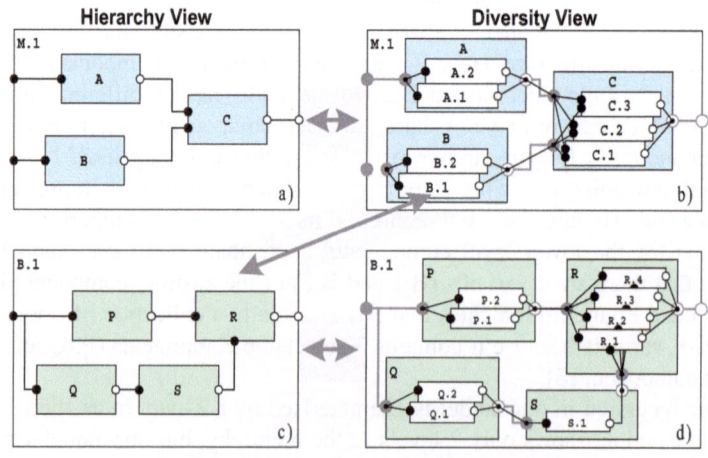

Figure 3 Adding interface information

possible configurations for product family M.1. E.g. our car model may come in 12 main variants involving 2 different chassis variants, 2 different transmissions and 3 different engines.

In practice, however, there may be all kinds of reasons that make particular combinations of components unfeasible. A common way to handle combinations is to use interface information: whether or not 2 components can be combined can often be related to their interfaces. To handle such cases we do not use the implicit connections between the abstract components (as shown in the diversity views of Figure 3). In our model, feasible combinations of component variants are expressed by explicitly connecting their interfaces as shown in Figure 4. Incompatible interfaces are simply not connected in the diversity view of a family (e.g. A.2 and C.2 cannot be combined).

Although this mechanism is intuitive and handles many of the restrictions found in practice, it cannot handle situations where components do not have a common interface (e.g. A and B in Figure 4) or where more than two components are involved. To handle such cases, we have

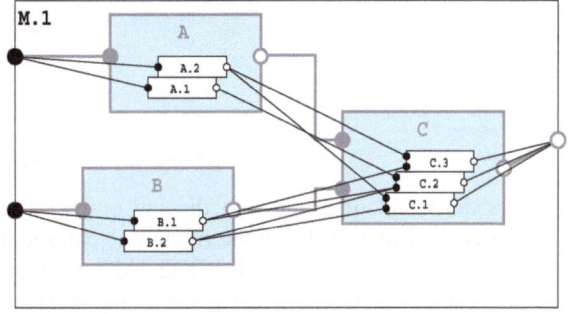

Figure 4 Feasible Component Combinations

added simple rules called *constraints* to our model. A constraint can express for example that certain component variants must always occur in combination or may never occur in combination. E.g. the automatic transmission variant may never be combined with the simple chassis variant. Note that there is no graphical notation for constraints in our model. The scope of this paper does not allow us to discuss constraints in more detail.

2.5   Individual Configurations

The graphical representation of a product family architecture in our model can also be used nicely to "browse" or "query" the architecture, assuming that the model is supported by a tool. One such query could be to show or highlight the component variants that together constitute a particular configuration. Figure 5

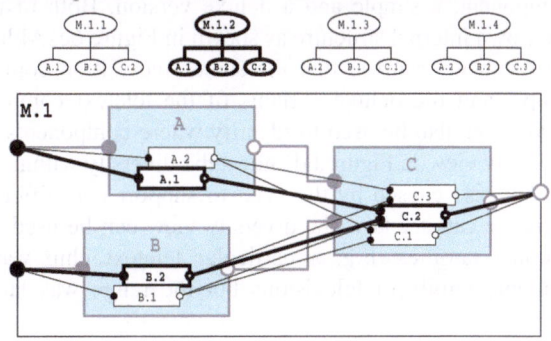

Figure 5 Highlighting an Individual Configuration

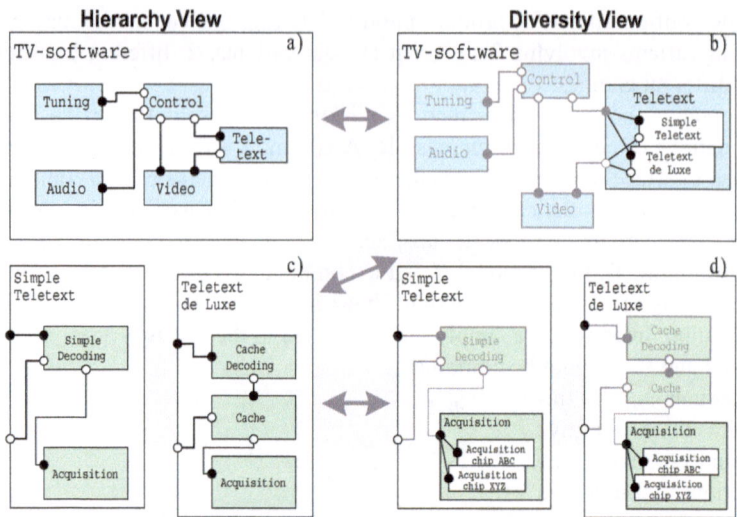

Figure 6 Diversity in TV Control Software

shows the result of a query to display or highlight configuration M.1.2 in the diversity view of M.1. From the figure one can see that this configuration consists of component variants A.1, B.2 and C.2. Another query could be to show all configurations in which a particular component variant or combination of two variants occurs.

3. A Software Example

Figure 6 shows an extremely simplified version of the control software for a family of television sets. For simplicity, only the diversity in the teletext[1] component is shown. Obviously, in practice diversity will also be present in many other components as well.

Figure 6a shows the most abstract level of the TV control software architecture. Moving to the diversity view in Figure 6b we see the diversity of the teletext component. It can be seen that there are two variants of the teletext component, a simple and a deluxe version. Both of these variants have in turn their own internal structure as shown in Figure 6c. Although their architectures are different, we can see that the same Acquisition component is used in both the simple and the deluxe variants of the teletext component. In other words, our model can also be used to identify where components can be *reused*. Finally, the diversity view in Figure 6d shows the diversity within the Acquisition component, in this case caused by the need to support two different types of teletext chips. Here we can see how the diversity view can be used to support the *evolution* of product families. E.g. a particular teletext chip was initially chosen for our example family of televisions but the range was later extended using a more

---

[1] Teletext is a system to transmit data (text and graphics) together with a TV picture.

advanced chip. By making both the architecture and the diversity explicit one can show the impact this has on the software, as well as help document the rationale behind the decision.

4. Discussion and Conclusions

Figure 6 above is just a simple example of how hierarchy and diversity can be integrated but should be sufficient to show how we have solved the first of the goals listed in the introduction. Our model allows hierarchical levels to be added in both directions: upwards and downwards. Extra levels can be added downwards to cope with complexity in the software, or upwards to describe a complete *system* as the top of the hierarchy. Further, by applying the model to cover other disciplines as well, the complete hardware and software architecture of a product family can be communicated and managed in a similar way (goal 6). In fact, the underlying ideas behind this paper, that both the hierarchy and diversity of a product family should be made explicit and that they should be handled recursively, were originally related to electronics development for consumer products.

Our approach differs from the idea of *variation points* as introduced by Jacobson et.al. [8]. Variation points serve another goal than we are aiming at. In particular the diversity supported by the variation points is hidden by the components themselves. One component may have several variation points and each may be designed in its own way. The variation points do not provide the hooks for managing the diversity of a complete product family. Our main point is to integrate the aspects of diversity and hierarchy to manage product families. We can imagine, however, that at the moment of design, variation points will be useful in expressing how the implementations of the components are related to each other, and how the recognised variation takes form.

In most approaches, e.g. [5][6][10][12], a software family architecture represents only a single hierarchy, where the variation is seen as an add-on feature. Often variation is modelled through inheritance, simple parameters, and/or optional parts. In our approach each variant gives rise to a complete sub-hierarchy. These sub-hierarchies may differ for each variant.

The GenVoca approach [2][3] separates between provides and requires interfaces. The requires interfaces are called the component parameters. Components that provides the same interface comprise a realm. By (recursively giving values to parameters hierarchical systems (including recursivity) may be built. Restrictions may be formulated that restrict the number of combinations that may be formed.

All these ingredients can be used to build systems described in our model. However, our approach is different from that of GenVoca, as follows. First, our aim is to put emphasis upon local views of the proposed and developed systems in the family. We show at each level what are the connections between the components that make up a higher level component. Thereby, our requires and provides interfaces differ from those of GenVoca. We use these interfaces for connections of components that build up a component of a higher level. A realm in the sense of GenVoca is equivalent to the kind of information showed in our diversity view. We do not use the term provides interface in that context.

We do not propose a general grammar view for our descriptions, as GenVoca proposes. Although we do not forbid recursive structure we also do not want to recommend them. We are usually dealing with systems with a fixed depth, the recursion is always limited. As with GenVoca we agree that we cannot use standard interfaces (our kind of interfaces!). We do not like to use an attribute grammar approach, as our model is aimed to facilitate the architect/developer, but not on automating the checks. Therefore, for us local view are crucial. We have presented here the most simple kind of restrictions, viz. those that can be visualised. Other restrictions can be described, but should preferably be described locally, and they should only be used with care.

Finally, our approach resembles the way in which integrated circuits are modelled in VHDL [1], a major hardware description language. In VHDL, the term "Entity" represents a design with a well-defined interface. An Entity can have one or more models (called "Architectures") which typically represent the Entity at different levels of abstraction (e.g. behaviour, register transfer, or gate level). An Architecture can contain component Entities. Although both models are structurally isomorphic on this point, VHDL deals with *alternative levels of abstraction* of a design ("views" in [7]) while our model covers intended to achieve diversity ("variants" in [7]).

One particularly important area for future work is investigating ways in which these ideas can be practised using mainstream development methods, such as UML, rather than using a specialised Architecture Description Language (goal 5). As explained by Robbins et. al. [11], while ADL's provide a great deal of expressive power, they are not well integrated with mainstream development methods. Consequently, if one describes the architecture using a dedicated ADL and, as we suggest here, continues the diversity analysis deep into the development phase, two different methods and notations will have to be used in parallel. This is not only *inefficient*, since the same information will have to be documented twice, it is also prone to *inconsistencies*, which is *unacceptable*. One solution would be to instigate consistency checking across the two methods but our preferred approach is to utilise and extend existing facilities within the mainstream development methods to model the diversity. A detailed discussion of this issue falls outside the scope of the paper.

Another issue that falls largely outside the scope of this paper is the impact that the approach has on the software development process and on the product creation process (goal 3). However, we would like to discuss two particular aspects in more detail. As mentioned above, the model is recursive, so one is able to work in either a top-down and a bottom-up manner. In practice these two approaches will be combined. On the one hand, new ideas will typically be developed in a top-down manner, starting with a fairly abstract idea and then adding the details. On the other hand certain features that have been developed for previous product families are already well understood so the details are known immediately, i.e. one can work in a bottom-up fashion, starting with the details and then working towards a complete system description.

Also, by explicitly managing the variants of a particular component, the idea of relatively independent development processes can be introduced. This is already common practice when one integrates 3rd party software, such as databases, into the product, but can now also be applied to proprietary reusable components.

Regarding goal 2, we have eliminated certain types of ambiguity by formalising [13] the structure of our model using semantic information modelling techniques [4].

Finally, we leave it to the reader to decide to what degree we have succeeded in achieving our goal 4 of intuitiveness and clarity.

5. References

[1]   Peter J. Ashenden, *The VHDL Cookbook*, First Edition, Dept. Computer Science, University of Adelaide, South Australia, July 1990

[2]   Don Batory, Sean O'Malley, *The Design and Implementation of Hierarchical Software Systems with Reusable Components*, ACM Transactions on Software Engineering and Methodology, 1 no. 4, pp. 355-398 (October 1992)

[3]   Don Batory, Bart J. Geraci, *Composition Validation and Subjectivity in GenVoca Generators*, IEEE Transactions on Software Engineering 23 no. 2, pp. 67-83 (February 1997)

[4]   J.H. ter Bekke, *Semantic Data Modelling*, Prentice Hall, ISBN 0-13-806050-9

[5]   Christina Gacek, Ahmed Abd-Allah, Bradford Clark, Barry Boehm, *On the Definition of Software System Architecture*, ICSE 17 Software Architecture Workshop (1995)

[6]   Hassan Gomaa, Reusable Software *Requirements and Architecture for Families of Systems*, J. System Software **28**, pp. 189-202 (1995)

[7]   P. van den Hamer, K. Lepoeter, *Managing Design Data: The Five Dimensions of CAD Frameworks, Configuration Management and Product Data Management*, Proceedings of the IEEE, **84** no. 1 (January 1996)

[8]   Ivar Jacobson, Martin Griss, Patrick Jonsson, *Software Reuse*, Addison Wesley (1997)

[9]   Jeff Magee, Naranker Dulay, Suzan Eisenbach, Jeff Kramer, *Specifying Distributed Software Architectures*, Wilhelm Schäfer, Pere Botella (eds.) Proceedings ESEC'95, pp. 137-153 (1995), Springer Verlag LNCS 989

[10]   A. Spencer Peterson and Jay L. Stanley, Jr., *Maping a Domain Model and Architecture to a Generic Design*, Technical Report CMU/SEI-94-TR-8, Software Engineering Institute, Carnegie Mellon University (May 1994)

[11]   Jason E. Robbins, Nenad Medvidovic, David F. Redmiles, David S. Rosenblum, *Integrating Architecture Description Languages with a Standard Design Method*, Dept. of Information and Computer Science, University of California, Irvine (1997)

[12]   Wilhelm Rossak, Vassilka Kirova, Leon Jololian, Harold Lawson, Tamar Zemel, *A Generic Model for Software Architectures*, IEEE Software, pp. 84-92 (July/August 1997)

[13]   G.H. te Sligte, A. Saunders, P. van den Hamer, *A graphical User Interface Design for an Architecture and Diversity Database*, Philips Research Internal Report, TN 054/97

Koala, a Component Model for Consumer Electronics Product Software[1]

Rob van Ommering

Philips Research Eindhoven
The Netherlands
ommering@natlab.research.philips.com

Abstract. We introduce a component model with an architectural description language that helps to manage the growing complexity and diversity of software in consumer electronics products. The model supports flexible instantiation and late binding of components at an absolute minimum of product costs (code size and speed). The model is being used in the production of the next generation of mid to high-end television sets.

1. Introduction

In consumer electronics products such as TVs and VCRs, software roughly doubles in size every two years [1]. Control functions become more complex, signal processing tasks shift from hardware to software, software intensive features emerge (Electronic Programming Guide), products are integrated (TV-VCR), and software functions typical for the computer domain are added (Internet). Next to this, the market demands a higher variety of products at a higher introduction rate, urging us to create even more software in less time. We shall deal with two fundamental software development problems in this paper: how to manage the growing *complexity* of the software and how to manage the required *diversity*.

Our first problem is to manage the increasing *complexity* of the software. In practice this means that the *actual* architecture (i.e. the structure of the code) must be managed, not the *intended* one (which can be found in the architecture documents). Previously, we utilized an architecture verification paradigm by extracting the structure from the code and comparing it with the intended structure [2]. We now want to tackle the problem by its roots and define the structure in an architectural language, thus equating *intended* and *actual*.

Our second problem is to manage *diversity*. We cannot handle the exponential growth of software with a similar growth of development teams. Instead we must reuse software within product families (TV), between product families (TV-VCR) and from other domains (computing). This implies that we must separate components and configurations; components must be completely configuration independent, and we must have flexible mechanisms to instantiate components and bind them into configurations.

---

[1] This work has been performed within the ESPRIT project 20477, ARES: Architectural Reasoning for Embedded Systems

Frank v. d. Linden (Ed.): ARES '98, LNCS 1429, pp. 76-86, 1998.
© Springer-Verlag Berlin Heidelberg 1998

Various component technologies are available in the world (e.g. COM [3]), and the same holds for architectural languages (e.g. Darwin [4]). Unfortunately, the computing hardware in high-end CE products of today resembles personal computers of ten years ago: 16 bit micro controllers operating at 20 MHz, 10-100 Kbytes of RAM and 100-1000 Kbytes of ROM. Therefore, though we can use the *concepts* of modern technology, we have to choose our own *implementation techniques* to support this. The rest of this paper will explain how we achieve this.

2. The Koala Component Model

We shall explain components, interfaces, configurations and binding in this section, and go into more detail in the next sections.

Components

A *component* is an encapsulated piece of software. It is a unit of development and a unit of architectural design. A component is non-trivial in size, yet sufficiently self-contained and configuration independent to be a reusable asset.

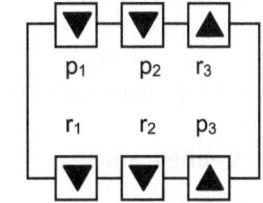

Figure 1 An example component

A component can communicate with its environment through *interfaces*. A component *provides* functionality through interfaces, and in order to do so it *requires* functionality through interfaces. All external functionality is required through interfaces, even access to the operating system or other general services. Note that in COM, most required functionality is implicit in the code, with the exception of connectable interfaces.

We draw components as rectangles and interfaces as small squares containing triangles (see Figure 1). The triangle designates the direction of function call. The similarity with integrated circuits is intentional: people in the TV domain will readily understand such pictures, and also we tribute the hardware reuse that has already taken place for years.

Let us be somewhat more precise. A *component type* is a reusable component in isolation; a *component instance* is an occurrence of such a component in a particular configuration. Components are by default single instantiatable, i.e. they can occur only once in a single configuration, but they can be made multiply instantiatable as well (see section 0).

2.1 Interfaces

We choose to describe connections between components at a level higher than that of single functions. An *interface* is a small set of semantically related functions (like in COM). To be more precise (again), an *interface type* is a syntactic and semantic description of an interface, and an *interface instance* is an interface occurring in a component.

```
interface VolumeControl {
    void setVolume(Volume v);
    Volume getVolume(void);
}
```

Figure 2 An interface definition

An interface type is described in an interface description language. We use a simple IDL, resembling COM and Java interface descriptions, in which we list the function prototypes in a C syntax (see Figure 2). Our interfaces contain functions only. Types are automatically made available wherever they occur in interfaces. Constants are treated as functions.

A component type is described in a component description language (CDL, see Figure 3). We list the types and instance names of the provides and requires interfaces. Note that the interface instance names are unique for a component, whereas component and interface type names must be globally unique.

```
Component Amplifier {
    provides VolumeControl vol;
    requires VolumeControl drv;
}
```

Figure 3 A component definition

2.2   Configurations

We construct configurations by instantiating components and connecting their interfaces. A requires interface must always be bound to precisely one provides interface, but a provides interface may be bound to more than one (or zero) requires interfaces.

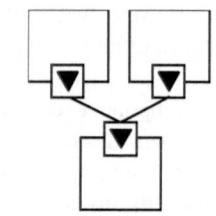

Figure 4 A configuration

A configuration is described in the component description language as well (see Figure 5). The description contains two sections, one declaring the component instances and one connecting their interfaces. Needless to say, the description closely resembles hardware parts and net lists. Note that component instances have names unique to the configuration in which they are instantiated.

2.3   Implementation

We shall now describe some implementation aspects. We implement components in C (and not e.g. C++, remember our resource constraints). A component is a set of C and header files in a single directory, which may freely include and use each other but may not have any reference to any file outside of the

```
component System {
    contains Amplifier a;
             AmpDriver d;
    connects a.drv = d.vol;
}
```

Figure 5 A configuration definition

directory. Next to a globally unique type name (the *long name*), each component type has a globally unique *short name*, consisting of say 4 characters.

A function f in a provides interface p of a component C with short name c is implemented in C as c_p_f. A function f in a requires interface r of a component is called as r_f. How does a call of r_f in one component arrive at c_p_f in another component? Simply by a:

```
#define   r_f(...)   c_p_f(...)
```

Such statements are generated by a small tool called Koala that reads CDL and IDL and produces header files to be included by component implementations. Note that the name c_p_f must be globally unique (hence the use of c), but the name r_f has as scope only the calling component (and is within that scope unique). See [5] where the same technique is being used. We find this technique very useful in our current applications (10^6 lines of code).

3. Extensions to the Model

The model described in the previous section is sufficient to build complete systems, but for practical use some more features are required.

3.1 Compound Components

When building large systems consisting of hundreds of components, it becomes unfeasible to interconnect them in a single description: the description gets too large to be understandable, cannot be easily maintained by a team of people, and different expertise areas are needed for different parts of the configuration. Therefore we make the component model recursive: any combination of components can again be viewed as a component with provides and requires interfaces.

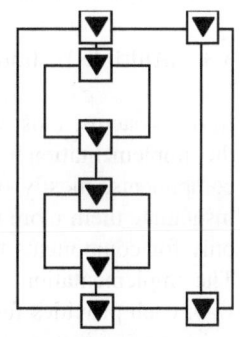

Figure 6 A compound component

Note that connections between interfaces can now be routed in more ways than described before. We find it easier to state that the tip of each triangle (drawn in an interface) must be connected to precisely one base, and that each base may be connected to zero or more tips. This allows for shortcuts between interfaces on the border of the component, a facility that can be used to obey strict layering conventions without any implementation overhead.

3.2   Gluing Interfaces

A direct connection between interfaces is not always
sufficient. It assumes that components are completely tuned
to each other in their interfaces, and this is often not the case
in the evolution of our software over the years. Moreover,
consider OCX components which are (claimed to be) highly
reusable but which must be glued with Visual Basic. We can
define glue *components*, but the managerial overhead of that
is just too large. Therefore we introduce *modules*.

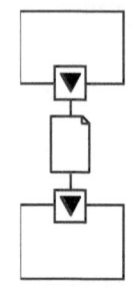

A module has a name unique for the component type in
which it occurs. If a tip of an interface is connected to a
module, then its functions are implemented in that module. If

Figure 7 Gluing

a base of an interface is connected to a module, then those functions are (possibly)
used by the module. The naming conventions are extended to cope with this new
situation, but we shall not discuss that here.

Koala generates for each module a header file. The component designer adds
one (or more) C files to implement the respective functions. This mechanism is
also used to implement basic components (that contain no instances of other
components): by connecting provides and requires interfaces to one or modules,
the designer can control the generation of header files.

3.3   Multiple Instantiation

In our systems, most components occur only once in a single configuration, and
the implementation techniques described above are then sufficient. For some
components, mostly of a service nature, it would be convenient to be able to
instantiate them more than once. Our language and binding tool supports this, but
only for components that are explicitly declared as multiply instantiatable (MI).
The implementation conventions (still in C) are extended in a straightforward
way: each provides function in an MI component has as extra (first) parameter a
pointer to an instance data structure. All binding is done at the instance level, so
that in calls to functions in requires interfaces these pointers are not seen. Instead,
Koala adds them in the appropriate #define statements. Koala also creates the
instance structures. Note that we mimic C^{++} implementation techniques for classes
and instances here.

3.4   Packages

We assume that component type and interface type names are globally unique.
This is not a necessary element of our approach: it is relatively simple to add the
notion of a package with private and public types and with import statements (as
in Java). We shall do this in due time.

4. Diversity

The use of components with explicit interfaces and an architectural description language serves our first purpose: to manage complexity. How do we manage diversity? First of all, the strict separation between components and configurations already allows us to create a multitude of configurations with a single set of components, adding glue wherever necessary to match the components. In this section we extend our model with several other features. We shall both deal with *internal diversity* (within components) and with *structural diversity* (between components).

4.1 Interface Compatibility

We follow the COM convention that an interface type, once defined, may never be changed anymore. Still, new generations of components may require the definition of new interface types that are small extensions of existing types. Of course, we can bind a requires interface of type I1 to a provides interface of type I2 (consisting of all the functions in I1 plus a few extra) by inserting a glue module, but the syntactic and code overhead of this is quite large. Therefore we allow the tip of an interface to be bound to the base of another interface if the first interface is of a *subtype* of the second. This is the case if the set of functions in I1 is a subset of that of I2.

4.2 Diversity Interfaces

We believe that components can only be made reusable if they are 'heavily parameterized' (compare the long property lists of Visual Basic components). Traditionally, this results in components using lots of RAM and ROM. In resource constrained systems, we can only parameterize our components 'heavily' if we have a way of removing undesired flexibility when inserting the component in a configuration. The parameterization is necessary for the *family* of products, and not for *individual* products.

In our component model, diversity parameters are declared as functions in requires interfaces. Note that this implies that their implementation lies *outside* of the component (as opposed to Visual Basic, where properties are implemented

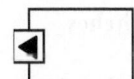

Figure 8 A diversity interface

within the component). The reason for this will become apparent in the next section. Requires interfaces containing diversity functions are called *diversity interfaces* (though in the model, diversity functions can be (and are) freely intermixed with 'normal' requires functions). Note that our mechanism in fact unifies the notions of parameterisation and binding, by reducing the component parameter assignment to a binding operation.

4.3   Late Binding

The trend in binding techniques is to shift the moment of binding from compile time to link time to initialization time to run time. Our model supports various forms of late binding, but to explain this, we must introduce another time scale, relevant for the development of embedded software.

Consider the binding and instantiation decisions that have to be made in order to get a running system. A number of decisions can be made at *component design time*. As we strive for configuration independent components, a (large) number of decisions must be postponed to *configuration time*. Even then, not all decisions can be made, as it is common to generate a single ROM mask to support a variety of products. Option bits in a non-volatile memory (set in the factory) can then be used at *run time* to complete the binding decisions.

The strength of our approach is first of all that configuration time binding is not equated to link time binding, and secondly that the component designer need not know beforehand whether 'non component design time decisions' are made at configuration time or at run time. We achieve this as follows.

Each diversity parameter is defined by a C macro within the component (following our binding implementation conventions). A component designer may treat such a parameter as a normal function, and write for instance:

```
if ( div_param() ) { do_something(); }
```

The parameter may be set to false at configuration time. The system can then be (re-) compiled, and the compiler will throw away the 'do something' clause, resulting in optimal code. The parameter may also be defined as a run-time function. This will then result in run time diversity resolution.

As most compilers are not able to remove unused variables and unused local functions, a second facility can be used by the component designer to aid the compiler. A special macro is generated if the diversity parameter is assigned a constant at configuration time. This can be used to guard certain constructs with #ifdef statements.

4.4   Switches

Diversity interfaces can be used to control the *internal diversity* of components. What about *structural diversity*?

Suppose that a component A uses B1 in one product, and B2 in another product. We can simply define two configurations to implement this, but A may be part of a complex compound component, and we do not want to duplicate the rest of that. Our basic solution is to insert a module between the requires interface of A and the provides

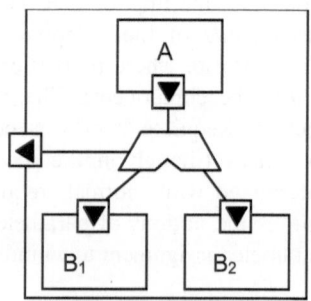

Figure 9 A switch

interfaces of B1 and B2. As this is a re-occuring pattern, we introduce a special concept for this.

A *switch* is an element that can be used to route connections between interfaces. Its top must be connected to the tip of one interface, and each of its 'bottoms' can be connected to the base of a different interface. The switch setting is controlled through a diversity interface.

Our binding tool Koala knows about switches. If a switch is set at configuration time to a certain position, then the other component is removed from the configuration (if it has no other connections), and the connection to the remaining component is just as in the case of static binding (with zero overhead). If the switch setting is not known at configuration time, then some form of code is generated (e.g. a set of if statements or a VTable technique) to connect the interfaces, and all components are included in the configuration. Naturally, this process is executed recursively for compound components.

4.5 Function Binding

How can individual diversity parameters be set to a constant value at configuration time? An interface is connected with its tip to perhaps other interfaces, but ultimately through a chain of such bindings to a module. In this module, the function can be implemented in C, but then Koala has no knowledge of it and cannot optimize.

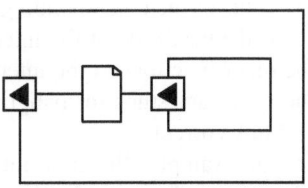

Figure 10 Function binding

Functions in modules can also be implemented in CDL in a subset of the C expression language, using constants, operators and functions available through other interfaces. This allows Koala to perform optimizations such as constant expression folding.

This mechanism enables a very convenient treatment of diversity parameters. Diversity parameters of inner components can be calculated using expressions containing constants and outer diversity parameters (the flow of information is (usually) inwards). In other words, we obtain an object-oriented spreadsheet of diversity parameters. This allows us to express diversity in different terms at different levels of aggregation.

An interesting side effect of this spread-sheet approach is that Koala can calculate certain design properties such as memory usage at configurations, if basic components export this information through provides interfaces and compound components perform the correct calculation and export it again.

4.6   Optional Interfaces

Suppose that a new version of a component supports
a new provides interface and needs a new requires
interface. We can give the new component (type) a
new unique name, but then the component is not
automatically inserted into existing configurations.
Instead, we allow the addition of interfaces to
existing components, provided that they are
declared *optional* (and drawn dashed, see Figure
11). Our treatment of optional interfaces resembles
the COM Query Interface mechanism.

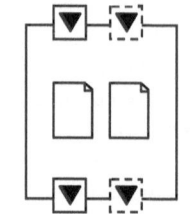

Figure 11 Optional Interfaces

An optional interface has an implicit extra function called iPresent, which acts
as a boolean diversity parameter. It is true if the tip of the interface is connected to
a non optional interface, false if the tip is not connected at all, and defined within
the module if the tip is connected to a module. If the optional interface is
connected to the base of another optional interface, the iPresent function inherits
the value of the corresponding function in the other interface.

At the base side of the interface, the function can be used to establish whether
the other functions in the interface may be called at run time. Koala will generate
the necessary stubs for dangling interfaces to ensure that the software is compile
and link correct.

In our example, the new interfaces may be connected to a new module, and
iPresent of the provides interface may be equated to iPresent of the requires
interface. If the component is used without connecting the optional requires
interface, then the optionally provided functionality is not available.

5. Execution Architecture

The basic rule in our approach is to make components configuration independent
as much as possible. As an illustration, we shall show in this section how we
define the execution architecture. Our approach is to define components in such a
way that the actual execution architecture can be established at configuration time.

5.1   Events

First of all, how do we deal with events? Instead of defining some event handling
mechanism in our model, we just advise component designers to *signal* events
through outgoing (*requires*) interfaces (just like in Visual Basic). Another
component that uses services of the component can provide an event-*handling*
interface that can be connected to the event-signaling interface. In a multi-
threaded system, functions in event interfaces are called on the thread of the
component raising the event, so the general rule is that the handling must be quick
and non-blocking.

We do not advise basic component builders to include event subscription
mechanisms in their components (though it's not in conflict with the model), as in

our systems there is usually one (product specific) destination for events. Instead, we implement event multicasting and subscription at the configuration level, using glue modules wherever possible.

5.2 Threads and Tasks

Our systems consist of many components but few threads (remember the resource constraints). We therefore advise not to declare threads in basic components, but instead declare them at the configuration level. Each component may implement its time consuming activities in terms of tasks, which are scheduled synchronously by a task manager running in a global thread. To do so, a component requires a thread ID through a *virtual thread* interface, and creates its tasks on such virtual threads. At configuration time, the (many) virtual threads are mapped to the (few) physical threads, thus enabling Gomaa's principle of Task Inversion (sometimes called thread sharing) [6].

A component may have tasks that operate on different time scales, and thus have to be implemented in different physical threads. It then requires two (or more) virtual thread interfaces, which will be mapped to different physical threads at configuration time. In this case, the component must make sure that internally the different activities are properly synchronized.

The rules stated above are not absolute. We propagate an SDL style of programming for simple activities, but for activities for which the Ada style of programming is more appropriate, a thread may be created within a component.

6. Concluding Remarks

We have introduced a component model and an architectural language optimized for resource constrained systems. Roughly spoken, the component model allows us to manage diversity, and the architectural language to manage complexity. At a number of points we deviate from existing approaches:

- we make all requires interfaces explicit (including the use of standard services), thus making connectable interfaces a natural element of our model;
- we treat component parameterization as a binding issue, by defining diversity interfaces;
- we support configuration time and run time binding, but do not equate configuration time binding to link time binding;
- we support internal and structural diversity, but regard structural diversity as internal diversity at a compound level;
- we provide a spreadsheet-like approach towards diversity parameters, where the parameters of inner components can be calculated in terms of parameters of compound components.

A small number of extensions to this model are still possible. The model is being used in the development of our next generation television sets. Ultimately, we want to be able to incorporate third party software (such as Internet browsers) in our products. We therefore plan an evolution of our component model towards emerging standards in this field. We believe that our model is flexible enough to be used in combination with COM and JavaBeans, and we plan to demonstrate this in the near future.

7. Acknowledgments

The component model was inspired by the work of Jeff Kramer and Jeff Magee (Imperial College London), and intensively discussed with them. The model was created by Hans Jonkers and the author (Philips Research), together with Aad Droppert and Marc Loos, working for the Philips Television product group. The Koala tool was implemented by Hans van Antwerpen and Maarten Pennings (Philips Research).

8. References

[1]   Remi Bourgonjon, *The Evolution of Embedded Software in Consumer Products*, International Conference on Engineering of Complex Computer Systems, (unpublished keynote address), Ft. Lauderdale, FL (1995)

[2]   Loe Feijs, Rob van Ommering, *Architecture Visualisation and Analysis: Motivation and Example*, Ares workshop Las Navas, Spain, November 18-19 (1996)

[3]   The Microsoft COM model, http://www.microsoft.com/com

[4]   Jeff Magee, Naranker Dulay, Susan Eisenbach, Jeff Kramer, *Specifying Distributed Software Architectures*, Proc. ESEC'95, Wilhelm Scha"fer, Pere Botella (Eds.) Springer LNCS 989 pp. 137-153 (1995)

[5]   Don Batory, Sean O'Malley, *The Design and Implementation of Hierarchical Software Systems with Reusable Components*, ACM Transactions on Software Engineering and Methodology, 1 no. 4, pp. 355-398 (October 1992)

[6]   Hassan Gomaa, *Software Design Methods for Concurrent and Real-Time Systems*, Addison Wesley (1993)

Session 3: Architecture Recovery

Jean-Marc DeBaud[1], Mehdi Jazayeri[2]

[1]Fraunhofer Institute for Experimental Software Engineering, Sauerwiesen 6
D-67661 Kaiserslautern, Germany
debaud@iese.fhg.de

[2]Vienna University of Technology, Distributed Systems Group,
Argentinierstrasse 8/184-1, A-1040 Vienna, Austria
M.Jazayeri@infosys.tuwien.ac.at

Architecture recovery is concerned with deriving high-level architectural information from the information available about a system. The available information usually consists of the source code of the system, various documents, and possibly domain and application experts. Most architecture recovery efforts aim to use automatic tools as much as possible. In many cases the goal of architecture recovery is to produce the architecture of one or more existing, successful, systems in order to use it as the basis for developing a family architecture for a product family.

The session started with the following initial set of issue to be addressed:

1. What roles do tools play in architecture recovery and are they adequate? What new tools are needed?

2. How to describe the results of architecture recovery? This issue addresses the relationship between architecture recovery and description techniques.

3. Is it possible to recover dynamic aspects of an architecture such as interprocess communication behavior of a system?

4. In the context of product families, how can architecture recovery take advantage of, and integrate, domain knowledge in the process.

The presentations of the papers in the session addressed most of these issues. Wolfgang Eixelsberger described the experience of recovering the architecture of a family of train protection systems. Johannes Weidl described the use of a specialized tool to recover implementations of state machines in the source code and describe them in a generic way. Nabor Mendonca described an experiment to address recovery of dynamic structure by applying architecture recovery to a client server system. Nelson Weiderman discussed the use of middleware for systematically evolving the architecture of legacy systems into distributed systems.

A lively discussion ensued in which even the idea of architecture recovery was questioned. One participant stated that in his organization they cannot afford the time to do architecture recovery: they have to produce and ship a new product every few months. Another participant stated that it is simply impossible to find enough skilled architects; therefore the more you can find about architecture of systems by automatic means, the better off you are. It was clear that how much architecture recovery you do depends on your application and domain area.

Frank v. d. Linden (Ed.): ARES '98, LNCS 1429, pp. 87-88, 1998.
© Springer-Verlag Berlin Heidelberg 1998

Other interesting issues raised during the discussion were:

1. Alexander Ran pointed out that architecture recovery is akin to porting an operating system. During the port, you discover the assumptions that were made about the environment. Nelson Weiderman pointed out that the year 2k problem is the same: we are trying to find out what assumptions the designers have made and modify them. In these tasks, the more modern software engineering techniques make it easier to do recovery.

2. Bob Balzer observed that rather than try to recover the architecture of several systems and combine them into a family architecture, you should try to recover the variability mechanisms already in the system and use those as a basis for developing the family architecture.

3. Dave Weiss stated that it is important to decide what assumptions are being made about the product line and what changes are expected. Sometimes you are stuck with some decisions. Therefore, it is important to document and classify your assumptions.

There seemed to be some general consensus on a few issues at the end:

1. The purpose of architecture recovery is to understand what is there already. Usually this is done on a successful system and therefore we also would like to understand why the system is successful.

2. Human intervention is necessary in reverse engineering and in architecture recovery.

Recovery of Architectural Structure: A Case Study[*]

Wolfgang Eixelsberger[1], Manfred Kalan[1], Michaela Ogris[1], Håkon Beckman[1],
Berndt Bellay[2], Harald Gall[2]

[1]ABB Corporate Research, N-1361 Billingstad, Bergerveien 12
{wolfgang,hb}@nocrc.abb.no
[2]Vienna University of Technology, Distributed Systems Group
A-1040 Vienna, Argentinierstrasse 8/184-1
{H.Gall,B.Bellay}@infosys.tuwien.ac.at

Abstract. Industrial software development is often an evolutionary
process. Software products are developed for one specific customer and
later on refined for other customers with different requirements in terms of
a product family. Refinements happen at the implementation level
(algorithms and data structures) and on the architectural level (the overall
system structure). Recovery of architectural information is necessary to
build up a complete and unambiguous description of the architecture of a
system. In this paper, we describe an approach for the recovery of
architectural structure that focuses on component and connector
identification. We describe different strategies to define components and
connectors of the system. The examples given in the paper were developed
out of an industrial case study, a real-time Train Control System. The
recovered architectural description allows reasoning about the quality of
the system architecture: The description of the architectural structure
revealed hardware-dependent components that in case of a hardware
change would have to be changed completely. Therefore, our
investigations showed that such a recovery of architectural structure is
important to reduce future efforts in the development and maintenance of
product lines.

1. 1.   Introduction

Software architecture, a concept for focusing on different properties of a system
has become one of the most interesting and compelling software engineering
research topics in the last years. David Garlan and Dewayne Perry gave a
definition that is a compromise to many interpretations of the term: "The structure
of the components of a program/system, their interrelationships, and principles
and guidelines governing their design and evolution over time." [1]

The structural issues of a software architecture "include the organization of a
system as a composition of components; global control structures; the protocols

---

[*] The architecture recovery process discussed in this paper is research work within the
ESPRIT project ARES (Architectural Reasoning for Embedded Systems). ARES is
supported by the European Commission under ESPRIT framework IV contract no.
20477.

Frank v. d. Linden (Ed.): ARES '98, LNCS 1429, pp. 89-96, 1998.
© Springer-Verlag Berlin Heidelberg 1998

for communication, synchronization, and data access; the assignment of functionality to design elements; the composition of design elements; physical distribution; scaling and performance; dimensions of evolution; and selection among design alternatives." [2]

1.1 Software Architecture Recovery

Software architecture related activities are often purely seen as forward engineering activities. However, many applications are not developed from scratch but derived from existing systems. Application development in industry is often an evolutionary process building on knowledge and reusable code of previous versions of the software systems successfully in use. The available information about previous systems is however often incomplete and inconsistent, especially when it comes to software architecture information. Complete and consistent architectural information of these systems is therefore of special interest and has to be recovered by using re-engineering concepts.

Therefore, architectural information of legacy systems has to be extracted from source code, documentation or other sources of information.

In the ARES project, we are currently developing a methodology to recover architectural information from legacy systems. Figure 1 gives an overview of the framework of our architecture recovery strategy.

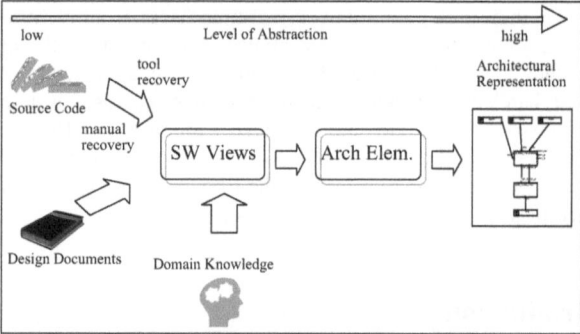

Fig. 1. Architecture Recovery Strategy

The input to the recovery process are various software views from the legacy system, for example, call graphs, file views etc. The level of abstraction of the software views (documents, source code, etc.) is low. In a stepwise manner the level of abstraction is raised to the architectural level. The recovery process will be applied on a number of members of the product family. The common architecture will be derived in a final step from the various architectural representations.

1.2 Related Work

In reverse engineering existing systems are analyzed to identify its components and interrelationships. The aim is to represent the system at higher levels of abstraction. Reverse engineering is therefore an important step in the architecture recovery process. However, architecture recovery goes beyond the identification of components and interrelationships [3], [4]. Architecture recovery means re-engineering of different properties of the software system, among which are the global control structure, the synchronization and communication protocol and information about physical distribution and performance. In [5] a framework is presented that integrates reverse engineering technology and architectural style representations to recover architectural representations from source code.

Design patterns describe solutions to recurring design problems [6]. Design patterns are a promising approach for defining a vocabulary for expressing software design concepts. Architectural patterns provide a set of predefined subsystems, specify the responsibilities of the subsystems, and describe rules and guidelines for organizing the relationships between the subsystems [6].

A product line (program family) is a group of software applications sharing a common set of features. The members of a product line share a common software architecture and are built from a common set of components. Architecture recovery of product lines focuses on the identification of structural commonality among members of a program family. The architecture of a product line describes architectural decisions inherent in each member of the program family. Identifying, assessing and describing the common architecture of a product line supports low-cost production and maintenance of applications [7].

1.3 Architectural Description

Software architects often use block-line diagrams for representing the architecture of a system. Such block-line diagrams are highly ambiguous. Architectural Description Languages (ADLs) are formal languages used to represent the architecture of a software system so that they can be communicated to other system stakeholders in an unambiguous way. To describe the components in our case study , we used the Darwin language and the supporting tool "Software Architects Assistant (SAA)" [8], [9] developed by Imperial College London. The Darwin language is based on the π-calculus and was originally used as a configuration management tool. This section gives a very brief introduction to Darwin, for more information see [10].

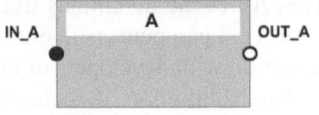

Fig. 2. Component A

Figure 2 shows a component displayed with the help of the SAA tool. OUT_A is the provided output port of the component. An output of a component is defined by a white dot. IN_A is the required input of the component and is defined with a black dot. Components communicate through ports with other components. Component A is a compound component with two sub-components B and C.

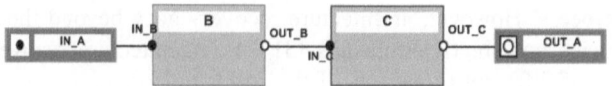

Fig. 3. The two sub-components of component A

Figure 3 describes the two sub-components of component A. The input (IN_B) to component B is through the IN_A port of the component A. The output (OUT_C) from component C is through the OUT_A port of the component A.

2. The Case Study

The case study, a Train Control System (TCS) system, is an embedded real-time system successfully in use in different countries. The TCS system forms a family of systems that has been specialized for different national railway companies. The members of the program family have to be maintained and further members of the program family have to be developed in a continuous process. The case study is a medium-size software application with around 150 kLOC (Lines of Code) implemented in C and Assembler. The Train Control System is executed on two different hardware platforms and is controlled by an in-house developed monitor. Future family members may be developed for different hardware platforms and/or different operating systems.

3. Recovering Architectural Structure

Component and connector identification is of central importance in the architecture recovery process. Components and connectors are the basis for the overall system structure and therefore represent an important part of the software architecture.

A number of definitions exist for the term 'software component.' Gregory Abowd defined components as "primary computations of the application" [11]. Mary Shaw defines components as "such things as clients and servers, databases, filters, and layers in a hierarchical system." [12] Paul Kogut gives a code-oriented definition of components: "Components can be small pieces of code (such as modules) or larger chunks (such as stand alone programs like database management systems)."[13] All of the definitions were suitable for other systems under consideration. But what are components in our specific system?

After discussing this question with developers of the Train Control System, we agreed on a function-oriented definition. A component is a set of functions, performing defined tasks in the system. Tasks are main requirements of the system consisting of a set of sub-tasks.

Inherent module or component concepts are missing in both programming languages used in the case study (C, Assembly). Component identification and recovery in the case study can therefore not be based on language concepts.

Thus, a number of possible *component identification* strategies were considered:

File structure — Functions and data structures collected in files are natural candidates for components since the reason for collecting functions in a file is often functional dependency.

Diversified software — The case study is a safety critical application in which software diversity is used to ensure fail safety. All safety critical parts of the system are implemented by an A,B,C style. A and B is software developed by different groups based on the same requirements, B uses however inverted data for safety reasons. C synchronizes, distributes and votes results from A and B. The A,B,C parts of the system are natural candidates for components.

Coupling - Coupling is the measure of interconnection among functions in a software system. High degree of coupling between functions could be an indication that the functions belong to the same component. Low degree of coupling could accordingly indicate that the functions belong to different components.

Design documentation — Design documents of the case study contain block-line diagrams that give indication about the existing architecture. Indicators are also the table of contents, since components are often described in subchapters.

Monitor - The software execution of the case study is controlled by a software monitor. The scheduling approach is a modified round-robin algorithm. The monitor tasks implement functionality that has to be completely performed within a specific time-frame to ensure correct execution. The monitor tasks are therefore component candidates.

The recovery work started by analyzing the design documentation. At first we identified that the overall system consists of a hierarchy of components. Components on the highest level were identified with help of the documentation. The block-line diagrams and the document structure with sub-chapters were clear indications for components. The components on the next lower level were mainly identified by analyzing the monitor that schedules tasks that perform a specific functionality and divide thereby the super-component into non-overlapping sub-components. On the next lower level, components were identified based on the diversified software principle: The A, B and C parts form according components.

The component identification process was an iterative process with a number of processing loops and feedback rounds with the developers.

The *connector identification* process was therefore closely related to the component identification process. Each component was analyzed concerning interactions with the environment (other components). Interaction in the case study is mainly based on shared-memory and function calls.

4. Result - The Identified Architecture

The recovered architectural information was described using the ADL Darwin.

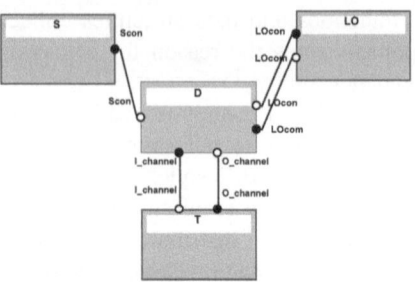

Fig. 4. Components of the case study

Figure 4 shows the highest hierarchy level of the system. The components contain again sub-components. Components are related to different hardware platforms. The D, S and LO components are related to the same hardware platform, the T component is related to another hardware platform. The HW-platforms are connected through a serial link. This information is however not expressible with DARWIN.

Components of the case study play different roles. The T component works as a server for the D component. The D component as a client sends commands through the O_channel and receives data through the l_channel from the server T. Towards the S component the D component plays the role of a producer. The connections between them are based on shared memory and function calls. Towards the LO component, D plays the role of a server and LO is accordingly the client.

Figure 5 describes the sub-components of component D.

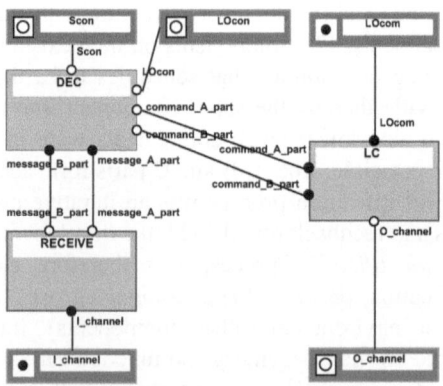

Fig. 5. The sub-components of D

The DEC and LC component are scheduled by a monitor. The connections between the components are shared memory.

The DEC component is a fail-safe component which consists of A, B and C components. The DEC component has therefore A and B inputs and outputs. The A and B parts of DEC controls the T component through the LC component.

In case further versions of the system will be developed for one hardware platform, some of the components have to be changed or removed. For example, components handling the data transmission between the HW platform would disappear.

The recovery of the architectural structure of the case study led to the following results:

- Hardware dependent components that might be subject to changes in future family members were identified.
- Darwin and the Software Architect's Assistant were well suited for the identification and representation of components and connectors.
- The architecture recovery resulted in descriptions of the structural architecture; other architectural properties such as communication protocols or data access need to be further investigated.
- Implications on further family members became evident from the architectural perspective on the system. We identified problems in the overall system structure that will be avoided in future products. Typical communication patterns were identified and will be analyzed with focus on performance and timing constraints.

5. Future Work

Complete architecture descriptions go beyond the architectural structure (components and connectors) and the global control structure. Our future work will therefore concentrate on other architectural properties as the communication protocols, the data access, the architectural style and performance aspects. Work presented in this paper results from analyzing one member of a product line. Other product line members will also be analyzed and the general software architecture will be recovered. Finally, a reference architecture will be build, consisting of a composition of generic and abstract components. The component of the reference architecture will be replaced by 'real' components when the architecture is instantiated for a real system.

6. Conclusion

Recovery of architectural information is a promising approach for gaining control over the evolution of existing software systems. Architectural descriptions allow reasoning about the quality of systems and will lead to reduced development and maintenance costs.

In this paper, we presented an approach for recovery of structural architectural information. The approach was developed while working on a real-time system family that is successfully in use in different countries. Components, connectors and the global control structure of the system were identified. The system structure (components, connectors) was described using the architecture description language Darwin together with the Software Architect's Assistant. In future work, additional architectural information such as the communication protocols and the reference architecture of the product line will be recovered.

7. Acknowledgments

The authors would like to thank the ARES consortium and especially our colleague Keng Ng at Imperial College London for his support on Darwin and the Software Architect's Assistant.

References

[1]   D. Garlan and D.E. Perry, "Introduction to the special issue on software architecture," IEEE Trans. on Software Eng., Vol. 21, No. 4, pp. 269-274, April 1995.

[2]   M. Shaw and D. Garlan, Software architecture: perspectives on an emerging discipline, Prentice-Hall, 1996.

[3]   T. Wiggerts, H. Bosma, and E. Fielt, "Scenarios for the Identification of Objects in Legacy Systems," Fourth Working Conference on Reverse Engineering. Amsterdam, The Netherlands, October 1997.

[4]   W. Eixelsberger, L. Warholm, R. Klösch, and H. Gall, "Software architecture recovery of embedded software," 19th International Conference on Software Engineering, Boston, USA, pp. 558-9, May 1997.

[5]   D.R. Harris, H.B. Reubenstein, and A.S. Yeh. "Recognizers for extracting architectural features from source code." Second Working Conference on Reverse Engineering, Toronto, Canada, pp. 252-261, July 1995.

[6]   F. Buschmann, R. Meunier, H. Rohnert, P. Sommerlad, M. Stal, Pattern-Oriented Software Architecture - A System of Patterns, Wiley and Sons Ltd., 1996.

[7]   D. Dikel, D. Kane, S. Ornburne, W. Loftus, and J. Wilson, "Applying Software Product-Line Architecture," IEEE Computer, Vol. 30, No. 8, August 1997.

[8]   K. Ng, J. Kramer, and J. Magee, "A CASE Tool for Software Architecture Design," Journal of Automated Software Engineering, Vol. 3, No. 3/4, Kluwer Academic Publishers, pp. 261-284, 1996.

[9]   J. Magee, N. Dulay, and J. Kramer, "Regis: A Constructive Development Environment for Distributed Programs," IEE/IOP/BCS Distributed Systems Engineering, Vol. 1, No. 5, pp. 304-312, September 1994.

[10]   M. Radestock, S. Eisenbach, "Formalizing system structure," 8th International Workshop on Software Specification and Design (IWSSD8), 1996.

[11]   G. Abowd, R. Allen, and D. Garlan, "Formalizing Style to Understand Descriptions of Software Architecture," ACM Transactions on Software Engineering and Methodology (TOSEM), Vol. 4, No. 4, pp. 319-364, October 1995.

[12]   M. Shaw and D. Garlan, "Formulations and Formalisms in Software Architecture," in Computer Science Today: Recent Trends and Developments. Lecture Notes in Computer Science, Vol. 1000, pp. 307-323, 1995.

[13]   P. Kogut and P. Clements, "The Software Architecture Renaissance," Crosstalk - The Journal of Defense Software Engineering, Vol. 7, No. 11, November 1994.

Reengineering C/C++ Source Code by Transforming State Machines*

Roland Knor, Georg Trausmuth, and Johannes Weidl

Technical University of Vienna, Distributed Systems Group,
Argentinierstr. 8/184-1, A-1040 Vienna, Austria, Europe,
{knor, trausmuth, weidl}@infosys.tuwien.ac.at,
WWW home page: http://www.infosys.tuwien.ac.at

Abstract. State transition mechanisms are widely used in software engineering to implement state/event-dependent behavior. In C/C++, the implementation of state machines using 'switch/case' or 'if' statements causes problems in readability, understandability, maintainability, and modification. We have developed both a source code pattern searching tool capable of searching for state machine occurrences and a design pattern to replace state machines with C++ generic components. With 'ESPaRT' (Enhanced String Pattern Recognition Tool) we search for state machines in the source code. Examples of patterns for state machine detection are given in the paper. The state machine information is extracted and the state machine code is replaced by generic components following the 'generic Harel State Machine Engine' (HSME) design pattern.

1 Introduction

A common and widely used technique to implement the dynamic behavior of reactive systems—and especially embedded systems—is the use of state machines. Depending on the current system state and incoming events issued by a source in the *environment*, a well-defined action (sequence of program instructions) is carried out and a new system state is set[1]. In automata theory, a finite state machine (FSM) is defined as a set of states, a set of events, an initial state, a set of final states, and a state transition function (for the formal definition see [10].) The state transition function determines for each valid pair (`current state`, `incoming event`) the system state to switch to. The visual counterpart of state machines—state transition diagrams—are used to model and simulate *reactive systems*[2].

---

* This work is funded by the European Commission under ESPRIT framework IV contract no. 20477 'Architectural Reasoning for Embedded Systems (ARES)' and is pursued by Nokia RC Finland, ABB Norway, Philips RC Holland, Imperial College, Technical University Madrid, and Technical University of Vienna.

[1] The *new* system state can be the same as the current.

[2] Reactive systems are systems that have continually to react to events from their environment.

Frank v. d. Linden (Ed.): ARES '98, LNCS 1429, pp. 97-105, 1998.

As with nearly every concept, there are many ways to implement a state machine in C/C++. The probably most common approach is utilizing the *switch/case* construct[3]. A so-called *state variable* is used to store the current state. If an event arrives, the current state is determined (using a *switch/case* construct.) Then, the event is determined (using another *switch/case* statement nested in the first) and the appropriate program code is executed in the corresponding case block. Usually, the last statement in the case block manipulates the current system state.

We argue, that such an implementation has deficiencies. In general, there is no separation of the code-parts processing the state machine (the so-called *state machine engine*), the state transition information and the code to be executed (the *actions.*) Furthermore, there is no explicit representation of the system states, events, and the state transition information. This can prevent a reader from understanding the dynamic behavior modeled with the state machine, especially if the state/event space[4] is large. Since readability and understandability are an essential basis for modification and enhancement of the state machine or for reverse engineering issues, we take effort to identify state machines in the source code and replace their implementation with an improved one.

Basically, such a venture has to offer three techniques. First, we must be able to identify state machines in the source code. We can look manually for state machine instances, use reverse engineering tools[5], or apply pattern searching tools such as 'grep' or more sophisticated ones that, for instance, parse the code to generate and use an abstract syntax tree (see [5].) Second, we have to analyze the state machine and identify the state and event space, the state transition function, and the actions executed at state transitions. This, as well, can be done manually or using an appropriate tool supporting the software engineer in the analysis task. Third, we have to replace the state machine implementation with a more sophisticated one, which remedies the deficiencies stated above, using the information of step two.

For the first task we use our pattern searching tool ESPaRT. We present the concepts of ESPaRT in Section 2 and explain how it can be used to detect state machines in the source code. For the third task, we have developed a set of C++ generic components in the HSME design pattern. Section 3 gives a short survey on the HSME components. In Section 4, we discuss the transformation process in detail and give an outlook on an appropriate tool supporting the task. Section 5 surveys work related, in Section 6 we draw some conclusions.

2   Finding State Machines Using ESPaRT

The simplest way of finding state machines in the source code is a manual search using an editor. However, a tool that is supporting the search for occurrences of

---

[3] Readers not familiar with C/C++ are referred to [7].

[4] The state space is the set of all possible states, analogously the event space is the set of all possible events.

[5] A comparison of reverse engineering tools can be found in [1].

state machines—or at least possible candidates—can speed up the overall conversion performance. Such a tool is *ESPaRT*.

ESPaRT was originally supposed to find duplicated statements in a code (like error handling, which often is added by a copy/paste procedure), with the requirement of being applicable to source code of different programming languages. The original idea was to use the UNIX tool *grep*. However, some source code variations, which were the result of later changes, could not be handled by *grep*. In the same way, the implementation of state machines—as high-level programming concepts—can vary in many ways, making the task of searching for state machine occurrences a non-trivial issue. To deal with variations, the Enhanced String Pattern Search Tool was built.

2.1 How Does ESPaRT Work?

ESPaRT is based on the idea of searching for characters rather than for tokens, i.e. the expression "if a > b then return a" will not be tokenized into "if — a — > — b — then — return — a", but it will be taken as a sentence which starts with an "if" and ends with an "a". *ESPaRT*'s pattern language is based on strings, but it is enhanced by *commands*, which overcome the restrictions of regular expressions by adding features of syntactic tools. Since the programming language *Perl* [9] offers a wide range of string manipulation functions, it has been used to implement *ESPaRT*.

ESPaRT is invoked by specifying a pattern file and the source code files. When a pattern is found, the line numbers and names of the files containing the match will be printed.

2.2 ESPaRT vs. Regular Expressions

ESPaRT is based on regular expressions, which can only be used for lexical matching. However, regular expressions do not satisfy several requirements that are needed to specify more complex patterns. To show the need of enhancing regular expressions to offer enough flexibility to the maintainer of a program, the enhancements of *ESPaRT* compared to regular expressions are summarized:

1. **Whitespace characters have to be expressed explicitly in regular expressions.** Using tabs accordingly can improve the readability of a code. However, in a search the amount of whitespace characters between two statements has to be considered in the regular expression pattern when using a tool like *grep*. *ESPaRT* uses a mechanism that allows the user to neglect the amount of tabs, blanks, or newlines between two expressions.

2. **Regular expressions cannot handle nested program blocks.** Blocks are considered the most basic components of high level programming languages. It is almost impossible to express a program block by regular expressions, since a block may recursively contain other blocks. Nested blocks can be handled by *ESPaRT*.

3. **Variable handling is unsatisfactory in regular expressions.** Though regular expressions allow the assignment of a match to a variable, they do not offer more flexible methods of assigning (variable) parts of a pattern to an identifier. In *ESPaRT*, these variable parts may not only be assigned to a identifier, but once a variable is instantiated, it may also be used later in the pattern.

4. **Regular expressions cannot handle variations of sequences.** If N statements may occur in a given order, $N!$ regular expressions are needed to specify all possible variations. The *SET* command of *ESPaRT* handles this case, because these statements only have to be listed once in the *SET* command.

5. ***ESPaRT* allows a more intuitive way of defining patterns.** A regular expression often has to be read twice before the pattern behind the expression can be recognized. In *ESPaRT*, patterns can be expressed by writing down the sequence of code the interpreter should look for. In the simplest case, fragments of the code could be copied into the pattern file and *ESPaRT* will look for other occurrences of this fragment.

2.3   State Machine Patterns

The problem of using search tools is to find the right pattern for the component that should be found. This means that a pattern for a particular state machine implementation will obviously not detect all state machines. In the following, an *ESPaRT* pattern will be presented assuming a particular implementation.

Switch/case Implementation Many state machines are implemented using *switch/case* statements. The *switch* statement contains the state and the *case* statement possible events or vice versa.

```
%MATCH%
        switch ($stateVar$)
                $BLOCK ("{" | "}" |)$
%END%

%SUBMATCH%
        case $event$ :
                $BLOCK ("{" | "}" | $stateVar$ = )$
%END%
```

The lines shown above have to be put into a pattern file that is interpreted by *ESPaRT*. The main pattern in the pattern file is enclosed by *%MATCH%* and *%END%*. Additionally, a subpattern may be specified to re-search the match from the main pattern for another pattern. Such a subpattern is enclosed by the keywords *%SUBMATCH%* and *%END%*. Once the main pattern can be matched against the source code, the lines in the code that caused the match will be searched again for occurrences of this subpattern.

Pattern Description The first line in the main pattern defines a *switch* statement that is based on a variable which itself is enclosed by parentheses. In the pattern, this variable is represented by the *ESPaRT* variable $stateVar$[6].

Thereafter, a block has to follow which (in C/C++) starts with "{" and ends with "}". This is expressed by using the $BLOCK()$ command of *ESPaRT* that takes three arguments which are separated by "|"s. The first two parameters define the start and end delimiter of the block[7]. The last parameter of $BLOCK()$, which is also an *ESPaRT* pattern, defines the contents of the block. If no third argument is specified, *ESPaRT* will not search the found block for a particular content.

After the the main pattern could be matched, the lines found in the code are re-searched for the subpattern. In our example, the subpattern consists of a *case* statement that is followed by a block containing an assignment to the state variable. This assignment can be seen as an important hint for a state machine.

The above pattern detects all *switch/case* expressions that contain a direct assignment to the *switch* variable.

2.4 Summary

The example given above does not cover all possible variations of state machines implemented by a *switch/case* structure. However, this is not necessary for a particular application, because parts of the pattern can be assumed not to change within the same collection of code. Moreover, state machines can also be implemented using other control structures (such as *if/else*.)

ESPaRT can be used to

1. Make an assumption about the implementation of a state machine (i.e. *switch/case*, *if/else*, assignment to a variable) expressed by an *ESPaRT* pattern.
2. Check whether the assumption (represented by that pattern) can be mapped against the code.

In applying *ESPaRT* several times, a collection of patterns will be created that can be used as a state machine pattern library. As this library grows, the probability to detect a state machine without *a priori* knowledge will increase.

3 The 'Generic Harel State Machine Engine' (HSME) Design Pattern

HSME was developed as a design pattern to apply the visual formalism of *statecharts* from specification to implementation of reactive systems (see [10] and

---

[6] Note, that expressions enclosed by two $ are *ESPaRT* expressions and everything else are statements taken from the source code.

[7] This parameters are necessary, because *ESPaRT* should also be applicable to other programming languages than C/C++.

[11].) Statecharts are an extension of the conventional state transition diagrams, e.g. allowing the modeling of concurrent states [3].

Following the idea of component programming (see [4]), the HSME state machine engine and state transition table both are instantiations of orthogonally designed generic components. This design offers some advantages: The generic state machine engine can execute all valid state machine descriptions provided by the user; the state transition information can be modified without going into low-level engine code; and the execution loop can be modified without unwillingly modifying state transition information (and vice versa.) Furthermore, to change the engine's functionality, the engine component code has to be modified only once and then has to be recompiled with all state-machine specifications concerned.

The components are C++ templates [7], so they are instantiated at compile time. The state transition information is stored in a table which is accessed by the state machine engine. Despite of the slightly longer execution time (table access and call overhead) and larger code size (C++ language mechanisms), our approach has has major advantages compared to a conventional implementation which were already mentioned. Because of the orthogonal component design and the template mechanism, we denote our components as 'generic', meaning that they are flexible and thus can be used in changing software environments by different instantiation, not by modifying their implementation.

This is a reasonable property concerning product families, where portions of the design of a family member are adapted to build a new one. HSME improves readability—and thus—understandability (see [12]) of state machines at the code level by explicitly representing states, events, and the state transition information. The explicit representation and the orthogonal design facilitates modification and enhancement when building a new family member.

Considering these HSME properties, it seems reasonable to replace conventionally coded state machines with generic components. The transformation process is discussed in the next section.

4   Replacing Conventional State Machine Implementations with Generic Components

Having both a flexible and configurable tool to search for state machine occurrences in the code and a set of generic components to replace the existing implementation, we will now discuss the actual transformation process. To carry out the replacement, we need all the information about the state machine. This information has to be extracted from the source code in a human-driven reverse engineering process. The different kind of information is discussed in the following enumeration.

1. **Position of the state machine in the source code.** With ESPaRT, we try to identify the location of state machine implementation parts in the source code. We do this by applying state machine patterns presented in

Section 2. Note, that the state machine parts can be distributed over the whole program.

2. **State variable.** ESPaRT can also give a hint to the state variable, since an assignment statement to a variable—the state variable—is usually part of the state machine pattern definition.

3. **State space.** Then, all the different states have to be identified. For example, in a *switch/case* construct, this can be done by examining all the case blocks that belong to the switch statement of the state variable. All possible states should be recorded together with semantically meaningful names. These names are used later in the HSME state transition table, providing a better understanding of the state machine functionality when reading the source code.

4. **Event space.** As a next step, the event space has to be identified. The detection of events in the source code can be difficult, because events are often modeled implicitly. Thus, application knowledge—such as where the events come from or where they are issued—gives a major advantage in the identification process. As with states, all identified events have to be recorded and named.

5. **State transition information.** Next, the state transition information has to be extracted. The next state is usually set by assigning a value to the state variable. The whole action block has to be searched for such an assignment following the call tree of all procedures invoked from the block. When no assignment is done, the next state will be the current state.

6. **Actions executed at state transitions.** Finally, the actions carried out at the single state transitions have to be identified, isolated, and the statements are summarized in a special HSME action function. These action functions are called by the state machine engine during execution. The local variables used by all the actions have to be identified, since there is a restricted scope for the statements now being encapsulated in an action function. The HSME engine provides references to those local variables during processing.

With this information at hand, the HSME forward engineering process can be started which is described in detail in [10]. The conventional code has to be substituted with the resulting HSME code. Since the generic state machine components are templates, the adapted source code has to be compiled with a C++ compiler. This may seem as a major drawback especially concerning efficiency important in embedded systems. However, our experience shows that with increasing speed and capacity of embedded system hardware many manufacturers are switching to C++, trying to profit from C++ concepts such as object-orientation and templates.

Of course, there is no way to guarantee that all the state machine information has been extracted and—thus—the transformation is functionality preserving. Obviously, a state transition diagram of the conventionally coded state machine, for example stemming from system design information, can be valuable in the reverse engineering process.

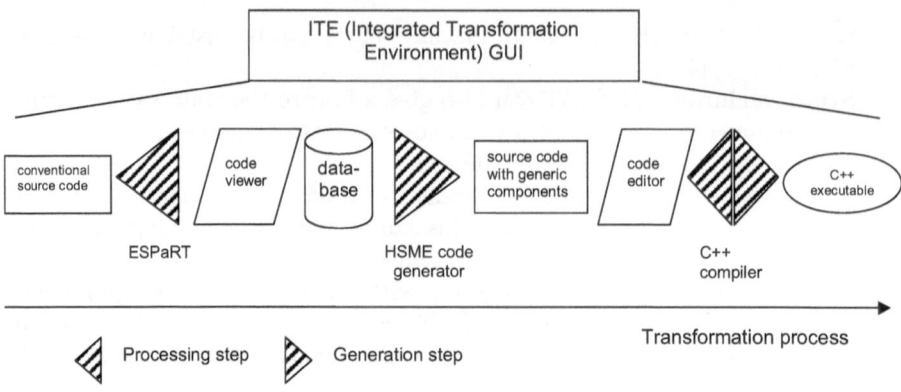

Fig. 1. The ITE tool structure

To support the reverse- and reengineering process, we will sketch a tool—further referred to as ITE (Integrated Transformation Environment)—which guides the software engineer throughout the whole process.

In a single GUI, ITE integrates the ESPaRT tool, an ESPaRT pattern editor, a code viewer and editor, a database for state/event/transition information, annotations, and patterns, a code generator producing HSME generic components, and an interface to a C++ compiler. Figure 1 shows the structure of ITE.

5   Related Work

A number of different approaches exist that implement state machines in C/C++ using high-level language facilities. For example, a pointer to a function pointer array can be used as the state variable. The function pointer array is called *jump table* and contains references to the event handler functions. In [2], the *behavioral* design pattern 'State' for the object-oriented modeling of state/event dependent behavior is presented. A similar object-oriented approach to model states as classes can be found in [6]. The design pattern 'Harel State' [10] is based on this approach to enable the processing of statecharts specifications.

6   Summary and Conclusions

In this paper, we discussed the transformation of conventionally coded state machines to generic components. Since the replacement process consists of a number of steps and involves the management of a considerable amount of data, tool support is essential. We discussed the structure of such a tool.

Today, the benefits of generic components, such as improved maintainability and reuse, are still under discussion but recognized. Since the transformation requires a reverse-engineering process that can be highly sophisticated, possibility for automation is limited and a high amount of human intervention is needed throughout the process. Neglecting the pattern search, tool support can mainly help in the process step integration, information management and organization. Since in C/C++ state machines can be implemented in manifold and sophisticated ways, the tradeoff improvement versa effort has to be concerned for each case separately.

References

1. B. Bellay and H. Gall. An Evaluation of Reverse Engineering Tools. Technical report TUV–1841–96–01. Distributed Systems Department, Technical University Vienna, December 1996.
2. E. Gamma, R. Helm, R. Johnson, and J. Vlissides. *Design patterns: elements of reusable object-oriented software*, Addison-Wesley professional computing series. Addison-Wesley, Reading, Mass. and London, 1995.
3. D. Harel. Statecharts: a visual formalism for complex systems. *Science of Computer Programming*, 8(3):231–74. North-Holland, Amsterdam, 1987.
4. M. Jazayeri. Component programming: a fresh look at software components. 5th *European Software Engineering Conference (ESEC '95)* (Sitges - Barcelona, Spain), pages 457–78, September 1995.
5. R. Knor. Converting data structures and algorithms from C to C++ applying the Standard Template Library. Technical report TUV-1841-97-16. Distributed Systems Group, Technical University of Vienna, November 1997.
6. A. Ran. Models for object-oriented design of state. In J. M. Vlissides, J. O. Coplien, and N. L. Kerth, editors, *Pattern Languages of Program Design 2*. Addison-Wesley, Reading, Mass. and London, 1996.
7. B. Stroustrup. *The C++ Programming Language, Third Edition*. Addison-Wesley, Reading, Mass. and London, 1997.
8. G. Trausmuth and R. Knor. Reengineering of C/C++ programs using generic components. 6th *European Software Engineering Conference (ESEC '97) - Workshop on Object-Oriented Reengineering* (Zurich, Switzerland). ACM SIGSOFT, August 1997.
9. L. Wall, R. L. Schwartz, and T. Christiansen. *Programming Perl*. O'Reilly & Association, Incorporated, 1996.
10. J. Weidl. Generic components for state machines. Technical report TUV-1841-96-04. Distributed Systems Group, Technical University of Vienna, December 1996. Master's thesis.
11. J. Weidl. Raising the source code abstraction level by using generic components for state machines. *International Workshop on Development and Evolution of Software Architectures for Product Families* (Las Navas del Marques, Avila, Spain), November 1996.
12. J. Weidl, R. Klösch, G. Trausmuth, and H. Gall. Facilitating program comprehension via generic components for state machines. 5th *International Workshop on Program Comprehension (IWPC '97)* (Dearborn, Michigan, USA), pages 118–27. IEEE Computer Society Press, May 1997.

An Experiment in Distributed Software Architecture Recovery

Nabor C. Mendonça* and Jeff Kramer

Dep. of Computing, Imperial College of Science, Technology and Medicine
180 Queen's Gate, London SW7 2BZ, U.K.
e-mail: {ndcm,jk}@doc.ic.ac.uk

Abstract. We describe an architecture recovery experiment performed on a distributed software system. Our main aim was to identify those situations in which existing reverse engineering techniques could be satisfactorily applied and those situations where such techniques would produce only limited or inaccurate results. Based on this experience, we propose ways in which these techniques can be improved.

1 Introduction

Most of the current work in the area of *software architecture* [12] addresses issues related to the early stages of the software life-cycle, such as specification, analysis and development. Very little is concerned with existing (legacy) systems for which high-level architecture descriptions are usually missing or inaccurate. To help in the process of extracting the architecture of existing software systems, tools and techniques are being developed for *architecture recovery* [3, 7]. Among other benefits, architecture recovery technologies can facilitate system understanding and maintenance, help in the identification of commonalities within a family of related systems, and also raise the possibility of reusing system structure and components in the development of new systems.

However, the usual discrepancy between code and architectural abstractions makes architecture recovery a rather difficult task. This task is exacerbated in the case of distributed environments, where typical architecture elements such as components, interaction mechanisms and configuration are generally not explicitly supported by the underlying programming language and are therefore difficult to identify in a typical distributed system source code [11].

With the aim of investigating the extent to which current reverse engineering technologies can (and cannot) be used to help understanding the architecture of distributed software, we carried out a detailed recovery experiment on the source code of an existing distributed software system. To verify the accuracy of the techniques used, we analysed source code small enough to be manually and thoroughly understood prior to the experiment, yet complex enough to highlight many of the difficulties involved in reverse engineering non-trivial software. This

---

* Supported by the National Council for Scientific and Technological Development of Brazil (CNPq) under grant No 200603/94-9.

Frank v. d. Linden (Ed.): ARES '98, LNCS 1429, pp. 106-114, 1998.

decision allowed us to compare the results produced using existing reverse engineering techniques with the abstractions that we had manually recovered, in addition to those described in the software documentation. Based on this experience, we propose new methods through which the results produced by the existing techniques used—and the techniques themselves—can be improved. All techniques employed during the experiment have been implemented and integrated with other off-the-shelf tools. Together these form the basis for an approach to the recovery of distributed software architectures that we are currently developing.

2   The Software

Our experiment was performed on the source code of ANIMAᴅO, a computer animation prototype [10]. The system is based on the client/server architectural style and written mostly in C, with a single utility class in C++, under an UNIX environment. Despite being relatively small, roughly 3,000 LOC, the software presents a non-trivial complexity: five independent executable components (namely INTEREXPSERV, EGESP, FRED, COLLISION and CONTROL) communicating through message exchange (implemented via UNIX *sockets*) and event notification (implemented via exchange of process *signals*). INTEREXPSERV stores all information regarding the animation process which is initially provided by the user in the form of an animation script. This component acts as the system server, accepting requests from the other components (or clients) to read or update the state of one or more animation objects. At each animation step the system updates the state of all objects and outputs the new states as an updated animation script. The set of all animation scripts generated this way can then be displayed by some compatible visualisation tool.[1]

The architecture of ANIMAᴅO, exactly as given in its documentation, is shown in Fig. 1. This architecture was verified to be accurate during our manual inspection of the code, and hence was used as our expected architecture with regards to the results to be produced by our techniques. In the following sections we describe several types of "high-level" abstractions or *views* that we were able to extract from the system source code during the experiment.

3   Modules and Subsystems

The system source code is spread over 8 header files and 11 source files or modules. As we are primarily interested in recovering system components as units of execution, we statically extracted information about all functions that each module defines and in which other modules those functions are called. This information revealed the system (static) inter-modular activation graph which is

---

[1] Due to space restrictions, in this paper we omit the description of the functionalities of the other components and report only on the issues related to recovery of socket-based interactions.

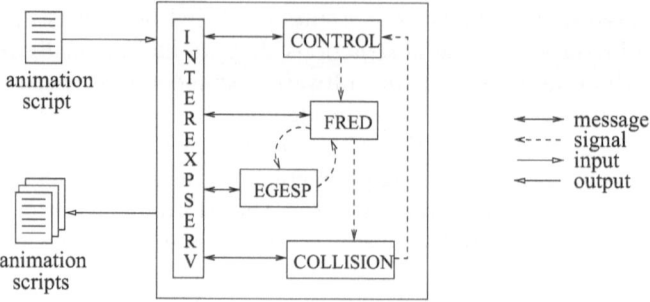

Fig. 1. Architecture of the ANIMADO computer animation system.

graphically represented in the *module view* depicted in Fig. 2(a). Since there are many more modules in the source code than components in the documented architecture, it is clear that modules are concepts not yet in the appropriate level of abstraction to be considered as representing system components. One way to assign modules to higher-level concepts is by clustering them into subsystems.

Among the many clustering techniques for subsystem classification that have been proposed in the literature, the technique proposed in [1] seemed to be the one that more closely satisfied our need for recovering components as high-level units of execution. In this technique, program units are clustered into higher-level units based on the concept of node dominance on the system activation graph. The technique can be applied to produce clusters of two types: one representing clusters containing units that would be part of the implementation of a more general system functionality, which we call here *entry* subsystems, and one representing clusters containing units that would be providing resources to other clusters, which we call *library* subsystems.

We implemented a modified version of this clustering technique and applied it to the system inter-modular activation graph. Six subsystems were identified and are represented in the *subsystem view* shown in Fig. 2(b). The subsystem containing only the message module is a library subsystem, and the other five ones are all entry subsystems. The effectiveness of this particular subsystem classification technique can, to some extent, be confirmed considering knowledge specific to the application domain. For example, routines provided by the stack and parser modules are clearly used by inter for interpretation of animation scripts. However, subsystems only partially match the abstractions described in the system architecture. For instance, we can associate code to components (the modules clustered inside each entry subsystem) but we can not say anything about servers, clients or message-based interactions. As a matter of fact, when it comes to architecture recovery, this mismatch between (recovered) code entities and architectural abstractions is the major obstacle faced by most traditional reverse engineering tools which rely only on structural software information.

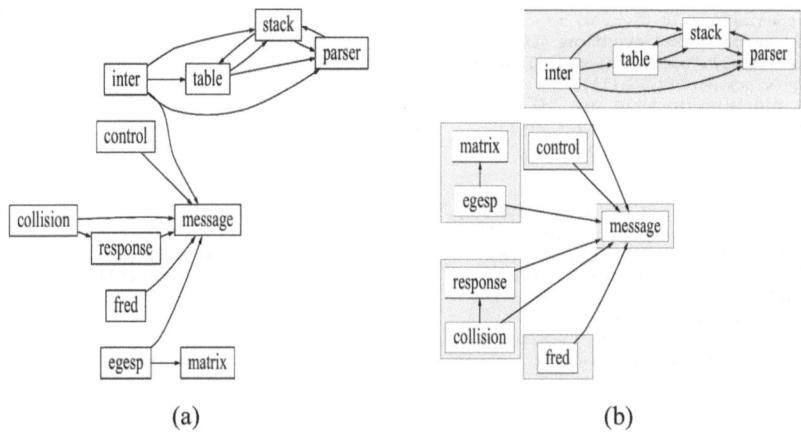

Fig. 2. The (a) module and (b) subsystem views.

4   Architectural Abstractions

Abstractions used in typical architecture descriptions vary substantially from one application or system domain to another. The identification of such abstractions in the system source code therefore requires some sort of previous domain knowledge (e.g., knowledge regarding the application, programming language and execution platform) stating how they are expected to be implemented. Two recent tools, ManSART [4] and ART [2], have started to address this issue in a fairly similar fashion [8]. Domain knowledge is expressed in the form of an architectural style library which contains information about several architectural styles and their elements, i.e., components and interaction mechanisms. This information includes a description of program patterns or *clichés* [9] through which some architectural elements are expected to be implemented in a traditional programming language. A search engine then attempts to match a given pattern against portions of the abstract syntax tree (AST) generated from an existing system source code.

During our experiment we implemented a similar mechanism on top of a Prolog environment. The AST representation, pattern notation and search engine, as well the clustering technique described in the previous section, all are implemented as Prolog predicates.[2] Figure 3(a) shows an example of an architectural pattern specified in our Prolog-based notation. This pattern states how the creation of a server-side socket is expected to be implemented under the C/UNIX domain using AST structural and traversal constructs.[3]

---

[2] In addition to the Prolog environment, we also use other off-the-shelf tools such as program analysers for parsing and source model extraction, and an automatic layout tool for graphical visualisation of recovered elements.

[3] Our pattern notation follows the notation used in ART which is in turn based on the formalism proposed in [5]. In contrast to ART, our notation does not (yet) support constraints expressed in terms of data/control flow links between statements.

```
socket_opening(SockId,CSockId) :-
  %%%% server socket creation %%%%
  fun_call(SCall,"socket",[Domain,Type,_]),
  assign(ASock,SockId,SCall),
  %%%% machine port set up %%%%
  member_ref(MRef,ServAddr,PortMember),
  obj_name(PortMember,"sin_port"),
  assign(APort,MRef,PortVal),
  %%%% socket binding %%%%
  fun_call(BCall,"bind",[SockId1,ServAddr,_]),
  %%%% listening for connections %%%%
  fun_call(LCall,"listen",[SockId2,_]),
  %%%% accepting connection %%%%
  fun_call(ACall,"accept",[SockId3,_,_]),
  assign(ACSock,CSockId,ACall),
  %%%% pattern constraints %%%%
  same_obj([SockId,SockId1,SockId2,SockId3]),
  before([ASock,APort],BCall),
  before([LCall],ACSock).
```

```
int server_socket(int *port)
{ ...
  sock = socket(AF_INET,SOCK_STREAM,0);
  ...
  server.sin_port = 0;
  if (bind(sock,(struct sockaddr*)&server,
           sizeof(server)) < 0){
    /* error ... */
  }
  ...
  *port = ntohs(server.sin_port);
  return sock;
}
```

(a)   (b)

Fig. 3. Example of (a) an architectural pattern described in Prolog and (b) a corresponding code fragment in the **message** module partially matching the pattern.

4.1   Searching for Code Patterns

We initially searched for this and a similar pattern describing the creation of a client-side socket. The results were two matches (one partial match and one full match) in the **message** module and one partial match in the **inter** module. Matches in **message** correspond to the initial creation of a server socket, as shown in Fig. 3(b), and a complete creation of client socket, respectively. The partial match in **inter** corresponds to a server socket waiting for and accepting client connections. We also searched for other possible variations for those two patterns but no reference to a function responsible for socket creation was found in any other module. From those three matches alone we can at best say that two sockets (of types server and client) are created in the **message** module, and that another server socket is possibly created in the **inter** module. No strong conclusion can be reached as to whether or not, for instance, sockets are created in other modules that could be associated with the implementation of clients such as **control** and **fred**. This situation is a typical example of the limitations of pattern-based approaches whose patterns are defined independently of the domain where they are used, as it is the case for ManSART and ART.

Clearly, the problem with those approaches is that they search for architectural abstractions without taking into account application specific domain knowledge. For example, from the subsystem view shown in Fig. 2(b) we know that the **message** module is actually a library providing resources to other modules. Since two types of sockets are created in this module, it may be that sockets are created in the other subsystems not only by means of the **socket** and related calls, as it is expected when only knowledge about the C/UNIX domain is considered, but rather by calling functions responsible for socket creation defined in the **message** module.

In order to check this hypothesis we augmented the client and server patterns to also include references to the `server_socket` and `client_socket` functions provided by the `message` module. A second search for these "refined" patterns confirmed that all entry subsystems do create sockets by calling either `server_socket` or `client_socket`. In this case, we can say that the `message` module is actually part of the implementation of the system *infrastructure* rather than the implementation of one of the system components. This distinction is important because code associated with the system infrastructure generally implements routines for components instantiation and connections and is mostly platform-dependent. On the other hand, code associated with components themselves is where the system behaviour is actually implemented and is (supposed to be) less dependent on platform-specific communication mechanisms. Thus, explicitly separating components and infrastructure code could be a significant contribution to facilitating system understanding and code reuse.

4.2   Components

The identification of code related to sockets creation finally allows the representation of the software under analysis in terms of architectural (rather than source code) abstractions. The first of these abstractions are *components*, which we represent following a notation similar to the graphical notation of *Darwin* [6], an architecture description language specifically created to describe distributed systems structure.

In our notation, each component encapsulates an entry subsystem and has an explicitly defined *interface* describing *services* that the component provides or requires. Services correspond to *interaction channels* (sockets, in the current experiment) created within the subsystem encapsulated by the component. Each service is associated with the respective code fragments implementing creation or use of its underlying interaction channel. Figure 4 shows how the INTEREXPSERV component is graphically represented according to this notation. In this view, the component is represented by a round-cornered rectangle and its service by a filled circle located at the component borderlines (which in turn represent the component interface). The filled circle means that the service is a provision, while an empty circle would mean a requirement. The source code units encapsulated by the component are represented by straight boxes inside the component's rectangle. Arrows represent "uses" relations between source code units. A bold line between a service and a code unit indicates that the code unit contains one or more code fragments creating or using that service. This explicit association of services to code units is important in that it bridges the gap between code and architectural abstractions and makes it easier to understand and visualise how a component implements a service it provides or uses a service it requires. Although in this particular view a service is only associated with modules, this association could be further refined to show how the service is implemented in terms of lower-level abstractions (e.g, function calls or even code fragments).

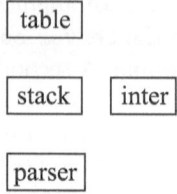

Fig. 4. The (recovered) INTEREXPSERV component.

4.3   Interactions

When an interaction channel is created by a component, the other potential users of that channel, besides the creator itself, can only be identified—if at all—by a careful analysis of the arguments passed to and returned from the calls responsible for the channel creation. In the case of sockets, the main parameter to be analysed is the machine *port* which is assigned to each socket created.[4] From Fig. 3(b) we can see that server sockets created by the function server_socket in the message module have their ports automatically defined by the system. This happens because the port number parameter (the field sin_port) is set to zero before the socket call. The actual port number, the one given by the operating system, is assigned to the incoming parameter of server_socket. This parameter is used to return the actual port number to the caller of server_socket. In the case of a client socket, the port number is taken directly from one of the incoming parameters of the function client_socket. The port number returned by server_socket is used only once, as a parameter for a fprintf call in the inter module. Inspection of modules which call client_socket showed that the value assigned to the port number parameter is always "atoi(argv[counter])", which means that the actual value is provided as an argument to the shell command which invokes the client program. Since no constant value can be identified in the code for any socket port, it is not possible to determine which sockets are connected to which other sockets. We are left to conclude then that information regarding interactions between ANIMADO components is not totally represented in the source code and therefore cannot be recovered without considering some other non-code source of information about the system.

In view of the mechanism that the system implements to establish its sockets connections (i.e., port numbers passed as arguments to invocation commands), one potential candidate for such a non-code artifact would be UNIX shell scripts. No shell script is included as part of the ANIMADO distribution package however. We raised this issue to one of the system's original developers and we were told that their original intention was to have the user him/herself manually configure the system. Their informal "script" is to first invoke INTEREXPSERV

---

[4] The *hostname* parameter indicating the machine where a server socket was created is also important, but we have deliberately omitted it from the current discussion for brevity.

which automatically outputs the port numbers assigned to each server socket created—this explains the port number value returned by the server_socket function being immediately passed to a fprintf call in the inter module. Each of these numbers can then be manually passed as the port number argument to the invocation of each client. This manual configuration procedure, albeit informal, is a crucial system artifact that confirmed the accuracy of the system's documented architecture.

5   Conclusion

This paper has described a controlled experiment performed with the aim of investigating the difficulties involved in the recovery of distributed software architectures. Although the experiment was restricted to a single and relatively small system, we believe that the characteristics and complexity of the software analysed provided us with interesting insights into the architecture recovery process as a whole. For example, although we recognised that it is important to identify architectural patterns in the code, it is equally important to identify whether matched code fragments can be associated with the implementation of a system component or with the implementation of the system infrastructure. Another insight is that the identification of potential system configurations, in terms of connections that might be established between components, can be more difficult than identifying components themselves. Also of interest was the confirmation that the analysis of non-code artifacts, even informal ones, may play an important role during the recovery process.

We are currently reorganising the techniques used in the experiment to form a new approach for the recovery of distributed software architectures. We then plan to perform further experiments to verify the applicability of this approach on systems of varying characteristics and sizes. With further experience, we expect to revise and improve our techniques and tools.

References

1. A. Cimitile and G. Visaggio. Software Salvaging and the Call Dominance Tree. *J. of Syst. and Software*, 28:117–127, 1995.
2. R. Fiutem, P. Tonella, G. Antoniol, and E. Merlo. A Cliché-Based Environment to Support Architectural Reverse Engineering. In *Proc. Int. Conf. Softw. Maint.*, pages 319–328. IEEE CS Press, Nov. 1996.
3. H. Gall, M. Jazayeri, R. Klösch, W. Lugmayr, and G. Trausmuth. Architecture Recovery in ARES. In *Proc. 2nd ACM SIGSOFT Int. Software Architecture Workshop*, pages 111–115, San Francisco, USA, Oct. 1996.
4. D. R. Harris, A. S. Yeh, and H. B. Reubenstein. Extracting Architectural Features from Source Code. *Aut. Softw. Eng. Journal*, 3(1-2):109–138, June 1996.
5. W. Kozaczynski, J. Q. Ning, and A. Engberts. Program Concept Recognition and Transformation. *IEEE Trans. Softw. Eng.*, 18(12):1065–1075, Dec. 1992.
6. J. Magee, N. Dulay, S. Eisenbach, and J. Kramer. Specifying Distributed Software Architectures. In *Proc. 5th Europ. Softw. Eng. Conf. (ESEC)*, LNCS 989, pages 137–153. Springer-Verlag, Sept. 1995.

7. N. C. Mendonça and J. Kramer. Requirements for an Effective Architecture Recovery Framework. In *Proc. 2nd ACM SIGSOFT Int. Software Architecture Workshop*, pages 101–105, San Francisco, USA, Oct. 1996.

8. N. C. Mendonça and J. Kramer. A Quality-Based Analysis of Architecture Recovery Environments. In *Proc. 1st Euromicro Conf. Softw. Maint. Reeng.*, pages 54–59, Berlin, Germany, Mar. 1997. IEEE CS Press.

9. C. Rich and L. M. Wills. Recognizing a Program's Design: A Graph-Parsing Approach. *IEEE Software*, 7(1):82–89, Jan. 1990.

10. M. A. F. Rodrigues. ANIMADO: An Animation System Prototype Using Dynamics. Master's thesis, State University of Campinas, Brazil, Department of Computing and Automation, Faculty of Electrical Engineering, July 1993. In Portuguese.

11. S. L. Schneberger. Software Maintenance in Distributed Computer Environments: System Complexity Versus Component Simplicity. In *Proc. Int. Conf. Softw. Maint.*, pages 304–313. IEEE CS Press, Sept. 1995.

12. A. L. Wolf. Succeedings of the Second International Software Architecture Worshop (ISAW-2). *ACM SIGSOFT Softw. Eng. Notes*, 22(1):42–56, Jan. 1997.

Reverse Engineering to Recover and Describe a System's Architecture[*]

Berndt Bellay and Harald Gall

Technical University of Vienna, Distributed Systems Group
Argentinierstrasse 8/184-1, A-1040 Vienna, Austria, Europe
Phone: +43 1 58801 4412
{bellay, gall}@infosys.tuwien.ac.at

Abstract. The increasing interest in the software architecture of systems stems from the need to generate product families, to facilitate the reuse of components, to better understand systems and to redocument them. This paper introduces our approach to recover and describe a system's architecture: different aspects of a system (i.e. architectural properties) are recovered and then described. The recovery process focuses on architectural properties, such as safety and variance and their description, but not on the recovery of a complete system's architecture. Such a property-driven recovery allows to incrementally investigate those aspects of a system that are of special interest for the recovery purpose. Additionally the paper presents our architecture recovery framework and process, and an example illustrating the applicability of our framework.

1   Introduction

The work on software architectures developed out of design abstractions and high-level structural descriptions of software systems. Currently, there is no clear distinction between what is referred to as high-level design and software architecture.

Software architecture has been approached from different directions: architecture definition (e.g. [7], [13], [14], [17]), architecture description (e.g. [10], [15]), domain-specific software architectures (e.g. [16]), architecture development environments (e.g. Aesop [6] or Darwin [12]), architecture description languages (e.g. [11]), and also architecture recovery (e.g. [4], [8], [18]).

We define software architecture on the basis of architectural properties that are beyond design descriptions and usually not explicitly represented in a design. Properties, such as safety can be described by a set of implementation techniques (e.g. redundancy, checksums, etc.). The identification of architectural properties is a key issue in the process of architecture recovery. This approach proved to be especially helpful in recovering the architecture of the TCS (Train control system) case study

---

[*] This work was supported by the European Commission within the ESPRIT Framework IV project ARES (Architectural Reasoning for Embedded Systems).

Frank v. d. Linden (Ed.): ARES '98, LNCS 1429, pp. 115-122, 1998.

because it is easier to recover architectural properties seperately. As a result, we defined architecture recovery as the recovery of architectural properties and their associated architectural descriptions that are relevant to a specific system.

The paper is organized as follows. In Section 2 we give a short description of the case study examined. Section 3 introduces our architecture recovery framework. Section 4 describes the architecture recovery process based on architectural properties and gives an illustrative example. Finally, we give some concluding remarks and an overview of future work.

2   Case study: Train Control System (TCS)

The Train Control System represents an embedded software system implemented in C and assembler to check signal information for speed control of locomotives. The signals are received via the antenna of the locomotive and processed by TCS.

The main system characteristics of TCS are: safety and fault-tolerance, embedded real-time system, two programming languages (C, Assembler), different development and target environments, and represents a member of a family of systems. The code size of the recovered part is approximately 150K LOC (Lines of Code) of C.

3   The Architecture Recovery Framework

In this section, we describe our architecture recovery framework. Architecture recovery is defined as the recovery of all architectural properties and their associated architectural descriptions that are relevant to a specific software system.

First we present architectural properties and their categorization. Then we give an overview of architectural descriptions and discuss their applicability to different architectural properties. We continue the presentation of the framework with a discussion of architecture recovery methods and tools.

3.1   Architectural Properties

We view software architecture as a set of architectural properties that influence and limit the degrees of freedom in the design process.

An *architectural property* (AP) represents a specific design decision related to a functional or non-functional requirement, and may be described using different architectural descriptions. Each architectural property is realized by a set of implementation techniques in the software system (e.g. redundancy, hardware tests, time-outs, or checksums for the architectural property "safety")

The investigations of the case study revealed several architectural properties that were not explicitly expressed in the design. We generalized the architectural properties and completed them with other related properties not originally found in the case study. Finally, we came up with the following categorization of architectural properties:

1. Information exchange
2. System control
3. Dynamic behavior
4. System structure
5. Safety
6. Security
7. Variance

Note that this categorization is not complete and might be extended.

The examples given for the implementation techniques result from recovering the architecture of TCS and do not represent a domain-independent description of architectural properties. An example for the resulting categorization is shown in Table 1 for the architectural properties safety and variance.

Table 1. Categorization of architectural properties

Architectural properties		implementation techniques
safety	type of safety	fail-stop fail-operational
	safety mechanisms	redundancy (dynamic/static) hardware tests (runtime/startup) time-outs checksums
variance	type of variance	standards customer need hardware platforms
	implementation	defines, files, variables run-time/compile-time

A more elaborate description of the architectural properties and the related implementation techniques as well as examples from the case study can be found in [2].

3.2   Architectural Descriptions

Each architectural property can be described using one or more notations. For example, implementations of the architectural property "information exchange" could be described using a component/connector description type, or an architecture description language (ADL). There is no single view or notation that is best suited for a particular architecture description. There may be advantages or disadvantages of one architectural description over the other: the best suited description of an architectural property is system dependent and has to be determined by the system architect.

3.3   Architecture Recovery Methods

Architecture recovery methods may be appropriate for one or more specific architectural properties. From our experience with the case study we concluded that there exists no single method that is best suited for the recovery of all architectural properties. Furthermore, an architecture recovery method may be appropriate and well-suited for one system, but this may not be the case for another system. For our architecture recovery framework we provide a list of methods to recover each of the previously defined architectural properties. For the architecture recovery of TCS we applied:

–   code browsing (manual/tool-supported),
    reverse engineering tools (to recover different software views) [1],
    additional tools (ImagParse, ParDsp, which are self developed tools to recover specific information from other sources [3]),
    view integration and combination (to generate extended and new views from recovered software views) [3],
    the "Hot-spots" technique (a combination of reverse engineering tools and application domain knowledge) [5], and
    the "ESPaRT" tool (for recovering similar string patterns in the source code) [9].

For the architecture recovery process of the case study, the following system information was available: source code, system documentation, domain knowledge, and application specific knowledge.

4   The Architecture Recovery Process

In this section, we present the principles of our framework and—based on these principles—the architecture recovery process.

4.1   Principles of the Framework

From the experiences of the architecture recovery of the TCS system we developed our architecture recovery framework. We base the framework on the following principles:

Architectural properties: We recover architectural properties, since:
    architectural properties are manageable units for architectural reasoning.
    there is no single view that describes a software architecture completely, and
    it is easier to recover the software architecture of a system in parts (separation of concerns),

Architectural descriptions: We use more than one architectural description because there is no single view or notation that is best suited for a particular software architecture description (see Section 3.2).

Recovery methods: There exists no single method that is best suited for the recovery of all architectural properties. We suggest to choose the best-suited method from a list of methods (see Section 3.3). The method to choose depends on:
    the architectural property to identify and recover, or the missing relationships to recover.
    the available system information,
    the task: identify and recover an architectural property, or recover missing relationships to build an architectural description, and

Case study: Depending on the case study different architectural properties are of interest, different architectural descriptions are required, and the system information to recover the software architecture vary.

4.2   Architecture Recovery Process

The following describes the architecture recovery process (see Figure 2):

I.   Select candidates of architectural properties
   A. Identify architectural properties (*AP*) that are of interest for the recovery
   B. Use Table 1 to find implementation techniques associated to AP′s
   C. Select candidates for architectural properties and related implementation techniques based on system information of the system under study (*Case study*)

II. Identify architectural properties in the system (*Identify & recover AP (X)*)
   A. Choose an appropriate method for each implementation technique to identify it in the system based on the available information (*M*)
   B. Search for the implementations representing the architectural properties using the recovery methods
   C. Add additional implementation techniques that are directly found in the system, and were not candidates (as said before, our list of implementation techniques as well as architectural properties may be incomplete)
   D. Recover the implementatios of the architectural properties, and thus the AP′s, identified in B) and C), from the system
   E. Put identified and recovered architectural properties into the set of architectural properties of the system (*AP (X)*)

III. Choose appropriate architectural description(s) for the architectural properties found from *AD*

IV. Build the architectural descriptions of the APs identified (*Build AD (X)*)
   A. Choose an appropriate method (M) for each AD to recover the missing relationships and to build the AD based on the information available and the architectural description to recover
   B. Build the architectural description(s) of the system (*AD (X)*)

The recovered architectural properties (*AP (X)*) and architectural descriptions (*AD (X)*) are denoted as the software architecture of the system X (*System X's architecture*)

4.3   An Architecture Recovery Example

The following provides an example of a recovery process using our architecture recovery framework:

Step I.: We identify the architectural property "safety" as one of the essential parts of the system, because TCS is a system for automatic train control which has to be realized with various safety features.

For this example we are only interested in the "safety mechanisms" (see Table 1). We used Table 1 to find the associated implementation techniques for this property.

The next three steps are only examplified by the implementation of "redundancy", but are essentially the same for others.

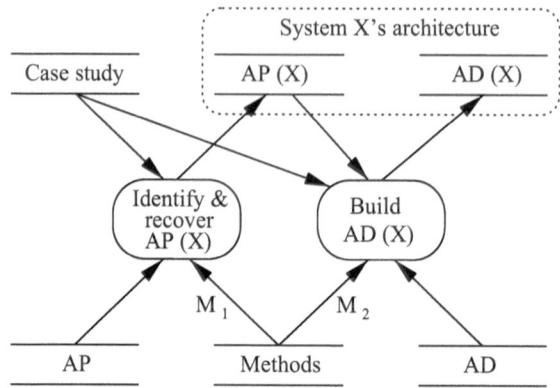

Fig. 1. Architecture recovery process

Step II.: Before we choose an appropriate method to find the implementation of "redundancy" that represents the architectural property "safety" we identify what information is available to find this property.

The available information states that the following parts specific to the redundancy implementation have to be found in the source code:

- redundant parts (e.g. functional parts, data structures, algorithms) and, additionally,

  either a component representing a "voter" in case of static redundancy,

  or a component that monitors the occurrence of errors and a watch-dog timer in case of dynamic redundancy.

To find redundant parts we used the capabilities of reverse engineering tools to identify similar functions and variables. In the case study it turns out that the naming conventions already hint at redundant parts (almost identical names with different prefixes for files, functions, types, and variables). After studying these parts we identified that the system uses static redundancy based on 2-version programming (functions and variables) and a voter which in this case performs comparisons.

Step III.: After identifying the implementation of "static redundancy" and thus a part of the AP "safety," an architectural description for the property has to be chosen. Possible architectural descriptions for this architectural property are, e.g. textual (e.g. descriptional text, tables) or graphical (e.g. system structure) descriptions. We choose a graphical description: a simple boxes-and-arrows diagram that shows a simplified data flow diagram. The reason for this choice is that it shows additional parts of interest.

Step IV.: To recover the data flow diagram we again choose a reverse engineering tool. By browsing the source code we build the data flow diagram (see Step II.) around the recovered types of functions (functions of the same type called in sequence were grouped together) and by adding information about data usage.

5   Summary and Conclusions

In this paper, we described our approach to software architecture based on architectural properties and a framework to recover and describe a system's architecture based on reverse engineering technology. The result of this architecture recovery process are the systems's architectural properties and their architectural descriptions. These architectural properties and their descriptions represent the architecture of a specific system.

By basing the software architecture on architectural properties, the architecture recovery process benefits from separation of concerns: architectural properties are manageable units for architectural reasoning; it is easier to recover the software architecture in parts; different views and different recovery methods can be used depending on the property to be recovered.

The current architecture recovery framework supports the task of recovering the architecture of single systems. A further step will be to extend the framework to cope with several members of a product family to recover their family architecture.

Acknowledgements

We are grateful to Mehdi Jazayeri, Vesna Hassler, Georg Trausmuth, and René Klösch for the stimulating discussions on architectural properties, and to Wolfgang Eixelsberger, Lasse Warholm and Haakon Beckman for their support in analyzing the case study.

References

1. B. Bellay and H. Gall. A Comparison of four Reverse Engineering Tools. *4th Working Conference on Reverse Engineering* (Amsterdam, NL), October 1997.

2. B. Bellay, H. Gall, V. Hassler, W. Eixelsberger. Architecture recovery based on architectural concepts. Technical Report TUV 1841-97-13, *Distributed Systems Department, Technical University of Vienna*, 1997.

3. B. Bellay and H. Gall. View integration and combination. Technical Report, *Distributed Systems Department, Technical University of Vienna*, 1997.

4. W. Eixelsberger, L. Warholm, R. Klösch, and H. Gall. Software architecture recovery of embedded software. *Proceedings of the 19th International Conference on Software Engineering* (Boston, USA), pp. 558-9, May 1997.

5. H. Gall and B. Bellay. The Hot-Spots technique to scavenge for architectural elements. Technical Report TUV-1841-97-11, *Distributed Systems Department, Technical University of Vienna*, 1997.

6. D. Garlan. An introduction to the Aesop system, School of Computer Science, CMU, July 1995.

7. D. Garlan and M. Shaw. An introduction to software architecture. In V. Ambriola and G. Tortora, editors, *Advances in Software Engineering and Knowledge Engineering*, volume 1, 1993.

8. D.R. Harris, H.B. Reubenstein, and A.S. Yeh. Reverse engineering to the architectural level. *Proceedings of the 17th International Conference on Software Engineering* (Seattle, USA), pp. 186-95, April 1995.

9. R. Knor, and G. Trausmuth. Converting data structures and algorithms from C to C++ applying the satndard template library. Technical Report TUV 1841-97-16, *Distributed Systems Department, Technical University of Vienna*, 1997.

10. B. Kruchten. The 4+1 View Model of Architecture. *IEEE Transactions on Software Engineering*, pp. 42-50. IEEE, November 1995.

11. D.C. Luckham and J. Vera. An event-based architecture definition language. *IEEE Transactions on Software Engineering*, 21(9), pp. 717-34. IEEE, September 1995.

12. J. Magee, N. Dulay, S. Eisenbach, and J. Kramer. Specifying Distributed Software Architectures. *Proceedings of the 5th European Software Engineering Conference* (Sitges, Spain). Published as *LNCS*, 989, pp. 137-53. Springer-Verlag, 1995.

13. D.E. Perry and A.L. Wolf. Foundations for the study of software architecture. *ACM SIGSOFT Software Engineering Notes*, 17(4), pp. 40-52, October 1992.

14. M. Shaw, R. DeLine, D.V. Klein, T.L. Ross, D.M. Young, and G. Zelesnik. Abstractions for software architecture and tools to support them. *IEEE Transactions on Software Engineering*, 21(4), pp. 314-35, April 1995.

15. D. Soni, R.L. Nord, and C. Hofmeister. Software Architecture in Industrial Applications. *Proceedings of the 17th International Conference on Software Engineering* (Seattle, USA), pp. 196-207, April 1995.

16. W. Tracz, L. Coglianese, and P. Young. Domain-Specific Software Architecture Engineering Process Guidelines. Technical report ADAGE-IBM-92-02. IBM Corp., 1992.

17. D.I. Witt, F.T. Baker, and E.W. Merritt. Software Architecture and Design Principles, Models, and Methods. Van Nostrand Reinholt, 1994.

18. A.S. Yeh, D.R. Harris, and M.P. Chase. Manipulating recovered software architecture views. *Proceedings of the 19th International Conference on Software Engineering* (Boston, USA), pp. 184-94, May1997.

Can Legacy Systems Beget Product Lines?

Nelson Weiderman, John Bergey, Dennis Smith, Scott Tilley
Software Engineering Institute
Carnegie Mellon University
Pittsburgh, PA, USA
{nhw,jkb,dbs,stilley}@sei.cmu.edu

Abstract. In many respects it is easier to formulate an architecture for a family of products if one assumes that the systems are being developed from scratch. But the vast majority of systems development efforts today start from a cornucopia of legacy systems. Significant progress in component-based architecture, system understanding, object-technology, and net-centric computing now makes it possible to evolve these legacy systems to a state in which they exhibit many of the characteristics of product lines. Systems in well-established domains are migrating to distributed object systems that exhibit large-scale reuse from a core set of assets while keeping the legacy systems largely intact. Many of these systems have evolved without overtly using product line terminology or practices and have been off the radar screen of the product line community as a starting point for product families. The advocates of product lines need to recognize this "distributed legacy evolution model" as an integral part of their practices for developing information systems.

1. Introduction

Legacy systems have usually been thought of as an albatross rather than an asset when it comes to evolving to more modern, productive, and useful systems. Software developers and software researchers have tended to focus their attention on "better, cheaper, faster" ways to build new systems rather than on evolution paths for heritage applications. They were justified in this focus since the stovepipe systems built in the past were virtually intractable in the face of available program understanding and integration technology. The emphasis on component-based architecture and product lines has clearly raised the state of the practice for developing new systems from scratch, but has contributed far less to the practice of evolving legacy systems.

The bad news is that there are few developments today that have the luxury of starting from scratch because of the huge investments in, and reliance on, legacy

Frank v. d. Linden (Ed.): ARES '98, LNCS 1429, pp. 123-131, 1998.
© Springer-Verlag Berlin Heidelberg 1998

systems. The good news is that there are new technologies and practices that make the migration path more tractable.

One of the reasons that the situation is changing so rapidly is the emergence of integrating infrastructures. With improved integration we have seen the the World Wide Web (the Web) and electronic commerce flourish. Where once information systems were isolated and difficult to access, they can now be accessed using the Web and its interfacing software.

The Internet is being used in a number of innovative ways to connect users and their stovepipe systems both inside organizations and between organizations. Within organizations, the Web is not only being used to connect departments such as marketing, sales, and engineering, but also to connect teams of software developers around the world working around-the-clock on the same project. Between organizations, the Web is being used to connect businesses with their suppliers and their customers. It is becoming a medium for placing orders, receiving delivery, and checking status.

There are many ways of evolving to product lines. Regardless of the starting point, the goal is to develop higher quality systems, faster, with higher productivity and improved efficiency. Product lines accomplish this goal by facilitating the systematic reuse of software assets. The emphasis is on strategic, coarse-grained reuse that leverages models, architectures, designs, documentation, testing artifacts, people, processes, and implementations.

The leverage of product lines is that software assets can be reused in different contexts. The cost of producing consecutive systems with the same asset base decreases over time. The domain model is reused from one application to the next and the productivity of the software development staff increases proportionately and hence the assets have a greater return on investment over time.

On the other hand, unintegrated (stovepipe) software assets that are not used for continuous production of additional assets become stale and require more and more resources to maintain them. Hence their value may decrease over time and eventually there may be more cost associated with their continued maintenance than benefit from their continued use. At that point the software becomes a liability with no leverage. Until recently this was the end of the story.

Now, it is becoming possible to leveraging software assets either at conception of the development of a product line or after the fact by extracting the necessary components from existing legacy assets. New product starts should plan for this reuse of software assets in advance. In fact, some plans for product lines arise out of expediency when it becomes apparent that the resources are not available to construct two similar systems without exploiting commonality [3]. A priori development of systems using a product line practice approach is an active research area and deserves continuing attention. For example see [1]. But the substantial contributions to migrating stovepipe legacy systems to product lines have gone largely unrecognized by the product line community and needs further attention.

We take the position that starting a product line effort with legacy assets is not only possible, but is in most cases preferable to starting from scratch. We posit that this leveraging of legacy assets is enabled through the convergence of a set of practices that we try to illuminate at a high level. We make our case by elaborating on a distributed legacy evolution model [10] with the following components:

- an enterprise approach for guiding decision making for system evolution,
- developing a technical understanding of systems at a high level of abstraction,
- using distributed object technology and wrapping for system evolution, and
- using network-centric computing for system evolution.

We also present credible evidence of progress and experience that supports this approach. While the range of application for these ideas may not include all classes of systems (real-time embedded applications may be one such exception), we believed that applicable scope is quite broad.

2. Using an Enterprise Approach for Decision Making

System evolution and technology insertion do not take place in a vacuum. Many attempts at evolution and migration fail because they concentrate on a narrow set of software issues without considering the broader set of management and technical issues. Evolution takes place in the context of an organizational setting that varies considerably in terms of the culture and the readiness to incorporate change. While there may be many complex technical problems that are largely unprecedented, a focus on the technical problems to the exclusion of the enterprise problems is a recipe for disaster. Hence it is crucial to plan for change in the context of the enterprise.

The Software Engineering Institute has developed an "Enterprise Framework for the Disciplined Evolution of Legacy Systems [2] as a guide for organizations planning software evolution efforts, such as migrating legacy systems to more distributed open environments. This framework draws out the important global issues early in the planning cycle and provides insight and guidance for a disciplined evolution approach.

In addition to the software engineering and technology considerations, the enterprise approach addresses the needs of the customer, the organization's strategic goals and objectives, the operational context of the enterprise, as well as the current legacy systems and their operational environment. It recognizes the central importance of both software engineering and systems engineering (and their interplay) to the system evolution initiative. The seven elements of the framework are the organization, the legacy system, the target system, the project, systems engineering, software engineering, and technologies.

These elements are applicable to a wide class of system evolution initiatives. In practice, the specific composition of the framework and their interrelationships are a function of the enterprise, its culture, and its management and technical practices (lifecycle activities, processes, and work products that are used to carry out the tasks described in the project plan and migration strategy).

3. Developing High-Level System Understanding

Program understanding is the (ill-defined) deductive process of acquiring knowledge about a software artifact through analysis, abstraction, and generalization [5]. Clearly, program understanding is a prerequisite for software evolution. However, we assert that the nature of program understanding should change from an understanding of the internals of software modules (white-box reengineering) to an understanding of the interfaces between software modules (black-box reengineering). A more detailed explanation of this approach can be found in [9].

Understanding is critical to our ability to evolve unproductive legacy assets (e.g., obsolete, overly-constrained, or stagnating components) into reusable assets that can contribute to a product line approach. Legacy assets may be aging software systems that are constructed to run on various obsolescent hardware types, programmed in obsolete languages, and suffer from the fragility and brittleness that results from prolonged maintenance. As stovepipe software ages, the task of maintaining it becomes more complex and expensive and the asset becomes more of a liability than an asset. While bottom-up program understanding has its place, it is often the case that software and system engineers spend inordinate amounts of time trying to reproduce the system's high-level architecture from low-level source code.

Legacy code can be difficult to understand for many reasons. It may have been created using *ad hoc* methods and unstructured programming. It may have been maintained in crisis mode with no updates to the higher-level documentation. There may be little or no conceptual integrity of its architecture and design. But every system has an architecture even if it is not written down. It is this architecture and high level understanding of the structure of the legacy system that must be the focus of a program understanding effort.

Program understanding is a relatively immature field of research in which the terminology and focus are still evolving. Tilley and Smith [5] describe three promising lines of research: investigating cognitive aspects, developing support mechanisms, and maturing the practice. Each of these lines should be tailored to a high-level, white-box form of program understanding necessary for more rapid and cost-effective migration. Evidence that the high-level understanding approach bears fruit is given by the examples cited in Section 6.

4. Distributed Object Technology and Wrapping

The approaches for software evolution of legacy systems are being dramatically changed by distributed object technology and wrapping [8]. Traditionally, the approach taken to legacy systems reengineering has been to understand the system's structure and to extract its essential functionality so the whole system or a series of pieces of the system could be transformed into a more evolvable system over the long term. But distributed object technology is changing the nature and economics of legacy system reengineering.

Traditional reengineering is based on "deep" program understanding and reverse engineering. The cost/benefit ratio of this approach is staying the same in the face of new technologies such as CORBA, Java, and the Web because deep understanding is linear relative to the size of the program and the new technology provides no additional leverage. However, the benefits of "shallow" interface understanding and component wrapping using these distributed object technologies is rising rapidly relative to the replacement cost. As a result, the economic balance is changing from traditional transformation-based reengineering to wrapper-based reengineering [9]. These economic factors are having a significant impact on many organizations struggling with modernizing their systems.

Component-based architecture and product lines are concerned with design abstractions for system-level structure. By "system-level" we mean something larger than a single computer program. The significance of making distribution extensions to OT is that software designers and maintainers have at their disposal the means of expressing abstract system designs and, more importantly, have tools for quickly fabricating working versions of these designs. That is, there is a more direct path now than ever before from abstract architectural concepts to concrete implementation of these concepts using DOC.

5. Network-Centric Computing

As is evident from the examples cited in the next section, the Net[1] is causing a "sea change" in both the nature of enterprise applications and development methods used to create them. There are clear and well-documented major trends toward electronic commerce and network-based development and collaboration. The use of the network has expanded far beyond e-mail and access to vast information sources. It has become a universal medium for information exchange. The value of the Internet to software engineering and systems development must be recognized and exploited. The promise of product line development for distributed legacy evolution will not be achieved until this medium is used more effectively.

The influence of network-centric computing (NCC) on software evolution can be summarized in three words — universality, ubiquity, and access. Universality is provided by portable executable content, such as Java applets, which runs on multiple platforms and operating systems. Making established user interfaces, such as web browsers, available on almost any client provides ubiquity. Making vast quantities of corporate data, which previously were inaccessible in mainframe-based databases available on the Net to the ubiquitous client software, provides accessibility.

One of the primary drivers of NCC is economics. Because applications and data are downloaded from servers on demand, there is a potential reduction in the

---

[1] The term *Net* as used here includes the Internet (the global computer network), intranets (local networks that are usually isolated from the Internet by a firewall), and extranets (extensions of an intranet into the Internet in a secure manner).

cost and complexity for system administrators in managing a corporate network [6]. Maintenance can be done at one central location rather than at thousands of sites in the organization, thereby reducing total cost of ownership (TCO). The tradeoff is that the end-users lose control and customizability of the local machine. However, they may gain significantly by increasing their productivity in their primary tasks by not being responsible for application installation, system administration, and troubleshooting tasks. Thus, NCC leverages system administration resources.

NCC can also leverage software assets in a number of ways by making them available over the Net. In its simplest form, just the user interface might be changed. Instead of accessing the enterprise database through an idiosyncratic user interface, the database can be accessed through a network browser. This transition has been accomplished many times by many organizations and, by now, should no longer be considered a high-risk, unprecedented form of software evolution. Many enterprise-wide intranets have taken this approach without significantly changing the underlying software base.

The next level of complexity involves partitioning the application into separate components so that the new version of the system can operate in a client/server manner. Once this step has been taken, the software is more free to evolve the individual parts into a reusable set of components that can provide the basis for a product line. In the first case (changing the interface) the business benefits from the universality, ubiquity, and access, but does not reap the rewards of Business Process Reengineering (BPR). In the second case (restructuring), the leveraging of assets and return on investment becomes paramount.

6. Examples of Successful Legacy System Evolution

One example of a successful legacy evolution is Wells Fargo Bank's online electronic banking system. Wells Fargo started offering real-time access to account balances via the Web starting in May 1995 and has expanded those services since then to include transferring funds, seeing cleared checks, examining credit card charges and payments, downloading transaction files, requesting service transactions, and paying bills [11]. The system has 100,000 enrolled customers and was handling 200,000 business object invocations per day as of early 1997 [7].

Wells Fargo has accomplished this by leaving their legacy systems largely untouched while adding the CORBA middleware to create a three-tiered client server system. The "customer" object and the "account" object allow the definition of a customer relationship whereby the client can first get all information about the customer's relationship with the bank and then, for each account owned by the customer, get the relevant summary information. Wells Fargo found that the key to enabling reuse of legacy systems was in having, maintaining, and sharing a well-architected enterprise object model.

The centerpiece of each monthly issue of Distributed Object Computing (DOC) magazine is a deployed case study such as Wells Fargo. They describe the development, the business case for building and deploying the application, the laundry list of technology used on the project and, when available, the staffing and deployment information. In their first eight issues, they have featured a web-based banking system, an airline reservation system, a criminal justice suspect index system, a newsmedia system to provide personalized news and digital content, a 911 emergency response system, a management information system for monitoring and directing large projects, an electric power exchange system for the electric power industry, and an information system for a utility company. In most cases these development efforts made heavy use of legacy software assets.

As an example of the specific leverage provided by technologies such as CORBA and Java, Allied Signal Engines, a business unit of Allied Aerospace, has reported a cost savings of $750,000 per new application [4]. This was accomplished by moving to a component-based software architecture and by outsourcing a major portion of the actual coding effort to an offshore development company in India. They found that they could "raise the starting point for every application, reducing the cycle time and thereby reducing costs." Their wide-ranging development efforts were made possible, at least in part, by the network-centric computing models that were described in the previous section.

The common themes running through all these examples are rapid development (months rather than years), the use of DOC and the Web, component-based architecture, and the use of the previously existing legacy infrastructure. Domain analysis is not the issue it is for new development because the domain is well-established, but significant effort goes into defining new business objects and redefining the business goals. Clearly, these "makeovers" are the basis of product families in the sense that they result in a set of core assets (distributed objects) that form the basis of future product development.

7. Conclusions

The approaches to software evolution are changing rapidly along with the changing technology. The changing technology is pushing the evolution of systems in several ways. Two approaches to software evolution appear to be on the decline. First, it is rarely possible, because of huge investments in legacy systems that have evolved over many years, to replace those systems and start from scratch. So the "big bang" approach to software migration is not often feasible. Second, it is increasingly less attractive to continue maintaining traditional (functional) legacy systems at the lowest level of abstraction expecting them to evolve into maintainable assets. So the fine-grained maintenance approach is also undesirable because it neither adds value to the asset nor provides for future leverage.

The recommended approach for systems evolution can be summarized briefly as follows:
- Understand the goals and resources of the enterprise with respect to a system evolution project. Use a software evolution framework to plan a disciplined system evolution.
- Understand the legacy system at a high level of abstraction using system understanding technology paying particular attention to interfaces and

abstractions. Find the encapsulatable components of the legacy system upon which to build.

- Consider middleware and wrapping technologies for encapsulating subsystems and creating distributed objects that form the basis for product line systems. Apply those technologies in accordance with the framework.
- Consider using the World Wide Web for expanding the scope of the legacy system and as a development tool. Capitalize on the universality, ubiquity, and access that the Web provides.

As is so often the case in software engineering, this approach to software evolution raises the level of abstraction so that our resources are being used more effectively. Economic realities are pushing us from low-level maintenance activities to high-level transformations. A focus on architecture and product lines is facilitating large-scale reuse in construction where before we were satisfied with small-scale reuse.

The use of these new approaches is still somewhat risky and advanced, but by no means unprecedented. They have been employed in prototypes, tested in small systems, and used to transform large systems. Useful and production-quality tools are now available. New developments are occurring at "Internet speed". Product line advocates must diligently follow the developments in integration and web technologies as well as legacy system migration techniques. Failure to do so will make their work much less relevant to the practitioners who have no other choice but to start from their legacy systems.

8. References

[1]   Bass, Leonard; Clements, Paul; Cohen, Sholom; Northrop, Linda; & Withey, James. *Product Line Practice Workshop Report.* (CMU/SEI-97-TR-003). Pittsburgh, PA: Software Engineering Institute, Carnegie Mellon University, 1997.

[2]   Bergey, John; Northrop, Linda; & Smith, Dennis. *Enterprise Framework for the Disciplined Evolution of Legacy Systems.* (CMU/SEI-97-TR-007). Pittsburgh, PA: Software Engineering Institute, Carnegie Mellon University, 1997.

[3]   Brownsword, Lisa & Clements, Paul. *A Case Study in Successful Product Line Development.* (CMU/SEI-96-TR-016). Pittsburgh, PA: Software Engineering Institute, Carnegie Mellon University, 1996.

[4]   Gill, Philip J. "CORBA Proves Its Value." *Object Magazine* 7, 8 (October 1997): 10-11.

[5]   Tilley, Scott & Smith, Dennis. *Coming Attractions in Program Understanding* (CMU/SEI-96-TR-019). Pittsburgh, PA: Software Engineering Institute, Carnegie Mellon University, 1996.

[6]   Tilley, Scott & Smith, Dennis. *On Using the Web as Infrastructure for Reengineering.* Proceedings of the 5th Workshop on Program Comprehension, May 28-30, 1997, Dearborn, Michigan. IEEE Computer Society Press, pp 170-173, 1997.

[7]   Townsend, Erik S. "Wells Fargo's 'Object Express'." *Distributed Object Computing* 1, 1 (February 1997): 18-27.

[8]   Wallnau, Kurt; Weiderman, Nelson; Northrop, Linda. *Distributed Object Computing with CORBA and Java: Key Concepts and Implications.* (CMU/SEI-97-TR-004). Pittsburgh, PA: Software Engineering Institute, Carnegie Mellon University, 1997.

[9]   Weiderman, Nelson; Northrop, Linda; Smith, Dennis; Tilley, Scott; & Wallnau, Kurt. *Implications of Distributed Object Computing for Reengineering.* (CMU/SEI-97-TR-005). Pittsburgh, PA: Software Engineering Institute, Carnegie Mellon University, 1997.

[10]   Weiderman, Nelson; Bergey, John; Smith, Dennis; Tilley, Scott; & Wallnau, Kurt. *Approaches for Legacy System Evolution.* (CMU/SEI-97-TR-014). Pittsburgh, PA: Software Engineering Institute, Carnegie Mellon University, 1997.

[11]   Wells Fargo Bank. Wells Fargo's WWW Homepage [on-line]. Available WWW: <URL: http://www.wellsfargo.com> (1997).

The Relation between the Product Line Development Entry Points and Reengineering

Jean-Marc DeBaud and Jean-François Girard

Fraunhofer Institute for Experimental Software Engineering (IESE)
Sauerwiesen 6, D-67661 Kaiserslautern, Germany
Tel/Fax: (49) 6301 707 216/202
{debaud,girard}@iese.fhg.de

Abstract. The product line for software systems (PL) approach has been touted recently as one of the most promising development approach for gains in product quality, time to market and cost reduction. The approach is complex and must be tailorable to situations in which its characteristics may be of interest for adoption within a development environment.

We first present in this short position paper a succinct overview of the main entry points (context) for PL adoption experienced so far within our technology transfer context. We then put a particular emphasis on the reengineering entry point in which we describe what we think are the main possible adoption scenarios.

Throughout the paper we emphasize the contribution of (reference) software architectures so as to highlight the key enabling role it plays for the PL approach.

Keywords: Software product line, domain engineering, software reengineering.

1. Introduction

1. 1. The Problem

In the software domain, a large number of organizations develop at least one line of products. That is, a set of products that share a core set of similarities. A key problem is to manage, as efficiently as possible, the development and maintenance of the software variations that go into these similar, yet somewhat different products. Among the problems experienced in practice are the lack of economic instruments to plan for, or to manage the diversity among, the product variants; the unstructured reuse of analysis, design or code artifacts within the line; the difficulties to manage the configuration of multiple products.

These problems have well documented consequences: Multiple code-bases prolifer, little conceptual integrity can be insured and sharp software structure degradations occur. In brief, the design of new variants as well as the maintenance of previous ones becomes increasingly difficult. A situation familiar to many organizations.

1. 2. The Product Line Approach and Its Context

Product line for software systems (PL) builds upon the idea of product line widely found the hardware industry, i.e., it takes a domain-specific view of the world where economies of scale and scope can be realized. But because PL has to deal with a much greater diversity, it must use an oversight structure to codify and articulate that diversity. This is the role of a domain-specific (or reference) architecture.

Frank v. d. Linden (Ed.): ARES '98, LNCS 1429, pp. 132-139, 1998.

The principal role of such architecture is to present and articulate both the commonalities as well as the differences within a line of products and engineer them within a fully reusable, highly parametrized design. Benefits to the architecture approach to implement a PL include: a solid, high level view of the line with which to reason about the product variants, a solid medium upon which economic analyses can be performed and traceability actuated, a mechanism to reuse past development as well as anticipate future ones, and, a structure where quality attributes can be examined and enhanced.

Yet, for the promises of PL to be widely realized, the approach must be adopted and hence be transferable within a variety of organizational context. In general, we has experienced so far within our technology transfer activities three prototypical contexts apt for PL adoption. One occurs when a set of already existing sysbuilt and the organization realizes that the PL approach could be adopted to maximize efficiency; we term this context the *project integrating PL*. The last context is the 'epistemic', *pure PL* case when an organization may decide to start a PL effort from the beginning for a line of product it wants to development and produce.

Even though we chose, because of the constraints of this forum, to focus more deeply only on the reengineering-enabled PL context (the most widespread, we believe), we will see that the concept of (reference) architecture plays a key role in all three contexts.

1. 3. Related Work

Few directly relevant publications explicitly address the general contexts for PL adoption are known to us. Yet, there is an increasingly larger body of PL work where this information transpire indirectly: [1], [2], [3], [10], [11]. All contain references to one or many contexts of application, these fit within the three principal contexts elicited above. None focus specifically on the reengineering-enabled PL context.

The remainder of this position paper is organized as follows. Section two outlines the main entry points for adopting a PL approach. Section three focuses on the reengineering entry point. Section four present our conclusions.

2. Main Entry Points to Product Lines for Software Systems

In this section, we refine the three principal entry points for adopting a PL approach within a development environment. Figure 1 above presents a somewhat simplistic, high level view of the main PL entry points and will be used to illustrate our description.

2. 1. Pure PL

This context refers to an organization that decides to start a PL effort without any or much existing software assets after having positively assessed the line economic viability. This case is very similar to a pure domain engineering (DE) effort where a domain analysis is first performed which then leads to the definition of a PL asset base. Pure PL produces a asset base made of the reusable infrastructure (RI) -- a domain model (concepts and relationships), associated reference architecture and components -- together with an application engineering process tailored to the development environment. After each product instance construction, possible unsatisfied requirements, errors or adaptations must be resolved and integrated within a new version of the asset base.

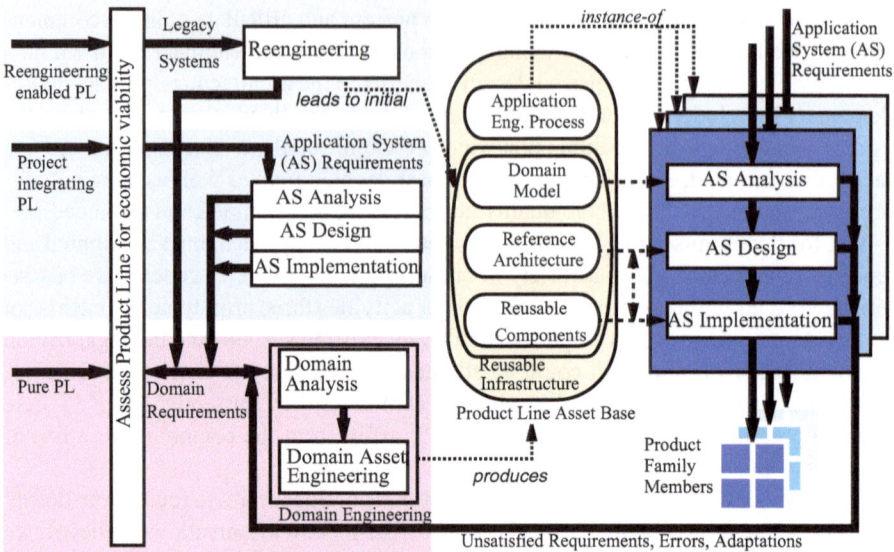

Figure 1: Product Line Development Entry

The domain model documents the reference architecture which itself articulate the executable components. A main elements of the reference architecture is a decision model which prescribes the dependencies among the reusable infrastructure artifacts and drives the instantiation process. The reference architecture should then be seen as highly coupled with the application engineering process.

In our description, we do use the word domain as possibly being of arbitrary size and denoting a collection of sub-domains (as in any interesting real world domain would).

2. 2. Project Integrating PL

The situation in this context is different from the pure PL case in the sense that some assets have already been produced within one or more running projects and a decision to adopt PL ideas is made. To introduce the PL, running projects must keep going while the PL asset base is developed. Yet, the integration between the asset base and the projects must be gradually completed and this is a difficult phase as the projects may have time-critical constraints among others.

The construction of the reusable infrastructure and in particular the reference architecture can play a critical role for this integration to happen.

The PL effort can start with the one or many of the architectures already developed by the projects and perform merge, extend and refine analyses to study how an integration could be done. This reference architecture can be used as a candidate or even the basis of the PL asset base.

This asset base can then serve as input to a pure PL development process such as the one described in the previous subsection so as to anticipate the future product variants.

This context process was of course prototypical in the sense that the degree of integration necessary as well as its precise occurrence in time can vary widely.

2. 3. Reengineering-enabled PL

Most organizations already possess application developed in their domains of expertise. Hence, we think this context is one of the most likely to be found in practice. Often, organizations come to the ideas of PL only after experiencing the pain of multiple, time-degraded code bases.

The challenge in this context is to start developing a PL asset base from the existing applications. It is in effect an attempt to re-understand the specifics of existing application and put this understanding in a form usable for a PL effort. Again, the notion of architecture is key.

It is our belief that any medium or large scale reengineering cannot succeed without a (domain-augmented) architecture recovery and redocumentation approach. Such architectures, coming from multiple existing systems, can then serves as one strong basis for development of a PL in a fashion largely similar to the one in the previous subsection. The importance and leverage given by an architecture-centric reengineering approach for the reengineering-enabled PL context is detailed at length in the next section.

3.   Reengineering as a Product Line Enabler

In this section, we introduce a process which applies reengineering on related systems with the goal of producing key initial PL assets. We termed this the reengineering enabled PL context. We first describe the recoverable asset types and their contributions towards a pure PL process. We then present the reengineering process to recover these assets. Last, we proceed by highlighting approaches which combine this assets recovery process with domain engineering so as to deliver a reusable infrastructure for a PL.

3. 1. Initial Product Line Assets

The proposed reengineering process produces the following assets:

- initial reference architecture
- recovered reusable components
- domain concepts and inter-relationships

The primary contribution of reengineering as enabler for PL is to recover architectural views of existing systems from the domain of interest and to associate with the logical components of this architecture the actual code implementing these components. These recovered architectural views are combined into an initial reference architecture. This architecture provides a good initial structure on which domain engineering can apply change and evolution scenarios to evaluate how well this architecture serves the needs of the PL.

The value of a reference architecture is more important if some of its key components are implemented and can be reused within a PL. By associating existing code which has been tested and validated by field usage with components of the initial reference architecture, the proposed process makes a first step in this direction. This code probably needs to be parametrized and generalized, but it shares with the initial reference architecture one important quality: they both come from existing systems from the domain which fulfil the needs of at least one instance of the intended PL.

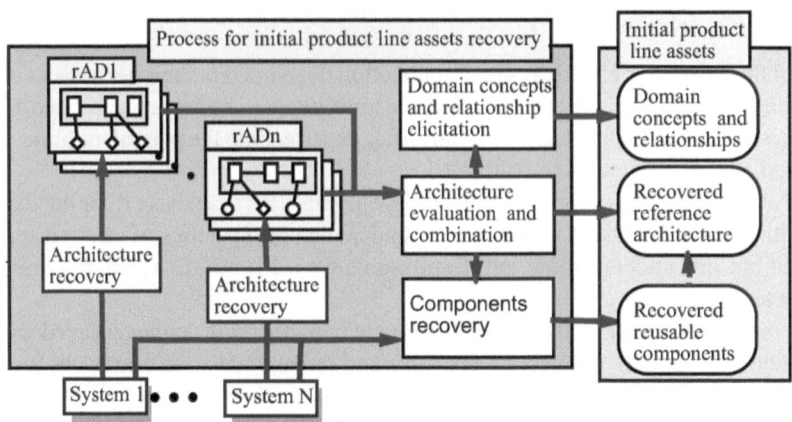

Figure 2: Process for Initial Product Line Assets Recovery

A secondary contribution of the reengineering process is to elicit of some key domain concepts and their inter-relationships. In a domain model built independently of existing systems, these concepts and relationships can point to gap in domain understanding.

Next we introduce the reengineering process which produces these initial assets.

3. 2. Process for PL Assets Recovery

Figure 2 illustrates the process for the recovery of the initial PL assets. It starts with architecture recovery, then proceeds with architecture evaluation and combination. While this evaluation and combination occurs, concepts elicitation implicitly take place. The process ends with component recovery.

Architecture Recovery

The architecture recovery can produce multiple views of each system using various component identification techniques which take into account different aspects of the system, like the call patterns [5], similarity in context [6],[13] and dynamic analysis [8]. Then communication patterns among these components can be identified, commonly with the support of data flow analysis [12] and cliche recognition [4]. The resulting views can be validated through feedback sessions with maintainers, designers and architects of the system.

Architecture Evaluation and Combination

The most relevant of these views are selected to perform architecture evaluation and combination. Here, we use scenarios which capture tasks performed by users in existing and forecasted applications (products), as well as maintenance and development roles to evaluate the relative ability of alternative architectures to support the needs of the PL. This evaluation is based on the structured scenarios used in the software architecture analysis method SAAM [9]. In the case where the decision to develop a PL stems from problems in adapting existing systems to new requirements, it is reasonable to expect that the main change and maintenance scenarios will be relatively easy to obtain.

When the original systems cover different aspects of the domain, these systems usually have complementary parts which do not excessively overlap and hence their parts may be more easily combined architecturally. The identification of these non-overlapping and complementary parts can be supported by techniques used to restructure systems while minimizing coupling. The final result of these evaluations and combinations is an initial reference architecture which can be improved upon during the later domain engineering phase.

Domain Concepts and Relationships

As the various views which compose the recovered architecture descriptions are validates and evaluated, some components will be associated with domain concepts by the system experts or the reengineers and the relations among these components (e.g. dependencies, communication, containments) will suggest relationships between domain concepts. These domain concepts and relationships are fundamental to the construction of the domain model.

Components Recovery

Once an initial reference architecture has emerged and the most valuable components are identified through architecture evaluation, we can focus our efforts in recovering and encapsulating these components. Using techniques used to identify small encapsulations [7], dependence analysis, dominance analysis and variable localization, it is possible to create initial reusable components which can be generalized, parametrized and improved upon during domain engineering.

3. 3. Assets Recovery & Product Line Engineering

This subsection highlights three scenarios for reengineering enabled PL - the sequential, parallel and hybrid scenario - to combine the assets recovery process presented above with domain engineering.

Sequential Scenario

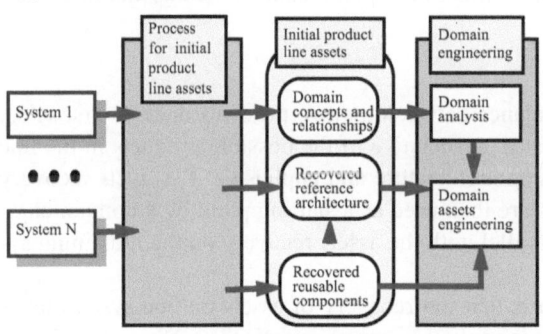

Figure 3: Sequential Scenario

The sequential scenario, depicted in Figure 3, performs architecture recovery on each of the systems, recovers the initial assets, and only when these initial assets are all available, the domain engineering does start. The main advantage of this scenario is that it provides the domain engineering with a clear view of what are available reusable assets.

Furthermore, it offers a clear decision point: After the asset recovery phase, one is in a better position to evaluate if there is already enough reusable assets and knowledge to support the creation of a PL. If the decision is to delay the introduction of the PL development, the recovered architectures are still valuable documentation of the existing systems. Similarly, the exercise of applying change scenarios to these architectures indicate to their respective maintainers valuable maintenance information.

Parallel Scenario

The parallel scenario, depicted in Figure 4, indicates that the domain engineering can proceed in parallel to the architecture recovery. The only information recovered from existing system which is concurrently provided to domain engineering is the domain concepts and their inter-relations. Otherwise the two activities proceed independently. Domain engineering produces an idealized reference architecture and reengineering produces an initial reference architecture. These two reference ar-

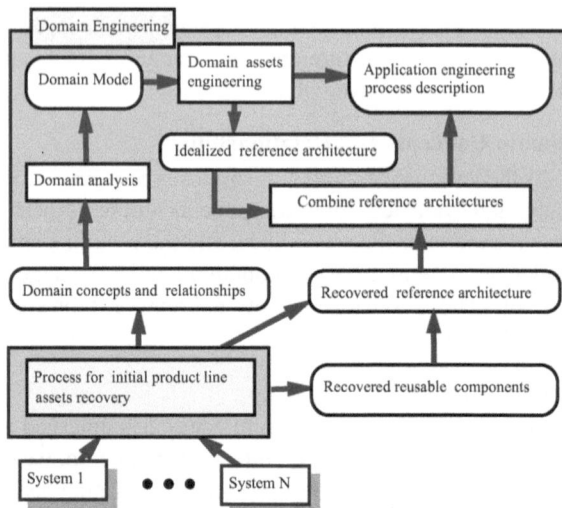

chitectures are then combined through a compromise between the idealized architecture developed with less historical constraints and an architecture which offers potentially more reusable components (of course, this scenario is a little schematic).

One advantage of this scenario is that the compromises in combining the reference architecture are made explicit. One knows the forecasted advantages of an architecture unconstrained by existing systems and one has a good estimate of the proportion of existing components which could be reusable. A second advantage is that domain engineering can start earlier than in the preceding scenario.

The main inconvenient is that it is likely that the combination of existing components within a reference architecture which was developed unconstrained by the history of existing systems may be difficult.

Hybrid Scenario

This scenario tries to strike a balance between the two previous ones. It first select one of the existing systems as most representative of the possible products in the line and the one with the most promising architecture and applies the PL assets recovery process on it. The initial PL assets are then used as a starting point by a domain engineering phase which proceed in parallel with the assets recovery on the remaining systems.

One advantage of this scenario is that the recovery of assets on one system takes considerably less time than when it is applied on many systems. Therefore, domain engineering can start earlier.

Generally, each of the three scenarios produces some (or many) elements of the reusable infrastructure used in the PL developments. That is a domain model, a reference architecture and some reusable components. However, it is clear to us that there is a trade-off between the freedom of defining a new reference architecture and the possibility to reuse components from existing systems. This trade-off is a strong, practical factor in the choice that an organization would make among the three scenarios.

4. Conclusions

We have presented in this position paper a description of three principal entry points to PL. We have paid particular attention to the one dealing with reengineering as we believe this case to be the most likely in real organization settings. A next step upon which we are endeavouring is the production of three guidebooks to document the processes we have outlined here in much better details.

Acknowledgement:

Oliver Flege graciously made available to us an initial version of the Figure 1 included in this position paper.

References

[1]   D. Bristow, B. Bulat, and R. Burton, Product-Line Process Development, Tech. rep., Software Technology for Adaptable, Reliable Systems (STARS), Feb. 1995.

[2]   L. Brownsword and P. Clements, A Case Study in Successful Product Line Development, Tech. Rep. CMU/SEI-96-TR-016, Carnegie Mellon Software Engineering Institute, 1996.

[3]   D. Dikel, D. Kane, S. Ornburn, W. Loftus, and J. Wilson, Applying Software Product-Line Architecture, IEEE Computer, pp. 49-55, Aug. 1997.

[4]   R. Fiutem, P. Tonella, G. Antoniol, and E. Merlo. A cliché-based environment to support architectural reverse engineering. In International Conference on Software Maintenance, pages 319–328, Monterey, Ca, Nov. 1996.

[5]   J.F Girard and R. Koschke. Finding components in a hierarchy of modules: a step towards architectural understanding. In International Conference on Software Maintenance, pages 66–75, Bari, September 1997.

[6]   J.F Girard and R. Koschke. A metric-based approach to detect abstract data types and abstract state encapsulation. In Automated Software Engineering Conference, pages 82–89, Nevada, USA, Nov 1997.

[7]   J.F Girard, R. Koschke, and G. Schied. Comparison of abstract data type and abstract state encapsulation detection techniques for architectural understanding. In Working Conference on Reverse Engineering, pages 66–75, Amsterdam, The Netherland, Oct 1997.

[8]   D. Jerding and S. Rugaber. Using Visualization for Architectural Localization and Extraction. In Working Conference on Reverse Engineering, 5 th, page unknown, October 1997.

[9]   R. Kazman, L. Bass, G. Abowd, and S.M. Webb. Saam: A method for analyzing the properties of software architecture. In International Conference on Software Engineering, pages 81–90, 1994.

[10] R. Macala, L. Stuckey, and D. Gross, Managing Domain-Specific, Product-Line Development, IEEE Software, May 1996.

[11] F. Maymir-Ducharme, The Product Line Business Model, in Proceedings of the Eighth Workshop on Institutionalizing Software Reuse, 1997.

[12] E. Merlo, J.F. Girard, L. Hendren, and R. De Mori. Multi-valued constant propagation for the reengineering of user interfaces. In *IEEE Conference on Software Maintenance*, pages 120–30, September 1993.

[13] R. W. Schwanke. An intelligent tool for re-engineering software modularity. In *International Conference on Software Engineering*, pages 83–92, May 1991.

Session 4: Analysis of Software Architectures

Paul C. Clements[1], Juan Antonio de la Puente[2]
[1]Software Engineering Institute, Carnegie Mellon University
Pittsburg, PA 15213, USA
clements@sei.cmu.edu
[2]Dep. Ingeniería de Sistemas Telemáticos, Universidad Politécnica de Madrid
E-28040 Madrid, Spain
jpuente@dit.upm.es

Introduction

Architectural analysis is a most important issue for an effective use of software architectures in the development of families of software products. Very often, architectural design deals with making decisions which can have an utmost impact on the system characteristics and quality. As the final system properties can only be observed when the system is at least partly implemented, finding ways of assessing the impact of architectural decisions early in the development cycle is vital to the industrial scale applicability of the architectural approach to software development.

The forth session of the ARES Workshop was devoted to this important subject. The session began with a general discussion about the goals of architectural analysis. This was followed by a short presentation of the papers that were submitted to the session. The discussion was resumed on the important issues of available technology for architectural analysis. The session ended with a summing up, where some conclusions were agreed upon by the participants.

The main points of discussion are summarized in the rest of this introduction.

Goals of architectural analysis

The goal of architectural analysis is to get measures of compliance with regard to some system properties. It is of crucial importance to identify which are the relevant properties for a given domain, and how analysis techniques can be applied to product families.

Some of the properties than can be analysed are quite general, e.g.:

- Performance, or satisfaction of real-time requirements.
- Safety, liveness, reliability, etc.

When dealing with product families, however, there are specific points that deserve special attention, e.g.:

- Time and cost of production for specific members of a family.
- Kinds of variation which can be covered by the architecture.
- Properties that are preserved for all variants of an architecture.
- Stability of interfaces with respect to evolution in products.

Frank v. d. Linden (Ed.): ARES '98, LNCS 1429, pp. 140-142, 1998.
© Springer-Verlag Berlin Heidelberg 1998

The issue of analysing the rationale of the architecture or the trade-offs it implies was recognized as an interesting, but considerably more difficult, one.

Another important issue is the role of analysis in an architecture oriented process, especially when reengineering an already existing product. In this case, architectural analysis can not only deal with architectural design issues, but with the results of other development phases as well, provided they can be referred to the product architecture.

Stakeholders

The identification of the main roles that take part in the process, and their different views, is an important issue that has a clear impact on the way the relevant system properties are defined. The discussion at the workshop revolved around those roles that are peculiar to a product line environment, and produced the following list:

- product line architect;
- builder of generic (core) assets;
- builder of product from generic assets;
- product line maintainer;
- marketer / funder of the product line

Listening to the stakeholders has been reported as one of the crucial issues in architectural assessment, which can be confirmed by the experience of the companies that are working in this area.

Techniques

A number of techniques for architectural analysis were described in the papers that were presented in the session. There was a general consensus that the field is not yet mature enough, and new techniques have to be developed which are specific to the architectural abstraction level, rather than just adapting design level methods. It was also recognized that architectural analysis techniques are application domain dependant, which makes it difficult to give general guidelines about which methods to use for a given product line.

The global perception is that companies using an architectural approach to product families development are currently using assessment methods based on meetings and reviews, rather than more formal techniques or automated tools.

Conclusion

The main conclusion of the session is that architectural analysis is a fundamental issue in putting architectures to work in industry. The field, however, is immature and more effort is required in order to identify the best approaches and techniques.

The relation between costs and benefits, and the stakeholders' views have been identified as important issues for discovering which are the relevant properties of an architecture, but a number of general properties, which seem to be of interest for different projects, have also been identified and listed.

Diagnostic Software Architectures

Richard T. Bechtold

George Mason University, 4400 University Drive
Fairfax, Virginia 22030-4444 USA
+1 703 993-1640
rbechtol@gmu.edu

Abstract. A critical distinguishing characteristic of architectures for families of embedded systems is their relative need for error-detection and -management. This need can range from extreme, as occurs with nearly all life-rated systems, to nominal, such as might occur with simple, inexpensive toys. Increasing a system's capability for error detection and management invariably results in increased complexity and an increased load on system resources. Consequently, even systems with extremely high error management capability sometimes demonstrate anomalous behavior. When this occurs, it is typically necessary to rapidly and effectively identify the source of the anomaly. Therefore, a key consideration when developing an architecture for a family of embedded systems is determining the scope and nature of the diagnostic requirements that will be placed on the architecture.

This paper discusses the value of diagnostic architectures, the construction of diagnostic architectures, and techniques for determining where diagnostic elements should be placed within an architecture. The paper also examines several specific diagnostic techniques and discusses tradeoffs between detail, data persistence, system performance, and system resources.

Keywords. Diagnostic Software Architectures, Error Management, Software Architectures, Embedded Systems, Software Families.

1. Introduction

There are essentially two types of embedded systems: those that are perfect, and those that are not. If it is possible that your system is less than perfect, then you need some means to diagnose the source of problems after they occur.

A common challenge in all embedded software systems is determining the ideal amount of internal error checking and management. The objective is to have a sufficient, but not excessive, amount of error management. Excessive error management typically causes unnecessary complexity, increased software size, and decreased software performance.

Frank v. d. Linden (Ed.): ARES '98, LNCS 1429, pp. 143-147, 1998.

Software systems are usually designed with error detection and management as an integral part of overall system functionality. To support insight into alternative error management approaches, analysts and designers might employ model-integrated environments [1], patterns [2, 3, 4, 5], and formal techniques [6]. Even with such techniques, very few systems can be asserted defect-free.

Therefore, as the architecture forms, most analysts and designers strive to ensure sufficient error management routines to accomplish two objectives. The first objective is to prevent errors from happening. The second objective is, if prevention fails, to manage the impact of errors as an expected part of overall system processing.

Outside of mission-critical, life-rated systems (flight-control being an excellent example) designers often fail to consider an equally important third objective. This objective is to design the software architecture to aggressively support after-the-fact identification and diagnosis of system errors and anomalous behavior. This diagnostic approach to software architectures provides the same type of recovery and corrective options to software development and maintenance personnel that diagnostic systems provide in mission-critical software systems and systems resulting from other engineering disciplines.

To summarize, in principle all systems should be designed to achieve perfect error detection and management. However, since there is a chance the actual system might be less than perfect, systems should also be based on architectures that help diagnose problems that were not successfully detected nor managed. In the event of anomalous system behavior a diagnostic architecture helps you rapidly focus the search for defects to the fewest modules, fewest objects, fewest lines of code, and fewest data elements possible.

Section 2 of this paper discusses the construction of diagnostic software architectures and presents techniques to use for determining where diagnostic elements should be placed within an architecture. Section 3 examines several specific diagnostic techniques and discusses tradeoffs between detail, data persistence, system performance, and system resources. Section 4 presents a summary and conclusions.

2. Constructing Diagnostic Software Architectures

When you, as a software project manager or engineer, are first informed of a problem in the performance of a software-intensive system you usually are given three types of information: (1) context--the system's general environment while executing, (2) sequence--the series of actions immediately prior to problem detection, and (3) consequence--the known and probable results of the problem. Therefore, a diagnostic architecture must augment the above information to provide the most comprehensive insight possible into the probable source of the problem.

Generally, insight regarding how best to augment problem information is achievable after preliminary system design, or after development of the system invention and design rules [7]. At this point the software architecture is beginning to take shape, and is primarily driven by key elements within both the problem domain and the solution domain. This is an ideal time to adjust the architecture so that it also supports diagnosis of system anomalies.

To identify where in the architecture you should consider making changes to accommodate diagnostic support, you ask the following four questions:

- Where can the most comprehensive insights be gained? (Breadth of insight.)
- Where can the most important insights be gained? (Depth of insight.)
- Which modules will dominate the behavior of the system? (Type of insight.)
- Which interfaces will reveal behavior? (Frequency of insight.)

A key principle in properly developing a diagnostic software architecture is that the diagnostics are intrinsic to the architecture, not to the code. That is, at certain locations within the overall system a call is made or message passed that results in the storage of diagnostic data (details on how this occurs are deferred until Section 3). Keeping the diagnostic algorithms out of the application code helps preserve maximum flexibility for modifying and updating the code without negatively impacting your ability to perform software diagnostics.

There are a variety of locations within the architecture that are good candidates for answering the four questions asked above. Consider, for example, using diagnostic routines:

- Immediately upon receiving data from external systems
- Immediately before passing data to external systems
- Upon exchange of data with persistent data stores
- Between major system states
- Before/after complex data manipulations
- Before/after high-visibility behavior
- Before/after critical no-visibility behavior

Note that some of the areas described above are usually well-protected by error detection and management routines. For example, checking data from external systems, and rejecting bad data, is a fairly common practice. However, if some of these areas are not well-protected then diagnostics could be critical when trying to isolate the source of system problems. As another example, any type of persistent data store is a candidate for diagnostics since sometimes these data stores are not nearly as persistent as originally designed.

In addition to determining how to adjust the architecture to support diagnostics, it is necessary to determine the most appropriate types of diagnostic techniques. This is discussed next.

3. Diagnostic Techniques

Diagnostic techniques can be classified using two characteristics: (1) what is being diagnosed, and (2) what are the limitations on the diagnosis?

With regard to the first, the two primary options are to diagnose the process or to diagnose the product. Process diagnosis generally consists of tracking the activation or invocation history of various objects, modules, subroutines, etc. Product diagnosis typically consists of tracking the creation, manipulation, storage, and destruction of data.

With regard to the second characteristic, limitations are usually a reflection of acceptable negative impact on available resources. Common limitation categories include:

- Frequency limitations (e.g., log no more than the last 100 change instances)
- Time limitations (e.g., log nothing older than the last 10 seconds)
- Activation limitations (e.g., only log data from the last 3 times the system was activated)
- Negative feedback loop limitations [8]. (e.g., limit when data recording threatens to result in excessive computational demand)
- No limitations (e.g., always record everything). Note: this is generally unrealistic.

After identifying areas in the software architecture that are candidates for diagnostic insight, it is then necessary to answer the two fundamental questions presented above: (1) what do I need to diagnose (process, product), and (2) what limitations exist regarding my ability to implement diagnostic intelligence (time, space, frequency, other)? By carefully considering the insights to be derived from using different diagnostic techniques at various places within the system, you can strive to have the most revealing and informative set of data while simultaneously minimizing negative performance impacts and the use of critical system resources. Properly designed diagnostic architectures may also yield highly reusable architectural components [9].

4. Summary and Conclusions

Due to market competition, innovation, technology advances, and other factors, embedded systems are often subject to considerable updating and evolutionary change. Ideally, the architecture for these systems are designed to anticipate, accommodate, and even facilitate rapid change. However, with the insertion of new or upgraded features there is always the possibility of inserting defects that result in system performance anomalies or outright failures.

Error capture and management routines are an essential part of even simple software systems. However, with increasing complexity it becomes progressively more difficult to determine if you have successfully implemented an appropriate amount of error management.

Although the ideal is for systems to always work perfectly, if your system ever starts exhibiting anomalous behavior, you must have the means to successfully conduct an investigation into the source of the anomalies. As presented in this paper, one means to improve your ability to conduct such investigations efficiently and successfully is to design the software architecture with the express purpose of supporting diagnosis of behavioral anomalies within the family of systems derived from the architecture.

5. References

[1]   Sztipanovits, Janos; *Safety Analysis and Diagnosis in a Model-Integrated Computing Framework.* Vanderbilt University. Technical Report MCSL-96-03. May 29, 1996. Also available at http://mcsl.vuse.vanderbilt.edu/ mgadocs/papers/mic96/micws/micws.html

[2]   Buschmann, Frank; Meunier, Regine; Rohnert, Hans, Sommerlad, Pet; *Pattern-Oriented Software Architecture: A System of Patterns.* John Wiley & Sons. July 1, 1996.

[3]   Fowler, Martin; *Analysis Patterns: Reusable Object Models.* Addison-Wesley Publishing Company; Addison-Wesley Object Technology: Addison-Wesley Object Technology Series. October, 1996.

[4]   Gabriel, Richard P.; *Patterns of Software: Tales from the Software Community.* Oxford University Press. August 1, 1996.

[5]   Vlissides, John M. (editor); Coplien, James O. (editor); Kerth, Norman L.; *Pattern Languages of Program Design 2.* Addison-Wesley Publishing Company. June 1, 1996.

[6]   Shaw, Mary; Garlan, David; *Software Architecture: Perspectives on an Emerging Discipline.* Prentice Hall. April, 1996.

[7]   Rechtin, Eberhardt; Maier, Mark W.; *The Art of Systems Architecting.* CRC Press, Systems Engineering Series. November, 1996.

[8]   Erickson, Jon D.; *A Software Architecture for Robust Hard Real Time Applications: Automatically Adapting System Activities to Available Computing Power.* NASA WWW site. http://tommy.jsc.nasa.gov/ARSD/ report_FY95/erickson_fy9513.html

[9]   *What is a Domain-Specific Architecture?* Honeywell WWW site. http://www.htc.honeywell.com/projects/ dssa/dssa_whatis.html

A Software Architecture Evaluation Model[1]

Juan C. Dueñas, William L. de Oliveira[2], Juan A. de la Puente

Department of Engineering of Telematic Systems,
Technical University of Madrid
ETSI Telecomunicación, Ciudad Universitaria, s/n, E-28040 Madrid
E-mail: {jcduenas, william, jpuente}@dit.upm.es

Abstract: The fulfilment of quality requirements is fundamental for the success of software-intensive systems. This fact forces companies to quantify the quality requirements at the moment of their specification, and to evaluate these requirements in all the results of the design process, both the by-products and the end system. The definition of the software architecture is one of the most important and early decisions of the design process, with a strong influence on the final quality of the product; therefore its evaluation should be made as early as possible, before the design is complete. This paper presents a software architecture evaluation model considering the software architecture as a final product itself and also as an intermediate product of the design process.

1. Introduction

The quality of equipment, services and systems is an essential element for the competition in the global market. Customers ask for increasingly more complex and demanding systems that must meet high quality standards. This fact drives software development companies to monitor the quality of both their products and their processes. Quality consists in the fulfilment of the system requirements, although as important as the "functional" aspect, is the fulfilment of other characteristics of its operation, more difficult to evaluate, such as the resource efficiency, the scalability, the maintainability, et cetera, that usually receive the name of "quality requirements".

[1] This work is partially funded by the ESPRIT program under contract EP20477, ARES project (Architectural Reasoning for Embedded Software), and by Spanish CICYT, under contract TIC96-0614.

[2] The work of William L. de Oliveira in the DIT/UPM is partially funded by CNPq-Brasil, with reference 260.022/95-0 and COPEL/LAC-Brasil.

Frank v. d. Linden (Ed.): ARES '98, LNCS 1429, pp. 148-157, 1998.

The scientific and industrial communities recognise that, in the case of software intensive systems, the first phases of the design and the decisions made then have a fundamental impact on the final quality. Not only because the errors made in the design cycle have more expensive reparation as they propagate, but because the early decisions will impose a strict threshold for the capacities and quality of the final system, especially in relation to these no-functional requirements. Being one of the first decisions made, the Software Architecture (SA) must be checked against these quality requirements. This approach is just to be applied in companies that design software systems with strict quality requirements.

A brief definition given by Garlan and Perry [9] establishes that SA is "the structure of components in a program or system, their interrelationships, and the principles and guides that control the design and evolution in time". This reveals the most important issues of SA:

- The focus on structural information, instead of algorithmic or behavioural models, because the approach is based on the definition and usage of high abstraction level components and their relationships (connectors in architectural terms).
- The information about "what to do" and "when" (i.e. the development process), is still part of the SA. This includes the know-how of the company about the product line.
- All the information included in the SA is oriented towards controlling the product evolution in time.

The draft-standard ISO/IEC 14598-1 specifies the elements required for quality evaluation of software: the quality model, the method for evaluation, the metrics and the supporting tools. Thus, in order to develop good software, quality requirements must be specified, the software quality assurance process should be planned, implemented and controlled, and all intermediate as well as end products must be evaluated. A suitable method to perform objective software quality evaluations is the measurement of the quality attributes of the software. This approach will be applied to the architecture of software systems: this article presents a quality model, methods for evaluation and metrics adapted to the assessment of SA: in the second section the general software quality assessment process is defined and in the third one the SA evaluation model. The article finishes with some comments about the current and future work in this area.

2. The General Software Quality Assessment Process

The result of any software development phase (including the last one) can be considered as a software product, with its own requirements that express the needs of its users, and that must be defined prior to the development. Besides, in the same way that global requirements evolve with respect to the development phase, they are also partitioned following the software product decomposition into its major components (which may require different evaluation criteria). An example of this at the SA level is the need for different quality requirements for the critical components in a hard real-time system, whose safety and predictability requirements are more strict than the requirements for the logging subsystems. Therefore, in order to keep consistent the quality specification for each subsystem with the one of the final product and throughout all the phases of the development process, quality requirements need to be specified in terms of a common quality model.

One available quality model is defined in the standard ISO/IEC Draft 9126-1 – Information technology – Software quality characteristics and metrics Part 1: Quality characteristics and sub-characteristics [7]. This part of ISO/IEC 9126 specifies a quality model that categorises software quality into six characteristics, which are further divided into sub-characteristics. These are defined by means of externally observable attributes for each software system. In order to ensure its general application, this standard does not cover which are these attributes, nor how can they be related to the sub-characteristics.

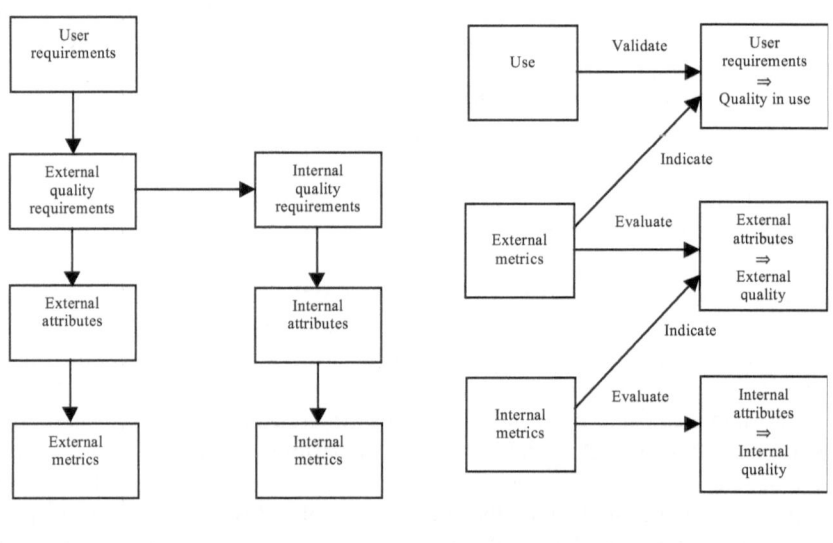

Definition view point   Evaluation view point

Figure 1: General quality process.

Once the quality model has been chosen, the general quality process starts (see Figure 1). The user requirements for the product (the result of any development phase) are studied by the development team, who specifies the product external quality requirements for each relevant quality characteristic, in order to establish the extent to which a product satisfies the user needs when used under specified conditions. A specific set of externally observable attributes (such as response time is used to define the efficiency of a computer system) are useful for this purpose. The completeness and correctness of the quality requirements specification need to be evaluated then to ensure that all the necessary requirements have been specified and unnecessary requirements excluded. The developers will evaluate the product against these requirements before delivery.

The external quality can be assessed by means of the external metrics applied under usage conditions. The external evaluation of the quality characteristics should therefore take place under conditions that emulate as closely as possible the expected conditions of use. It is important at this point to note that "metrics" in this context denote any kind of quantitative result that follows certain conditions about allowed values, scale and the measurement procedure. For example, the results of simulation, provided those items, can be categorised as metrics.

At next, the developers must specify the internal quality requirements of the product. The internal quality is the whole set of internal attributes of a product that determine its ability to satisfy its needs. The difference between external and internal attributes is that those reflect the influence of the environment of usage of the product, while internal ones focus only on intrinsic properties of the product (such as modularity and complexity), more related to its structure and to the way it is being built. In any case, the specification of the internal quality should use the same quality model used for the external quality specification, so the external and internal attributes are kept coherent.

The internal quality of each product can be evaluated by internal metrics, which measure these internal attributes. One of the most important usages of the internal quality evaluation is to help in choosing and improving the development process for a product line. Another main usages are the evaluation of internal attributes for technical decision making on several building options during development, and their usage like external quality indicators.

3. The Software Architecture Evaluation Model

Following these general considerations for the development and evaluation process, the specific process for the SA evaluation, shown in Figure 2, is based on the consideration that SA is a software product, and it should follow and adapt the general software quality process. In the next description, the taxonomy used for metric, measure, measurement, quality and attributes is that defined in [7].

3.1 Quality Specification

Following the definition given by the standard ISO 8402, the quality specification must contain the totality of characteristics of an entity that bear on its ability to satisfy stated and implied needs. The user view is expressed in the external quality specification and the developer view is expressed in the internal quality specification.

The external quality specification

The users and the developers specify the external quality of the final product or system and the external quality of the SA using the quality reference model presented in ISO/IEC 9126-1. The specifications must contain the selected quality characteristics and their optimum and allowed values under the user viewpoint. These requirements will be evaluated before the product delivery through testing techniques.

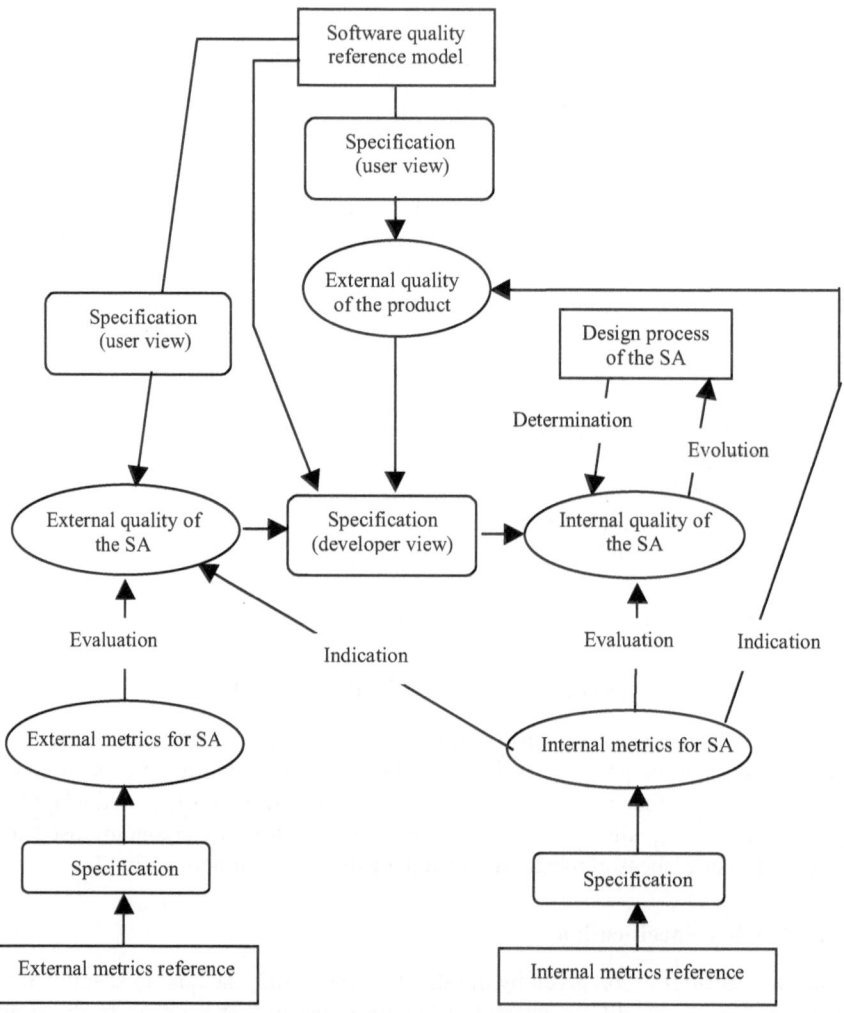

Figure 2: Quality evaluation model for SA.

The internal quality specification

The developers specify the internal quality of the SA based on the external quality of the product and the external quality of the SA, using the same quality reference model (ISO/IEC 9126-1) and by means of the definition of a set of software internal attributes. The specification must contain the software internal attributes selected for each quality characteristics and also their optimum and allowed ranges of values.

The developers need to decide how to particularise the specified quality requirements on the SA. For this purpose, they need to map these quality requirements to internal attributes that will be present on the SA. The mapping is based on the expert's knowledge or company accumulated data, depending on the maturity of the process implanted on the company.

The internal attributes are composed by special elements (such as functional elements or data elements) denoting quality characteristics, and intrinsic properties resulting from the development process (such as size, modularity, complexity, coupling and cohesion). For example, considering for analysability the following correspondence with internal attributes, the developers need to establish the relative importance between these attributes and their values. Some techniques such as the Quality Function Deployment (QFD) [8] are suitable for this purpose.

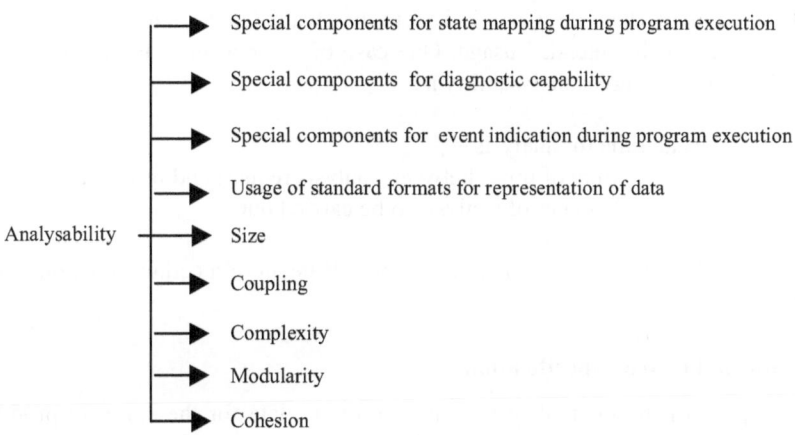

Analysability → Special components for state mapping during program execution
→ Special components for diagnostic capability
→ Special components for event indication during program execution
→ Usage of standard formats for representation of data
→ Size
→ Coupling
→ Complexity
→ Modularity
→ Cohesion

3.2   Metrics Specification

The metrics specification must contain: the selected measure for each specified quality characteristic and internal attribute, a measurement scale, and the set of available methods for measurement, including procedures to categorise qualitative data. The metrics will be external when evaluate the external quality or internal when evaluates the internal quality.

A particular measurement is useful when the measure helps in understanding a process, its resources, or any of its products [3]. Then, the assessment team must choose some of the available metrics (some will be presented in this section); or define new metrics following a certain reasoning process, such as the Goal-Question-Metric (GQM)[2], composed by several activities:

- The first step is to define the goal in terms of purpose, perspective and environment. In the present case, the purpose is related with the SA quality evaluation, indication and comparison, and the end product quality prediction. The perspective depends on the aims of the assessment and it is closely related to the role of the evaluation staff: developer, user, management, maintainer, et cetera. There are two suitable environments: the SA representation considered like an intermediate design product or like an end product itself.

- The second step is to establish the questions that indicate the attributes related with the goal.
- In the third step each question is answered, and a proposal for new or existing metrics is carried out.

The external metrics specification

The purpose of the external metrics is to provide data for the evaluation of SA as a product in itself, not related to the final product, but focusing on its usage during the development; its users are often the staff of the next development phase. External metrics depend on the real use of the SA (for example, for evolution analysis of a product line), so it has to be evaluated as part of a working environment for the intended usage. One case of external measure applicable to the SA for measuring its analysability is:

Mean time for analysis =
Sum of times between analysis request and its execution /
Number of analysis to be carried out

A common case of analysis is to trace the fulfilment of a certain function point in the SA.

The internal metrics specification

The purpose of the internal metrics is to provide data for the software product evaluation regardless its environment. Internal metrics provide users, evaluators, testers, or developers the chance to evaluate the product quality before its usage. Then, internal metrics can be used:

- to evaluate the SA internal quality.
- to indicate that the software satisfies external quality requirements.

The measurement of internal metrics often use figures of amount or frequency of appearance of special software elements in the product representation (such as graph representation or tables of control, data flow, state transition structure or documentation) and therefore the figures can be obtained without execution. However, few available metrics for SA have been found in the literature. Thus, some common metrics defined for design representation and source code must be adapted to the elements that appear in SA representations, that are expressed using an Architectural Description Language (ADL) [3] [4] [5] [6]. One common measurement procedure is the architectural walkthrough using the ADL model and the description of its components.

Some examples of measures that detect the presence or absence of special elements in the SA are:

- Security measure:
  Data encryption ratio =
  > Number of data components defined with data encryption-decryption facility in the SA /
  > Specified number of data components requiring data encryption-decryption facility in the internal quality specification.
- Analysability measure:
  Diagnostic functions ratio =
  > Number of diagnostic functional components in the SA /
  > Specified number of diagnostic functions in the internal quality specification.
- Changeability measure:
  Parameterisation ratio =
  > Number of parameterisation data components in the SA /
  > Specified number of parameterised data components in the internal quality specification.

The intrinsic properties (such as size, modularity, complexity, coupling and cohesion) are determined by combination of measures directly applied on the SA representation. These measures can be further divided into those referring to the number of interface and implementation elements, and those about the SA configuration, defined as counts of graphs and interaction elements in the model.

3.3   Quality Evaluation

The quality evaluation consists of the data collection, the measurement and the analysis of results.

The external quality evaluation

For external quality evaluation, the goal of metrics is to find the values specified in the external quality specification for each software characteristic. Then, an external quality specification must exist which defines the expected software characteristics with their values. The measures are applied and the results are compared with the expected values.

On the other hand, if there are no available specifications for external quality, the results of application of internal metrics on the SA can be used as an indication or foresight of the presence of a certain quality characteristic in the end product. The metrics are applied and the results identify the presence or value of an internal characteristics set (such as the presence of special function or size) that can be associated with some external quality characteristic (such as modularity and diagnostic function can be associated with maintainability).

The internal quality evaluation

For the internal quality evaluation, the goal of metrics is to find whether certain internal attributes meet the values specified in the internal quality specification for each software characteristic. Then, a previous internal quality specification must exist which defines the expected internal attributes with their values and their evaluation procedures. The measures are applied and the results are compared with the expected values.

The presence or absence of special elements is, usually, detected by several questioning techniques [1] (such as scenarios, questionnaires and checklists) and inspection techniques (such as SA models walkthrough). This information, usually, is not formalised in an ADL, but it is attached to the ADL model in the form of annotations, attributes or natural language descriptions. The intrinsic properties, however, can only be detected by measuring techniques [1] applied on the SA representation formalised through an ADL.

The SA development process used constraints the internal attributes of the SA, so the measurement result can be used as feedback for the improvement of the SA development process. Another peripheral use for software internal attribute measures is to normalise external measures in order to allow the comparison between SAs. For cxample, using the internal attribute "size" for normalisation of analysability measures:

> Analysability metric normalised by size:
> Density of time analysis = Mean time analysis / Size

4. Conclusion and Future Work

This paper presents a research work whose aim is to establish the basis for the SA quality evaluation and prediction of the final system quality, since it is accepted that SA, as a product of the design process, has a great influence onto the final product quality. For this purpose, a quality model based on well-know standards has been chosen, and a conceptual framework that relates quality requirements, metrics and internal attributes of the SA and final system has been proposed.

Additionally, a rigorous formalisation of the evaluation process of the quality requirements of the SA, especially in relation to metrics has been advanced. Although it is an especially novel work because of youth of the work area, the adoption of design models based on components (strongly based on the SA approach) will show in the future more work in the same line.

Same aspects that still need elaboration are:

- The formalisation of the relationship between internal quality attributes and quality characteristics/sub-characteristics, which must be studied for specific application domains, development processes and ADLs. QFD will be used to organise and identify the weighted relationship between quality characteristics and internal quality attributes, allowing to make the technical decisions more appropriate, even in presence of contradictory quality requirements and attributes.

- The definition of internal metrics for the internal attributes measurement. As mentioned, GQM will be used to identify the metrics from goals established with respect to internal quality attributes through a reasoning process.

An application experiment of these concepts for architectonic evaluation in the telecommunication system area is being carried out, after a previous phase of architectural recovery. Some metrics are being applied on the obtained SA. The measurement results will also be evaluated by system experts.

This work does not pretend to establish the optimal values for the internal quality attributes, because they are context-dependent, but to formalise a framework that provide the means to meet these values and the way for predicting the quality of the final product from the SA evaluation.

5. References

[1] G.Abowd, L.Bass, P.Clements, R.Kazman, L.Northrop, A.Zaremski, *Recommended Best Industrial Practice for Software Architecture Evaluation,* Technical Report CMU/SEI 96-TR-025 (1997).

[2] V.R.Basili, H.D. Rombach, *Goal/Question/Metric Paradigm: The TAME Project: Towards Improvement-Oriented Software Environments,* IEEE Transactions on Software Engineering, Vol. 14, n. 6 (1988).

[3] N.E.Fenton, S.L.Pfleeger, *Software Metrics – A Rigorous & Practical Approach – Second Edition,* International Thomson Computer Press (1997).

[4] IEEE Standard, *IEEE Std 1061 – Standard for a Software Metrics Methodology* (1992).

[5] IEEE Standard, *IEEE Std 982.1 – Standard Dictionary of Measures to Produce Reliable Software* (1988).

[6] IEEE Standard, *IEEE Std 982.2 – Guide for the Use of IEEE Standard Dictionary of Measures to Produce Reliable Software* (1988).

[7] ISO/IEC Standard, *ISO-9126 Software Product Evaluation - Quality Characteristics and Guideline for their Use* (1991).

[8] B.M.Reed, D.A.Jacobs, *Quality Function Deployment for Large Space Systems,* National Aeronautics and Space Administration, (1993).

[9] M. Shaw, D. Garlan, *Software Architecture. Perspectives on an Emerging Discipline,* Prentice Hall 1996.

An Architectural Infrastructure for Product Families

Robert Balzer

Information Sciences Institute, 4676 Admiralty Way
Marina del Rey, CA 90292
balzer@isi.edu

The whole idea of product families is building shared assets that can be leveraged to develop members of the product family. This has led product family developers to focus on three classes of shared assets because they knew how to leverage assets of those classes. These classes are reference architectures, reusable components, and component generators. Reference architectures define the span of a product family by providing a framework for obtaining the members through instantiation. The leverage gained from this class arises from shared structure, interaction protocols, services, interfaces, and components. Reusable components are generalized versions of components that can be specialized for particular family members through configuration and/or run-time parameters. The leverage gained from this class arises from avoiding the time and cost of rebuilding those components for each family member and from using more mature, higher quality, and better tested components. The structure, protocol, interface, and service restrictions specified in the reference architecture make it feasible to define the range that the components of that architecture must span. It can then be determined whether this space can be spanned through configuration and run-time parameterization. If so, prebuilt reusable components are the appropriate shared asset class. If not, generators must be employed to custom build each family member from specifications. The leverage gained from this third class is the same as the reusable component class, only the means of obtaining this shared asset is different.

Most of the research and practical experience in product families falls into these three areas. I propose adding a fourth: an infrastructure for monitoring, instrumenting, testing, and debugging the architectures of individual product family members. Such an infrastructure would enable developers determine whether a product family member was performing properly, how well it was performing, and the locale of any correctness or performance problems.

It is well known that for non-product family software that 50% or more of the effort is devoted to testing. One major reason is that there are no shared testing assets available (because it is not a product family member). The acceptance criteria, test plan, test cases, test drivers, and test analyzers all have to be developed anew. Moreover, much of the critical behavior of the system is not externally visible and can only be accessed and tested by placing probes on the

Frank v. d. Linden (Ed.): ARES '98, LNCS 1429, pp. 158-160, 1998.
© Springer-Verlag Berlin Heidelberg 1998

interfaces between components. Creating those probes and the instrumentation they contain is both labor intensive and error prone.

Product families provide an ideal opportunity for reversing this situation. Just as reference architectures provided the constraints that made component generators technically feasible and economically justifiable, these same constraints make it possible to create shared architecture level monitoring, instrumenting, testing, and debugging assets that are either applicable across the product family or easily specialized for individual family members. As with building component assets, one can either prebuild general assets that are specialized via parameter instantiation, or generate individualized specialized assets from specifications, as they are needed.

1. Instrumented Connectors

We have started to create an infrastructure for such architecture level monitoring, instrumenting, testing, and debugging assets. The centerpiece of this infrastructure is the capability to insert arbitrary programs into the communication paths provided by the architecture through which components interact with one another. This probe capability, called *instrumented connectors*, is both dynamic and transparent. It differs from previous probe technologies that operated at a single fixed level of abstraction, often the lowest. This meant that high level architectural behavior had to be inferred from the low-level events visible through the probes.

Instrumented Connectors instead employ the abstractions defined by an architecture. These can be high level and domain specific, especially in product family architectures. Thus, a financial product family architecture could be expected to define an account abstraction with an owner, a balance, and a set of operations for manipulating that account. Having access to the behavior of a system at these levels of abstraction make it much easier to monitor, instrument, test, and debug that system.

That is one of the main benefits provided by Instrumented Connectors. The other is ubiquity. Previous probe technology was usually tied to a single type of architectural interaction, such as remote procedure calls, network sockets, user interface messages, or operating system calls. Because most architectures employ a wide variety of such interaction mechanisms, probe technologies tied to a single type of architectural interaction could only provide a partial, and normally quite small, window into a system's behavior.

Instrumented Connectors

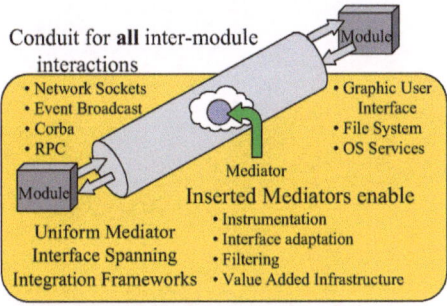

By contrast, Instrumented Connectors handle the full range of architectural interactions from very high level domain specific interactions defined by an architecture to the low level generic interactions defined by the operating system and windowing interface upon which that architecture runs.

This is possible because modern operating systems, such as UNIX and WINDOWS, have adopted a uniform mechanism for programs to obtain services from the operating system, from their own library, or from another program. This mechanism is calls to the functions in shared libraries. The level of abstraction used in those calls is defined by the shared library, and therefore, can become as high level and domain specific as the designers of those shared libraries desire. Thus, CORBA is packaged and accessed as a shared library, and the applications that use it employ the distributed object model it defines.

Instrumented Connectors are deployed by intercepting the calls to selected functions within one or more shared libraries. This interception is accomplished by a *Relinker* that dynamically redirects all calls to selected shared library functions to the probes being inserted. Those inserted probes call the original shared library functions before, during, or after their added monitoring, instrumenting, testing, or debugging.

Instrumented Connectors implementations have been built for SunOS 4.01, Windows95, and WindowsNT without modifying the operating systems or the applications being instrumented. The details of these implementations differ significantly because of the differences in how shared libraries are implemented and accessed on these operating systems. We believe this technique will work for other versions of Unix and Windows but have not yet done so.

2. Future Work

Currently the programs inserted into an instrumented connector, i.e. the replacements for particular shared library functions, are manually constructed for each use. We plan to design a specification language for these probes that utilizes the abstractions defined by the shared library, and a generator that produces the code for the probes from those specifications.

Assessment of Timing Properties of Family Products[1]

Alejandro Alonso, Marisol García-Valls, Juan A. de la Puente

Dept. Ingeniería de Sistemas Telemáticos
Universidad Politécnica de Madrid
Ciudad Universitaria s/n, E-28040 Madrid, Spain
{aalonso,mvalls,jpuente}@dit.upm.es

Abstract. This paper presents an approach to obtain the timing implications introduced by variations in new products of a family. This is carried out by building a global RMA model of a system from the individual models of its components. These individual models are integrated according to some interconnection information.

1. Introduction

The correctness of real-time systems depends not only on the logical correctness of the results, but on the time when they are produced as well. Sometimes, these systems are developed without considering the timing requirements until the implementation phase, where they are checked by measuring the execution time of the final code. This approach has been used because of the lack of expertise on these kinds of systems and the lack of appropriate tools and theory. Nowadays there are tools and methods that allow the checking of the fulfilment of the time requirements on earlier phases, based on the system structure and on estimations of the execution time of the code [1]. In addition, it is possible to check analytically the fulfilment of the time constraints. The most well known technique is rate monotonic analysis (RMA) [2] [3]. In the context of the ARES project, this technique has been used to evaluate some industrial case studies with time constraints. The approach taken has been twofold:

- Analyse the software platform of one of the case studies, in order to evaluate whether it is possible to derive real-time models for applications based on it [4].

[1] This work is partially funded by the ESPRIT program under contract EP20477, ARES project (Architectural Reasoning for Embedded Software), and by Spanish CICYT, under contract TIC96-0614.

Frank v. d. Linden (Ed.): ARES '98, LNCS 1429, pp. 161-169, 1998.
© Springer-Verlag Berlin Heidelberg 1998

- Derive RMA models from existing real-time applications. The goal is to develop a model which analysis gives results that match the behaviour of existing applications [5].

Although the results of this work are successful and useful for the associated companies, the final goal of the ARES project is to provide techniques for assessing properties of family products, an in particular their timing behaviour. For this purpose, a tool for this purpose has been designed. Its goal is to extract RMA models for different products, based on a set of basic components and the particular configurations of interconnection. In the relevant cases, the variation of products is mainly related with one or both of the following features:

- The use of different components for performing certain functions, depending on the final users of the product.

- Different physical models [6], i.e. different hardware architectures. The basic components are allocated to one or more processors, depending on the particular functional and time requirements for each product.

In these cases, a similar pattern is found for all the products of a family: there is a basic set of components that can be used to build a system and that can be interconnected in different ways. The current approach to extracting the RMA model of the system is to develop it more or less manually, based on the knowledge of each of the components. In order to deal with family products, the RMA approach can be generalised by providing means for generating automatically the RMA model of the whole system, based on the individual models of the components, their interconnections, the available resources, and the scheduling policies of the resources. This approach could improve the analysis of the timing properties of new products, allowing the developer to get a faster feedback on the timing behaviour of the whole system and to evaluate easily different design choices for a new product.

The work reported in this article is related with the development of a method and a framework for deriving RMA models of products based on the RMA models of the individual components.

2. An Overview of Rate-Monotonic Analysis

2.1 System Model

RMA is a collection of quantitative methods that enable real-time system developers to understand, analyse, and predict the timing behaviour of many real-time systems. RMA is based on fixed-priority scheduling theory [2]. A set of assumptions about the system are made. The following are the most relevant:

- Concurrent system composed by periodic and aperiodic tasks. Each task is characterised by its period, deadline and computation time.

- Based on a preemptive and priority-based scheduler (some extensions allow the analysis of other scheduling policies).

- Inter-task communication based on a suitable protocol for dealing with priority-inversion.

- No process may voluntarily suspend itself.

- All processes are released as soon as they arrive.

Any deviation from this behaviour implies that the RMA technique is not applicable or that the system worst-case execution time may be too high, as mentioned above.

2.2. Basic Concepts

Event sequences

Rate monotonic analysis starts by identifying *event sequences*. An *event* is an instantaneous change of state, and an event sequence is a succession of events of the same kind occurring at definite times. An event sequence is characterised by an *arrival pattern*. There are several kinds of arrival patterns, e.g.:

- **Periodic**: events are separated by equal intervals of time.

- **Irregular**: events are separated by unequal, but known, intervals.

- **Bounded**: an event cannot occur before a minimum separation time has elapsed after a previous event.

- **Bursty**: an event can occur arbitrarily close to the previous one, but the number of events over a specified interval is bounded.

- **Unbounded**: an event can occur at any time, with no restrictions or bounds.

Response to an event: actions and resources

Every time an event occurs the system performs some *actions* which, together, make up the *response* to the event. For this purpose, actions can be ordered in different ways: sequentially, parallel, etc.

Actions require some *resources* in order to be executed. Every time an action begins or ends, a scheduling decision has to be made in order to allocate resources to actions. The amount of resources required, and the duration of each action, are important scheduling parameters. Actions have some **attributes** that characterise their timing behaviour:

- **Priority**: this is a parameter that is generally related to the importance or urgency of an action, and can be used to resolve resource allocation conflicts.

- **Usage**: the amount of time that the action uses the resource(s).

- **Atomic**: an action is atomic if it must be executed from start to end without releasing the resource.

- **Jitter tolerance**: jitter is a deviation between the specified time for input or output action and the actual time it is performed. Jitter tolerance specifications may be *absolute* or *relative*.

Another important issue is the **allocation policy** being used for each resource. Although different policies can be accommodated, the most comprehensive temporal analysis techniques assume that a *fixed priority* allocation policy is used. For example, when dealing with CPUs, possible policies are fixed priority, dynamic priority, time slice, and cyclic executive.

Timing requirements

Responses can have *timing requirements*, which usually have the for a *time window* relative to the event arrival time, within which its actions must be performed. When the window starts at zero, the end of the window is called the *deadline* of the response. Timing requirements can be:

- **Hard**: The timing requirement must be met at all times. Failure to perform the response within the specified window, even a single time, is unacceptable.

- **Soft**: It is only required that the average response time being within the specified window.

- **Firm**: There are both a soft requirement (for a single response instance) and a hard requirement

A timing requirement is characterised by a *response interval*.

Once a model of the system including all the above elements has been built, a number of analysis techniques can be applied in order to assess whether the temporal requirements can be met or not. The technique range from simple utilisation bound analysis to response time computation under a variety of assumptions.

3. Generating a Global RMA Model

In this section, the main steps to follow in order to reach the global model need to be identified. In particular, the following steps are the most important:

- Determine the connections between the components, i.e. the dependencies between the events of the various subsystems.

- Specify a physical model [6] of the system determining the systems resources.

- Specify the allocation of components to resources. As a result, all the activities in the components have the appropriate resources from the physical model.

- Model the interconnections based on the resources.

- Assign priorities to the tasks according to some priority assignment policy.

The interconnection between models is, in most of the cases, based on the interconnection of events, i.e. one of the results of handling an event is to raise another event, which is handled in some other component. In order to support this it is necessary:

- To reflect this relation in the appropriate table. In some cases, the events' entries can be collapsed into one, which is fired by the initial event.

- The transmission of the event requires some resources. Taking into account this, it is necessary to include in the activities table, the appropriate activity and the required resources.

The way to model the interconnections between the system's components depends on the characteristics of the system under study:

- **Monoprocessor/distributed system.** In a monoprocessor system, dependent events belonging to different components are simply joined together by concatenating the respective action sequences. This is so because the signalling method is based on the use of shared memory or on operating system features. In this case, it is commonly considered that the time for signalling events in different components is negligible.

  In this case, the global RMA model contains the initial event with its new action sequence formed by concatenating the action sequences of the related events. The rest of the attributes of the new event are usually those associated to the initial one, although it is necessary to consider the attributes of the other events involved.

  In a distributed system, dependent events are connected by creating a new action sequence which is made of the action sequences of the dependent events plus some additional actions which reflect the communication between the events of components located in different resources (CPUs). In these cases, it is clear that the notification of an event to another component in a different CPU requires the use of the resources associated to the communication media.

- **Synchronous / asynchronous components.** To obtain a global RMA model, it is necessary to consider whether the interconnections are between synchronous or asynchronous components. To explain this, let us suppose that there is an external event, which is handled in a distributed fashion. This means that it starts executing on a given processor and continues executing on others. When the response in that same processor is completed, there might be different alternatives for continuing with the distributed response. If the processors where the subsystems are executed, are scheduled with different policies, it may not be possible to directly merge the stream of events. Let us suppose that a system is composed by two subsystems on different processors. The first one is based on fixed-priority while the second follows the cyclic executive policy. If the last action for an event is to raise another event in the second processor, the corresponding sequence of actions will not be activated immediately. It will be activated when the proper synchronous action checks for the occurrence of the event at the start of a new cycle.

- **Allocation policies of the resources.** As before, we can think of the distributed execution of an external event. If the processors where the response to the event occurs have different allocation policies, then in the global RMA model, the distributed response to the event will be broken down into separate responses to individual events on different processors. Otherwise, the dependent events will be joined into one event with an action sequence as the result of joining the action sequences related to the individual events.

- **Level of abstraction.** It is important to note that the level of abstraction at which the system is described influences the final RMA model of the system. If the system is described with a low level of abstraction, it is necessary to consider fine-grain activities that otherwise can be omitted.

4. Illustration of the Method

This section presents a simplified example (which relies on figure 1) to clarify the above concepts on how a global RMA model for a system can be built out of the individual models of the components.

Let us consider a system composed of components A and B. For the sake of simplicity, this example only deals with an event on each of the components. Then, it will be presented how it is possible to connect these components for different monoprocessor and distributed configurations.

In a monoprocessor system, it is assumed that the time taken by component A to signal B that it should initiate action a_2 is negligible. Therefore, the resulting action sequence is obtained by directly joining the action sequences of events e_1 and e_2, which is the complete response of the system to the occurrence of the external event e_1.

In a distributed system, where component B operates *asynchronously* (event e_2 is handled immediately after the completion of a_1), the resulting global RMA model contains just the external event e_1 with an extended action sequence. Being that components A and B execute on different CPUs, some means are needed for signalling to component B that it must initiate action a_2. As it can be seen in figure 1, this is carried out by adding action a_{msg}, which represents the sending of a message over a communication link. The time taken to transmit a message over a network cannot be considered negligible. Moreover, the global RMA model will contain the network media as a new resource and the possible access collisions should also be considered.

In a distributed system, where component B operates *synchronously* (event e_2 is initiated periodically), the resulting global RMA model contains the events as separate. Although e_2 depends on e_1, e_2 will execute periodically if the action sequence for e_1 has completed.

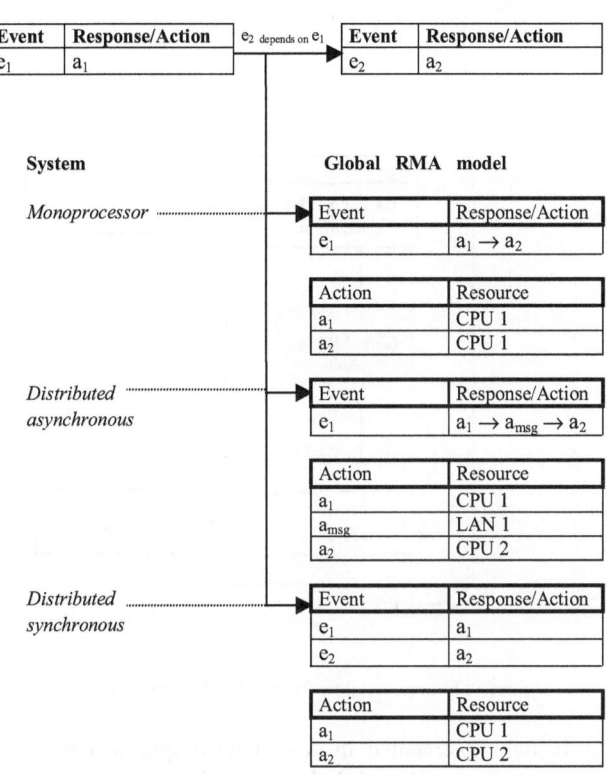

Figure 1: Possible types of connections of events

5. Tool Support

A new tool called TRASTO (Time Response AnalySis TOol) is being developed. Its purpose is to support the generation of global system models based on the RMA models of the system's components. The information flow of the process is shown in figure 2. This tool takes the required information from the situation table of each component. It also takes input information regarding the interconnection of the components of the system, its location and the physical model of the system.

The interconnection information is entered by the designer. It includes information such as dependencies between events on different components, specification of the components of the system and its location, policy for the communication media, and other information. By simply changing the interconnection information and a few other parameters it will be possible to compare the timing response of different alternatives for the design of a given product.

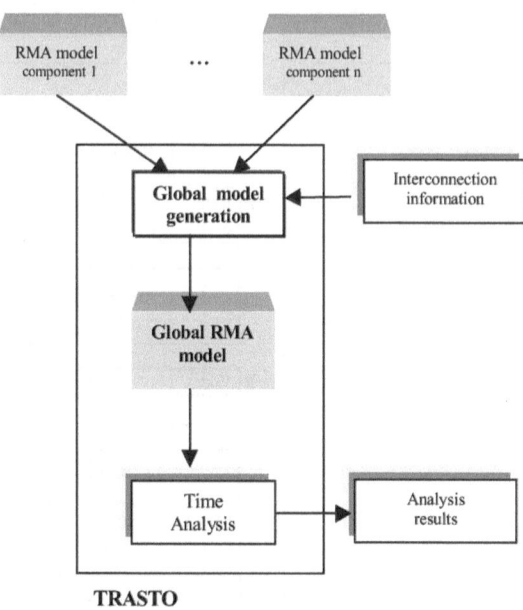

TRASTO

Figure 2: Information flow for the global model generation.

This tool is being implemented in Ada. One output will be a global RMA model of the whole system. This global model will be input to an analysis tool that will perform the schedulability analysis of the system.

6. Conclusions

So far, we have been working on applying RMA techniques to the different components of a system or product. However, it would be desirable to generalise this technique in order to support future product evolution with the minimum possible effort. Therefore, starting from the RMA models of each of the components of a system, it will be very useful to obtain a global RMA model of the overall system.

The idea behind this is to achieve a certain degree of automation when building the global RMA model from the models of the components of the system. This way, it will be possible to achieve a fast way to test the variations introduced by new products of a family, and decide whether they adjust to the expected behaviour and requirements.

By adding information about the interrelations of events of the blocks of a system, it is possible to automate the process of integration of these RMA models in order to obtain a global RMA model of the system. This will allow the user to have a more general view of the timing behaviour at the level of the whole system.

We are also developing a tool with which a good degree of automation in this process is achieved. The output of this tool is the global RMA model for a system, which can be input to an analysis tool to obtain measures of its schedulability.

7. Acknowledgements

The authors wish to acknowledge the participation of other DIT/UPM team members: Juan C. Dueñas, G. León y William Lopes, and other members of the ARES consortium in the development of this work. The ARES consortium is formed by NOKIA Corporation (Finland), PHILIPS (The Netherlands), ABB Corporate Research Norway (Norway), Imperial College (United Kingdom) and Technical University of Vienna (Austria).

8. References

[1]   N. Audsley, A. Burns, R. davis, K. Tindell, and A. J. Wellings, "Fixed Priority Preemptive scheduling: An Historical Perspective," *Real-Time Systems*, vol. 8, pp. 173--198, 1995.

[2]   M. H. Klein, T. Ralya, B. Pollack, R. Obenza, and M. González-Harbour, *A Practitioner's Handbook for Real-Time Analysis. Guide to Rate Monotonic   Analysis for Real-Time Systems.* Boston: Kluwer Academic Publishers, 1993.

[3]   J. A. de la Puente, "Rate Monotonic Analysis for Quantitative Evaluation of Embedded System Architectures," ARES ARES-TR151UPM, 1996.

[4]   A. Alonso, M. S. García-Valls, and H. Jonkers, "Analysis of the time response of CoCoNut based applications," ARES project ARES-TR472-UPM, 1997.

[5]   A. Alonso, M. García-Valls, H. Beckman, and W. Eixelberger, "Timing response assessment for the BTM model," ARES project ARES-TR124UPM, 1997.

[6]   P. Kruchten, "The 4+1 View Model of Architecture," *IEEE Software*, vol. 12, 1995.

Session 5: Development Process

David M. Weiss[1], and Frank J. van der Linden[2]

[1] Lucent Technologies Bell Laboratories, 1000 E. Warrenville Road
Naperville, IL 60566, USA
weiss@bell-labs.com
[2] Philips Research Laboratories, Prof. Holstlaan 4
5656 AA Eindhoven, The Netherlands
flinden@natlab.research.philips.com

1. Introduction

„Everything should be as simple as possible, but no simpler", *Albert Einstein*.

One of the aims of the ARES project is to „help to design reliable systems with embedded software that satisfy important quality requirements, evolve gracefully and may be built in-time and on-budget." The development process should be designed to support this. If we simplify enough, each development process for product families looks like this:

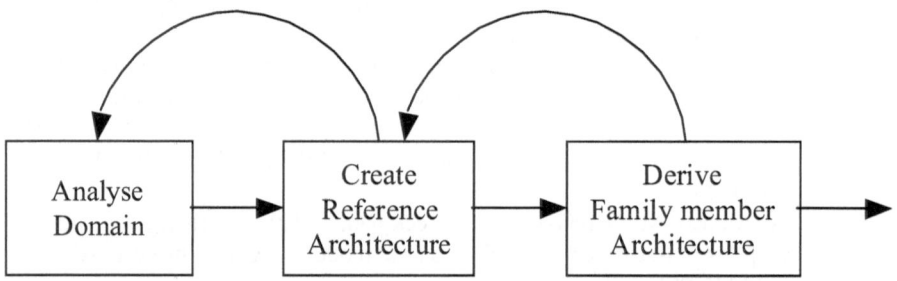

2. Issues

During this session the following issues were a guideline for the discussion. The first set is derived from general observations about the process of developing architectures of software for product families and product lines. The latter issues emerge from the submissions for this session.

1.   How well are current processes working?
   1.1.   What processes are currently in use for defining product lines and their architectures?
   1.2.   What successes and failures are people having with processes for creating product lines and product line architectures?

Frank v. d. Linden (Ed.): ARES '98, LNCS 1429, pp. 170-171, 1998.

1.3. What factors have led to or prevented success with product lines and product line architectures?

1.4. What measures of effectiveness have been proposed and used to determine whether or not product line architectures are successful?

1.5. What processes for creating product lines and product line designs are used in other engineering fields, such as electrical, mechanical, aerospace, and automotive?

2. Which stakeholders do we have and what are their concerns?

3. How should diversity be accommodated?

3.1. Inclusion of diversity and variation during domain analysis

3.2. How can we incorporate diversity already in the domain model. Possibilities are: inheritance, data-orientation, the use of frames, design spaces, axes of variability. What is the value of the variation points, introduced by the book Software reuse written by Jacobson, Griss, and Jonsson.

3.3. How to structure variation at the reference architecture level.

4. How to evolve legacy systems into product families?

3. Discussion

Issue 1 led to a discussion about the reasons for setting up a product line architecture. Mass customisation is a first reason for setting up architectures for product families. However, there were doubts whether customisation means having one (customisable) product or a family. The main reason for customisation is, however, keeping up the speed of change, not the amount of variation. The customers will not accept with a large amount of new products per year. We tried to get data about the effectiveness of using product line architectures, and for techniques deriving them. However, no one had such data.

Issue 2 is connected to the paper of Tom Dolan. He recognises several stakeholders, but non of them have specific stakes for dealing with product lines. This discussion lead to the question whether technical and organisational issues can be separated over the stakeholders. Note that such a separation exists within the academia. This discussion led to an agreement under most representatives that it is quite important to take organisational issues into account when one sets up a product family architecture.

Issue 3 did not led to a conclusive discussion. All kinds of techniques may help, they should be considered before they be applied. Localising may help, but is it always possible. Commonality analysis may be a first step towards localisation.

There was no time to discuss issue 4.

The session concluded with a citation from Isaac Newton:

"If I have seen farther than others, it is because I have stood on the shoulders of giants."

We all know on whose shoulders we stand on. On which shoulder will the future generation stand?

Stakeholders in Software-System Family Architectures

Tom Dolan[1,2], Ruud Weterings[1], Prof. J.C. Wortmann[2]

[1] Philips Medical Systems Nederland BV
[2] Eindhoven University of Technology

Abstract This paper identifies the requirements placed on software-system family architectures by the various stakeholders involved in software-system family development. The requirements are uncovered by analysing the *roles* of the various stakeholders in software-system family development. The stakeholders will have certain roles which pertain to the individual project/product and which are typical of all development paradigms. However, those in product family development will also have roles arising out of the fact that a family is being developed. An important task of the software-system family architecture is to support these family-related roles. The paper has a practical orientation, and concentrates on reporting research results. Further the paper provides an example of how the stakeholders and their roles may be allocated in a "real" organisation.

Keywords: Software System Architecture, Product Families, Stakeholders, Software Development.

1. Introduction

This paper is concerned with software-system family architectures. In particular it is motivated by two widely-held opinions in the software development research, and industrial communities:

- Architecture is a key determinant of successful product-family-oriented development;
- The explicit recognition and support of development-stakeholder concerns is regarded as an integral part of modern software-development methods.

The purpose of the paper is to identify the requirements placed on software-system family architectures by the various stakeholders[1] in software-system

---

[1] Stakeholders have been defined [Bennett, 1996] as: *"people or things* (e.g. other systems) *that have requirements or expectations about a system"*.

Frank v. d. Linden (Ed.): ARES '98, LNCS 1429, pp. 172-187, 1998.

family development. The requirements have been uncovered by analysing the *roles* of the various stakeholders in software-system family development. The task of the software-system family architecture is to support these roles.

The results reported in this paper are interim deliverables of ongoing PhD research by one of the authors in the area of Software-system family architecture assessment. The remainder of the paper is structured as follows:

- In section 2, product family development is briefly explained, and its dependence on multiple development disciplines and product architecture highlighted. Key characteristics which must be supported by the architecture are presented. Software-system family development is contrasted with more-traditional mechatronic[2] product families, and the additional challenges for software-system family architecture listed.

- In sections 3 and 4, the various stakeholders in software-system family development are identified using sources from literature and experience. Subsequently (and based on the findings from section 2) the roles of these stakeholders are divided into those that apply to product families and single products. Section 5 contains a practice-oriented example will be provided illustrating how the various stakeholders and their respective product-family roles may be implemented in a real organisation.

- Section 6 will present the conclusions of the work, and point to follow-on research in this area.

2. Software-System Family Development

2.1 Product Families

A product family has been defined by Meyer and Lopez [Meyer, 1995] as *"a set of products that share a common core technology and address a related set of market applications"*. They add that the commonality of technologies and markets leads to efficiencies and effectiveness in manufacturing, distribution and service, where the firm tailors each general capability to the needs of specific products or niches.

This important aspect of product families - accommodating specific needs within the general product framework - is made more explicit by [Erens, 1996], when defining a (mechatronic) ***product family*** as a *"product concept that is designed for a market but caters for the individual wishes of customers by introducing variety within a defined product architecture... "*.

Both of the previous definitions emphasise the important fact that product families must be defined based on similar market features *and* a similar technical platform supporting those features. The initial presence of such a defined technical platform generally means that product families require the existence of a

---

[2] This is an artificial word created in Japan in the 1970's by combining mechanics and electronics [Buur, 1989]. It describes the technologies used in products containing both mechanics and electronics, specifically where electronics and software are replacing mechanically-coupled mechanisms.

relatively mature product/market combination, where all involved parties have a good understanding of the market and technical basis of the product family [Wortmann *et. al.*, 1997].

Another very important aspect of product family development which has received more emphasis in the so-called "product line" research effort at the Software Engineering Institute [SEI, web], and by the work of Rob Sanchez in "strategic product design", is the long-term, strategic issues relating to the leveraging of current product design investments across other family members and indeed future generations of the family. In particular product family thinking seeks to use some component designs in many models and some components in successive generations of products [Sanchez, 1996] to:

- realise the economies of scale necessary to reduce such component manufacturing/development costs;
- increase component reliability through experience.

In simple terms, product-family-oriented development seeks to *explicitly* address the issue of how to maximise product-speciality for the customer while minimising the resultant variety (or rather its negative effects) for the provider. Additionally these issues must be addressed both within and between generations of the family. In so doing it is concerned on the one hand with *flexibility* (accommodating the various customer-specific requirements) and on the other with *reuse*.

2.2   Product Family – Caracteristics and Consequences

The following general characteristics of product families can be derived from the previous section:

1. product family producers are *market-oriented* rather than (single) *customer-oriented*;[3]
2. the provision of flexibility (to supply variety) within a reuse (to cover costs) context is the mantra of product family production;
3. the strategic alignment of commercial and technical product-family definitions is essential for success;

Looking at some selective consequences of these characteristics for the product family producer in turn:

The market-orientation of product families means that the organisation is directed towards satisfying multiple customers. Such organisations direct their sales, development and support activities by using *internal* representatives of the multiple *external* customers and users. The development activity must support all aspects of the system life-cycle; and therefore must *incorporate* the various stakeholders and their specialised skills.

Product families must provide both flexibility and reuse; and represent a balancing-act between a customised product and a mass-produced standard

---

[3] This does not mean that family-producers ignore customers; on the contrary they are highly customer-focused; but families are designed and built for multiple, *a-priori* unknown, customers (a market) in contrast to a single-product whose development is driven by an individual customer order. Single-products may be derived from a family.

product. The decision on where to be-flexible/reuse, and how much flexibility/reuse to provide, is typically complex and demands comprehensive analysis and acceptance by all stakeholders.

The successful alignment of the commercial and technical family-definition must be carried out in the context of multiple stakeholders and their extensive communication. The product family architecture is the technical-platform underlying the family; and must support the complex family-development activities of the various stakeholders.

Product family architecture is, therefore, (after [Clements, 1995]) an artefact to support the various stakeholders in:

- managing the complexity of the product family;
- co-ordinating their development activities.

Any useful study of product family architecture should address the concerns, roles, and responsibilities of the stakeholders.

2.3 Software-System Families

The principles of general product families have been extensively discussed above; this section deals with the family-aspects particular to those cases where the product is a software-system.

A system is defined [Rechtin, 1991] as *"a set of different elements so connected or related as to perform a unique function not performable by the elements alone"*. This broad definition allows the terms "system" and "product" to be used interchangeably; so a system can be regarded as a product in the previous discussion on product families. Further, we can regard a *software-system* as a specialisation of a more-general system, where some of the system elements comprise software, and this (software) aspect of the system is important for the individual dealing with the system. Thus, *A software system is a system containing significant (from the point-of-view of those involved with the system) software elements.*

The inherent flexibility of software is one of the main reasons for the incorporation of software elements in previously non-software system families. In fact, software is so flexible that one of the greatest challenges in developing software-intensive systems is managing the uncontrolled entrance of variety into the system both during and after development.

From the standpoint of the flexibility and reuse, the following significant challenges to product family development are particular to software:

- The widely-held perception that software is ultra-flexible, means that the expectations of users and customers as regards the flexibility that must be provided by the software-system family are very high.
- Software-systems increasingly find application in environments where interoperability with other software-systems is expected - this means that software producers must adopt a *systems-within-systems* view of their product, and must plan for standard interfacing to relevant external systems.
- An increasingly obvious *customer* needs the facility that he/she carry out future-proof, producer-independent modifications to the software-system after initial

purchase and installation. This need is not as great in mechatronic systems; where customisation is essentially the responsibility of the supplier, and the customer regards the system as a black-box. This fact is illustrated when one considers that customers (in general) expect mechatronic systems to be *replaced*; whereas they expect software-systems to be *upgraded*, thus preserving their own individual customisations.

- The demand (from both producer and customer) to recoup investments across system-upgrades; coupled with the dominance of development over production costs in software means the reuse *across* generations is more emphasised in software-systems. [Jacobsen *et. al.*, 1997] regard software reuse and family-oriented development as going hand-in-hand. The challenge of software reuse in product family development arises from the immaturity and flexibility of software, which has mitigated against off-the-shelf, catalogue-based development typical of non-software-component systems.

Some key aspects of software-system families surmised from the discussion sofar are:
- a broader range of "flexibilities" is demanded from software-system families; by both the customer (e.g. customisability, extensibility, interoperability) and the producer (e.g. configurability, upgradability);
- the customer has become a much more influential stakeholder;
- more attention has to be given to integrating with other systems.

These coupled with the reduced life-cycles typical of software products, means that a broader stakeholder discourse must occur, often under strict time-pressure.

2.4   Software-System Family Architectures

Thus far the focus has been on the business-related aspects of family development; but as the definitions and discussion has show there is a very important technical aspect to family development. The remainder of this section will explore the technical foundation (architecture) of the flexibility and reuse business drivers in the context of software-system family development.

Section 2.2 has described a system as a collection of interrelated components. The relationships between different elements are the key to the added value of systems, but are also the source of system complexity. Those developing systems need a (or a set of) representation(s) of the system which helps them to manage its complexity - a system architecture [Rechtin, 1991]. In general terms, architecture deals with *overall* system structuring issues such as the organisation of the elements into a composite whole, and system-wide control and communication (from [Shaw, 1996]). This "connected-elements" view of architecture is very common ([Perry and Wolf, 1992], [Kruchten, 1995], [Gacek, et.al., 1995]); and has been translated into the notions of "modules" (elements) and "interfaces" (connections) by the general software community. Extensive discussions on modules are provided by [Ulrich, 1991], [Erens, 1997] and [Berard, 1995]; interfacing is well addressed by [Bennett, 1996]; and [Jacobsen et. al., 1992], [Jacobsen et. al., 1997].

The authors have previously stated that the architecture was the technical basis of the software-system (product) family. Clements ([Clements, 1995]) says that the product architecture can allow or preclude many important quality aspects of the system:

- the modifiability of the system, for instance, depends on the degree of modularisation prescribed in the architecture;
- the reusability of common family-features depends on the coupling[4] (integration) between components;
- system performance is heavily influenced by the volume and complexity of inter-component communication across the various interfaces;
- interfacing also dictates how open the system is to integration with other systems in the users' environment.

Here clear dependencies are established between those key software-system family concepts listed in section 2.2 and the main architecture primitives.

The definition, development, and management of the modules and interfaces underlying the family is one of the core activities of software-system family development. Module/interface definition, therefore, must be framed in the context of the required flexibility it must provide and its role in supporting reuse of family elements. As mentioned previously product family development is very much focused on the long-term, and the definition of modules/interfaces must also account for the fact that the module/interface is regarded as a single unit of maintenance and upgrade. The challenge is to define and maintain these architectures in the face of complex requirements for flexibility and reuse and in the context of a multi-disciplinary organisation.

3.   A Stakeholder-Oriented Approach to Architecture

The fact that software-system family requirements are complex, (even contradictory), and embedded in a multi-stakeholder, interacting organisation means that the technical infrastructure of the family - the architecture - must be stakeholder-centric in order to accommodate the reality of family definition and maintenance. Among the many definitions of architecture in the literature (the breadth of which indicates the lack of maturity of the domain) that by Gacek has been selected as being most appropriate for product family-based development, and the most inclusive of the various accents emphasised by the architectural research community. [Gacek *et. al.*, 1995] states that a software-system architecture comprises:

- *a* collection *of software and system components, connections and constraints;*
- *a* collection *of system stakeholders' need statements;*

---

[4] Coupling (amount a single module "knows" about other modules, [Berard, 1995]) is a more-technical term used when describing the strength of connection or dependence among system components. Low coupling facilitates module reuse and replacement.

- *a rationale which demonstrates that the components, connections, and constraints* define *a system, that if implemented, would satisfy the collection of system stakeholders' need statements.*

The same authors further imply the need for architecture *representation schemes* to support reasoning about the architecture's ability to support stakeholder needs.

This broad definition of architecture, with reference to requirements and rationale, shall be interpreted for the *spirit* of the sentiment rather than the *literal* content - the authors regard system requirements as being a separate artefact from the system architecture; but the two are closely related and should support each other, the support being explicitly recorded in the "rationale" aspect of the architecture.

The most notable aspect of the definition is its strong emphasis on stakeholders; a pragmatic attempt to place people centre-stage in architecture. This is also a realisation of the strong relationship existing between architecture and organisation first expressed in Conway's Law[5]. [Clements, 1995] builds on this theme by reflecting on the important roles of architecture as :

- supporting *stakeholder communication* by providing abstractions to manage complexity and clearly separating areas to support decision-making;
- reflecting the development *organisation structure* (as seen in team structures, work assignments) - changes in one imply changes in the other;
- recording *design-decisions* to consolidate requirements, drive implementation and maintenance, and embodying these decisions in corporate memory so that they are reused throughout the family.

The philosophy in this paper is that before detailing views, representations and the various processes associated with architecture, the software-system stakeholders and their respective family-based requirements should be identified and used to derive the appropriate architectural properties to support them.

4. Software-System Family Stakeholders

Who are the stakeholders in software-system families?, and how do they interact with the architecture? - A non-trivial question given that architecture is all-pervasive throughout the development process (see e.g. [Hammer, 1996], [Bennett, 1996]). This section will identify the major software-system family stakeholders; and associate with the important family-aspects/activities identified earlier in sections 2 and 3. The method used in based on literature review, and practical observation from industry. In order to keep the results as general as possible, no pre-conceived family-development-method has been used - however as in all things organisational (as product families clearly are!) - some peculiarities in approach and

---

[5] Conway's Law: "Organisations which design systems are constrained to produce systems which are copies of the communication structures of the organisation." (Datamation 14, 4 April 1968).

terminology will inevitable creep-in, and readers are encouraged to actively edit findings to suit their own context.

Stakeholders are defined here as - *the set of people providing the organisational roles representing the interests of all those entities that have requirements or expectations about a system throughout its life-cycle.* This definition associates organisational roles to the various entities referred to by Bennett, [Bennett, 1996], recognising the fact that in market-led organisations, there must be *internal-*representatives not only for those entities involved in building the system, but also for those using the system.

Software-system stakeholders may be categorised by their "stake" in the system, Table 1 below identifies four categories of development stakeholder (based on [Macaulay, 1993]), and gives examples of possible stakeholders (and their roles in architecture) for each (from [Gacek et.al., 1995]).

Table 1: Stakeholder roles -initial

Stake (abbreviation)	Stakeholder	roles/concerns
Financial (F)	Customer	☐ schedule and budget tracking • risk assessment ☐ requirements traceability
Development (D)	Architect	• complete consistent architecture • requirements traceability • support for trade-off analysis
	S/W developer	• select/develop s/w components • maintain compatibility with existing systems
Support/customisation (S)	Maintainer	• maintain compatibility with existing systems • receive guidance on s/w modification and family evolution
Usage (U)	User	• performance, reliability, compatibility, usability,... • accommodate future requirements

The strong emphasis on requirements traceability, compatibility with *existing* systems, and accommodation of future needs is indicative of Gacek's rationale-based approach to architecture. This contribution has proven useful in identifying software-system stakeholders; and the explicit identification of roles is important and more revealing than a simple check-box. A feature of this, and indeed much other research in software architecture, is the emphasis on single-system development.

But reality bites! The approach towards identifying software-system family stakeholders and their roles must reflect the reality that family-oriented research is relatively sparse, and that most work is based on non-family environments. Further, most software companies (in reality) realise families through delivering contiguous product-lines or product-releases in the form of individual, operationally-managed, development projects. So most stakeholders experience development of families as a series of related product releases within a strategic family framework. For these reasons, the approach for the remainder of the paper will be to present the stakeholders and their roles/concerns from both a conventional product-development perspective and from the perspective of family-development. This will provide stakeholders with a link to their "product reality" while also clearly indicating those parts of their job are related to family issues.

The list in Table 2 below is an extension to Table 1 to address the family-aspects, and is based on: the characteristics of software-system families presented in sections 1-3; the collected experience of the authors; and various contributions from literature, notably [Hammer, 1996] and [Jacobsen et. al., 1992]. In the interests of brevity the list will provide keywords to identify roles. Rather than presenting an exhaustive set of arguments for all stakeholders and roles[6] - this paper will confine itself to abstracting the general method from that rationale for a specific stakeholder, to be provided later.

Table 2: Software-system Family Stakeholder roles

Stakeholder (S take)	Product roles/concern	Family roles/concerns
1. Customer (F)	•schedule and budget tracking	•strategic alliance •accommodate future requirements •flexibility (compatibility, scalabilty)
2. Customer (D)	•risk assessment •requirements traceability	•flexibility (interoperability, customisation, extensibility, industry-standards, state-of-the-art technology)
3. Customer (S)	•reliability •maintainability	•upgradeability •use of industry-standards
4. User (U)	•performance, reliability, interoperability, usability	•consistent features across family (e.g. UI) •increasing levels of performance and usability •correspondence between system and application domain
5. Business management (F)	•track individual product relative to policy/targets/roadmap	•Overall family **business policy/targets** •market segment •release policy/business roadmap •make-buy (outsourcing)decisions •strategic alliance management
6. Product management (F)	•derive individual product commercial targets; •product-content/priorities	•derive product roadmaps •defines commercial options/features •commercial configurations
7. Marketing/ Sales management (F)	•**represents Customer(F)** •individual product market/sales plan •product compatibilities and configurations	•**represents Customer(F)** •market family aspect •returns market info. on preferred options •must know current/future configurations and compatibilities

---

[6] This is reported in an internal research-project report, any specific cases may be discussed via correspondence with the authors.

Stakeholder	Product roles/concern	Family roles/concerns
8. Architecting (D)	**•represents Customer(D)** •specify design of product within family constraints •demonstrate requirements traceability and trade-offs	**•represents Customer(D)** •provide technology roadmap supporting business roadmap •provide for current/future requirements •satisfy flexibility and reuse requirements (rationale/assessment) •reference architecture for family evolution •technology watching to influence business roadmap
9. Customer support management (S)	**•represents Customer(S)** •guidance on software modification. •compatibility with existing systems. •product maintenance and customisation •testing	**•represents Customer(S)** •maintain compatibility with existing systems across upgrades •receive guidance on s/w modification and family evolution
10. Application specialism (U)	**•represents user (U)** •applicational integrity of product •defines user functions, use-cases •beta-testing •user-training	**•represents user (U)** •applicational integrity of family •reviews application domain model •indicates future requirements •context of family in user-environment •user-based options features/configurations
11. Development management (D)	•co-ordinate inter-project resources •provide development infrastructure •development personnel management	•matches development capabilities to family business strategy •state-of-the-art tools and techniques •evolution of development process. •standardise/reuses cpts/practices across families.
12. Development project Management (D)	•project schedule/budget/resource/quality •feedback to product/business management •formal project process	
13. Requirements analysis (D)	•analysis of stakeholder requirements for product •requirements specification/management/traceability	•application domain modelling •architecture assessment •analyse new requirements in family context
14. S/W design (D)	•select/develop/test s/w components to specs. •maintain compatibility with existing systems	•use state-of-the-art technology •balance of new and reused functions •communicate technical issues to business/technical management
15. Purchasing Management (F)	•co-ordinates project component/services supply	•assesses development partners •provide ideas to reuse/standardise purchases across families

The table above is very detailed, and is the result of much research and discussion. In order to provide an idea of the general process involved; the customer stakeholder (previously identified as very important in software-system families) will be examined in some detail here. The most obvious feature we see is that the customer is very prevalent throughout the list; how did this happen? The authors gathered the various possible stakes provided by [Macaulay, 1993]; and then went through sections 2 and 3 and isolated keywords from the text and (if mentioned) their associated characters. The fact that the customer has a financial stake (Customer(F)) is obvious. Section 2 however talks about "future-proof extensions at the customer site independent of the producer"; this is essentially development under the responsibility of the customer - so a development stake has been identified for the customer (Customer(D)). Similarly it was stated in section 2 that "customers wanted individual customisations preserved across upgrades"; concern with compatibility across upgrades is normally the task of support - hence Customer(S). This process is repeated until the candidate stakeholders have been covered. Hereafter remaining keywords are associated with new stakeholders.

Some of the most relevant issues from Table 2 are highlighted below:

- Almost all stakeholders have a role to play in family-development, relating the roles here to appropriate architectural representations/structures and discovering how these structures shall best support the role is the challenge to software-system family architecture.
- Internal stakeholders which represent the multiple external stakeholders (shaded grey) of market-oriented development are indicated e.g. Application specialists represent the multiple users of the system.
- The key-issues of software-system families raised in sections 2 and 3 (e.g. flexibilities, strategic planning, requirements traceability) have been allocated to stakeholders.
- a clear distinction between family and non-family activities and stakeholders (e.g. Development Project Management has no role in family) has been made.

The list of stakeholders and roles is long, and should be edited/interpreted by readers to suit their own organisational context. The next section will provide such an example-editing which maps the list to a more realistic organisational setting, indicating a generic combination of stakeholder roles for family management.

5. Software-System Family Stakeholders – A Practice-Oriented Reductionism

The number of stakeholders listed in Table 2 is relatively large[7] even considering the internal stakeholders who replace the customers and users (and could even be extended depending on individual organisation structures); particularly when one considers the practical concerns of running effective review/team meetings and structuring task forces/management-teams in an industrial context. This section presents a re-allocation of *internal* stakeholder-roles to reflect the fact that

---

[7] The list is also considered long in deference to George Miller's [Miller, 1956] "7 +/- 2" theory on the storage limit of short-term human memory.

individuals in *family*-management may fulfil multiple stakeholder-activities in a real organisation. These re-allocations are intended to:

- ease the mapping to common business management-team structures;
- be useful guidelines; not rigid rules.

The following combinations of stakeholders have been made from Table 2.

Table 3: practical reallocation Software-system Family Stakeholder roles

Stakeholder (S take)	Product roles/concern	Additional Family roles/concerns
1.Business management (F)	•as in Table 2	•represents Purchasing management(F)
2.Product management (F)	•as in Table 2	•represents marketing and sales management (F) •represents Customer (F) •represents Application specialism (U)
3.Customer support Management (S)	•as in Table 2	•represents Customer (S)
4.Development Management (D)	•as in Table 2	•represents Architecting (D) •represents Customer (D) •represents Requirements analysis (D) •represents s/w design (D)

The above re-allocation has mapped all internal and external stakeholder family-roles from Table 2 onto the 4 key-business stakeholders - Business management; Product management; customer support management; Development management. This is *a* realistic organisation of family responsibilities considering industrial family-management structures – there are of course others and individual organisations will establish their own mapping. As stated previously, regardless of the   number   of   people   involved,   the   important   point   is   that   the concerns/responsibilities of all stakeholders are addressed by the product family management-team. The message of Table 3 is that the key-family stakeholders listed must possess/have-access-to the skills of those other stakeholders they represent at the family-management table. Another important issues is that the various activities and responsibilities are *clearly allocated* to named individuals and that this allocation is communicated throughout the organisation.

6.   Conclusions and Directions

The intention of this paper has been to identify the:

- stakeholders important for software-system family development;
- the requirements imposed by those stakeholders on the software-system architecture.

both of these intentions have been met, as described in Table 2 above.

Additionally, the following important conclusions have been derived during the analysis described in this article:

- The system properties of flexibility and reuse are where software-system families differ most from traditional mechatronic product families. In software-system families the facts that:
  - customisation of the product, independent of the supplier, will be done throughout its life-cycle;
  - interoperability with third-party systems is a competitive necessity;
  - both customer and supplier are constrained to operate in an environment of ongoing product upgrades which must support backwards compatibility and provide a solid basis for future extensions;
  - porting products to different platforms is necessary to capture customer base and follow technical innovations;
  - development costs dominate over operational costs

  means that both flexibility *and* reuse are prime competitive strategies for marketing and developing software-system families. In particular, reuse of modules and interfaces between generations of a family is more important for software-system families than mechatronic families.
- A major challenge in software-system family development is managing the uncontrolled entrance of variety into the system during its life-cycle. The definition, development, and management of modules and interfaces to support flexibility and reuse lies at the heart of managed family evolution. The product of such activities is the system-family architecture.
- The fact that software-systems are subject to ongoing modifications throughout their life-cycles, and are increasingly expected to operate in close co-ordination with third-party systems means that system-wide qualities (the "ilities") have become very important business enablers. Extensibility, interoperability, reusability, scalability, portability are all key competitive aspects of software-system family business.
- Most work in architecture to date has concentrated on single-product development-oriented systems; work on market-oriented, product-family based systems is not so established, particularly with respect to the system characteristics mentioned previously.
- Software-system family development is a stakeholder-driven process; the software-system family architecture is the technical realisation of the family strategy, and consequently the family architecture should be stakeholder-oriented.
- Stakeholders can be classified according to the nature of their stake in the system (financial, development, support, usage)
- Those stakeholders important for software-system family development have been identified; and their family-level concerns described. Further, an allocation of activities to a reduced stakeholder-set has been performed in section 5 as a guideline towards achieving a manageable, adequately-skilled family organisation. These stakeholders and their associated activities represent the people and requirements respectively that must be supported by software-system family architectures. Determining what and how this support is provided is the topic of ongoing research by the authors.

The work reported here may also serve as a basis for other directions in ongoing/future research including:

- establishing rules/directions for the explicit mapping of the product family responsibilities indicated in this article to stakeholders. The product family organisation needs clearly defined roles and responsibilities in order to function effectively in light of the broad, interdisciplinary nature of the necessary interactions.
- relating the various stakeholders to the particular aspects of product family flexibility and reuse indicated in section 2 of most importance to them.

Authors' Affiliation

- **Tom Dolan** is employed by Philips Medical Systems Nederland BV, where he works as a Requirements Analyst in the development of Radiology Information Systems. He is also employed by the Eindhoven University of Technology where he is pursuing Ph.D. research in the area of Information System Architecture Assessment.
  - *email*: - t.j.dolan@tm.tue.nl
- **Ruud Weterings** is employed as an Application Architect by Philips Medical Systems Nederland BV. His responsibilities include the development of information architectures supporting multi-vendor interoperability in the domain of clinical radiology and cardiology.
- **Hans Wortmann** is professor of Industrial Information Systems at Eindhoven University of Technology. His research interests include Software Development; Information systems; and Logistics control; he has authored/co-authored more than 40 scientific publications and 4 books in the last decade. Prof. Wortmann is editor-in-chief of the international journal "Computers in Industry", and acts as reviewer/manager for many CEC-funded research projects. Hans is also active in consultancy for a wide range of industrial clients (e.g. AKZO, Stork, Philips, Volvo, DAF), and is a member of Baan's Innovation Board, and acts as a non-executive member of the Board of Directors of Baan.

6.1   References and Bibliography

[Bennett, 1996]
> Bennett, Douglas. W.; Designing Hard Software : the essential tasks; Manning   Publications Co.; Greenwich Connecticut; 1997; ISBN - 1-884777-21-X.

[Berard, 1995]
> Berard, Edward. V.; Basic Object-Oriented Concepts; The Object Agency Inc., 101 Lake Forest Boulevard, Suite 380, Gaithersburg, Maryland 20877; [Home Page: http://www.toa.com]; 1995.

[Buur, 1989]
> Buur J., Andreasen M.M.; "Design Models in Mechatronic Product Development"; *Design Studies;* Vol 10 No 3 July 1989; Butterworth & Co (Publishers) Ltd

[Clements, 1995]
> Clements, Paul C., Len Bass, Rick Kazman, and Gregory Abowd; *Predicting Software Quality By Architecture-Level Evaluation*; Fifth International Conference on Software Quality; Austin, Texas; 1995. (available to

download from :-
http://www.sei.cmu.edu/technology/architecture/projects.html)

[Erens, 1996]

Erens, Freek.; *The Synthesis of Variety - Developing Product Families*; Ph.D. Thesis; TU Eindhoven; 1996; ISBN 90-386-0195-6.

[Gacek *et. al.*, 1995]

Gacek, C., A. Abd-Allah, B. Clark, B. Boehm; "On the Definition of Software System Architecture"; *ICSE 17 Software Architecture Workshop*; April 1995.

[Hammer, 1996]

Hammer, Dieter K.; *IT-Architecture: A Challenging Mix of Aspects*; Workshop on Engineering of Computer-Based Systems (ECBS'96) - Architecture Metrics and Measurements; New Orleans, Louisiana, USA; October 1996.

[Jacobsen *et. al.*, 1992]

Jacobsen, Ivar. et. al., *Object Oriented Software Engineering - A Use Case Driven Approach*, Addison-Wesley, 1992.

[Jacobsen *et. al.*, 1997]

Jacobsen, Ivar., Martin Gris, Patrik Jonsson.; *Software Reuse - Architecture, Process, and Organisation for Business Success*; ACM Press; New York; 1997; ISBN 0-201-92476-5.

[Kruchten, 1995]

Philippe B. Kruchten; "The 4+1 View Model of Architecture"; *IEEE Software*; November 1995; pp. 42-50.

[Macaulay, 1993]

Macaulay, L. A.; "Requirements as a Cooperative Activity" *Proceedings of IEEE International Symposium on Requirements Engineering*; San Diego, California; IEEE Computer Society Press; Los Alamitos Cal.;1993.

[Meyer, 1995]

Meyer, Marc H., and Luis Lopez; "Technology Strategy in a Software Products Company"; *Journal of Product Innovation Management*; Vol. 12; pp. 294-306; 1995.

[Miller, 1956]

Miller, George; "The Magical Number Seven Plus or Minus Two"; *Psychological Review*, 63; 1956; pp81-97.

[Perry and Wolf, 1992]

D.E. Perry, and A.L. Wolf; "Foundations for the Study of Software Architecture"; *ACM Software Engineering Notes*; October 1992; pp. 40-52.

[Rechtin, 1991]

Rechtin, Eberhardt.; *Systems Architecting - Creating And Building Complex Systems*; PTR Prentice Hall; Englewood Cliffs; New Jersey; 1991; ISBN 0-13-880345-5.

[Sanchez, 1996],

Sanchez, Rob.; "Strategic Product Creation: Managing New Interactions of Technology, Markets, and Organisations"; *European Management Journal, Vol. 14 no. 2 April 1996*; pp121-138; Elsevier Science Ltd.; 1996.

[SEI, web]   http://www.sei.cmu.edu/technology/product_line_systems/

[Shaw, 1996]

Shaw, Mary and David Garlan; *Software Architecture - Perspectives on an Emerging Discipline*; Prentice Hall; Upper Saddle River; New Jersey; 1996 ISBN 0-13-182957-2

[Ulrich, 1991] Ulrich, K.T., Tung K.; "Fundamentals of Product Modularity"; *DE-Vol. 39 - Issues in Design Manufacture Integration* ; ASME; 1991.

[Wortmann *et. al.*, 1997]

Wortmann, J.C., D.R. Muntslag, and P.J.M. Timmermans; *Customer Driven Manufacturing*; Chapman & Hall; London; 1997; ISBN 0-412-5703-0-0.

Handling Variant Requirements in Software Architectures for Product Families

Cheong Chye Yu, Ananda L. Akkihebbal, and Stan Jarzabek

Department of Information Systems and Computer Science
National University of Singapore
Lower Kent Ridge Road, Singapore 119260
cheongyu@iscs.nus.edu.sg, ananda@iscs.nus.edu.sg, stan@iscs.nus.edu.sg

Abstract. A reference architecture implements features that can be reused, after possible customizations, across members of a system family. Family members display similarities but they also vary one from another in user, design or implementation requirements. In this paper, we describe techniques that allow us to handle certain classes of variations at the architecture level and to build systems by customizing the architecture rather than by implementing variations at the code level. To achieve this end, we model variations within a domain model and then define how variations in system requirements affect the configuration of a reference architecture at different levels of granularity and abstraction. During system engineering, we customize a reference architecture by selecting architecture components to be included into the target system, by customizing component interfaces and, finally, by modifying components at the code level. In this paper, we show how we model variations within a domain model and describe the mechanism for mapping variations into the architecture component interfaces. We applied described techniques in our domain engineering projects in the facility reservation and software project domains.

1. Introduction

Domain analysis results in understanding of commonalties and variations in a domain. A reference architecture implements common features to be reused across systems in a domain. Function and class libraries, packages (e.g., for financial systems), Object-Oriented frameworks [6], integration frameworks and program generators exemplify different types of a reference architectures that enable different forms of reuse. As systems may differ in certain requirements, a reference architecture must be customized to reflect variations.

There are a number of reasons why it is preferable to address variations at the architecture level rather than at the code level. It is more intuitive to think about variations at a high level first before addressing them at the code level later.

Frank v. d. Linden (Ed.): ARES '98, LNCS 1429, pp. 188-196, 1998.
© Springer-Verlag Berlin Heidelberg 1998

Business goals and constraints can thus be expressed more intuitively and developers need not be bogged down by low-level implementation details. Types of variations that had been addressed during architecture design, can be implemented by customizing architecture at the design level. Unexpected variations, can be either implemented in ad hoc way by modifying code or by evolving the architecture design. Finally, a variation at the architecture level may be equivalent to many variations at the code level. Thus, less work needs to be done if we can address variations at the architecture level.

Addressing variations at the design level poses, however, additional challenges for domain analysis, architecture design and documentation. During domain analysis, we must fully understand and precisely describe variant requirements. The very nature of a reference architecture compels us to precisely describe variant requirements. A reference architecture implements common features to be reused across systems in a domain. It is meant to be configurable to support variant requirements. A precise description of variant requirements will allow the reference architecture to take into account these variant requirements. Then, we need to provide the architecture with generic mechanisms to handle different classes of variations. Variations at the architecture level may constrain the range of lower-level variations. These constraints must be sufficiently documented to allow the developers to use the architecture properly.

The contribution of the work described in this paper lies primarily in novel domain analysis methods and software engineering techniques that make it possible to deal with variations at the design level. During system engineering, we customize a reference architecture by selecting architecture components to be included into the target system, by customizing component interfaces and, finally, by modifying components at the code level. In this paper, we concentrate on modeling variations and on the mechanism for mapping variations into the architecture component interfaces. We applied these techniques in domain engineering projects in facility reservation [2] and software project domains [5].

2. Modeling Variations during Domain Analysis

Requirements have often been categorized into mandatory (i.e. those that are supported in all systems in a domain), optional (i.e., those that are only required in some systems), and prerequisite requirements (i.e. those that are needed for other requirements) [4, 8, 9, 13]. Work has been done on developing various views to describe variant requirements. For example, in Gomma et al [4], aggregation hierarchies, object communication, generalization/specialization hierarchies and state transition diagrams have been extended to capture the similarities and variations in a family of systems. Parameterization has served as a useful tool for modeling variant requirements. For example, in Lam and McDermid [8], optional and variable domain elements are modeled using parameters. In Karhinen et al [7], a design overlay concept to model variant requirements is implemented by using SDL (System Definition Language) extended with named parameter slots. In Natori et al [9], specification patterns are used to represent the variant and common aspects of a domain. The notation used for these specification patterns uses parameterization.

Current domain modeling and requirement engineering methods seem to lack rigor in describing variant requirements. While formal approaches [3, 12] to producing a domain model facilitate automated generation of a target system, we believe that complementary graphical methods to represent variability and commonality in the domain are also necessary. We believe that this will give the right balance between ease of use and rigor. In our experience, modeling of dependencies among requirements in a domain is critical to understanding a domain.

In our domain analysis work on the FR (facilities reservation) domain, we have augmented the notations of various modeling notations to model variant requirements. For example, the ER (Entity-Relationship) model shown in Fig. 1 describes the FR domain in terms of the entities involved and the relationships among them. The usual ER notation has been augmented to show the mapping between variant requirements (e.g. Facility Group–OPT) and relationships (e.g. "consistsOf") in the ER model. In this and other notations, the notation we use to document variant requirements is based on [13].

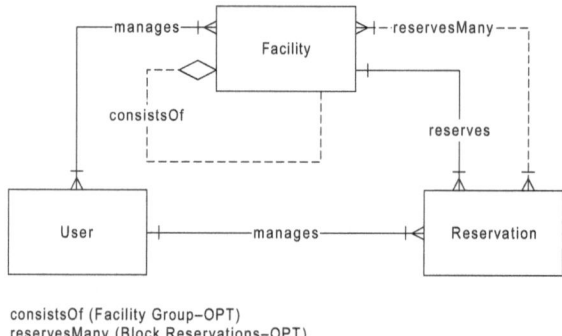

consistsOf (Facility Group–OPT)
reservesMany (Block Reservations–OPT)

Fig. 1. Entity-Relationship Model with Variant Requirements

Another aspect of the FR domain that is highly variable is the nature of permissions granted to various users of a facility reservation system (FRS) to reserve facilities. In some cases, permissions are given across the board to a whole group of users; at other times, there may be a need to individually specify the permissions that each user has. This is further complicated by the presence of middlemen in some FRSes. These FRSes require a middleman to vet certain user actions, such as the making of reservations. In other FRSes, users may be able to make reservations directly without any middlemen. Finally, there are FRSes that support both cases.

The ER model shown in Fig. 2 models variations in permissions. With this model, we can use the tuple (Permission, Owner, Middleman, Subject) to keep track of various permission-related relationships and associated entities (Fig. 3).

We have also augmented the usual state transition diagram notation to model variant requirements. Fig. 4 gives an example of how we use this augmented notation to show the change in the state of reservations over time. We have incorporated variant requirements (e.g. Confirmation by User–OPT) and how they are mapped onto variant states and transitions.

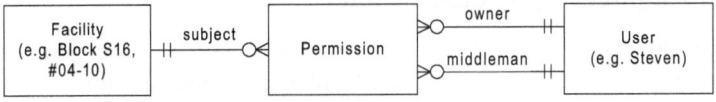

Fig. 2. Entity-Relationship Model showing Permissions

Requirement	Permission	Owner	Middleman	Subject
(ADD_RES_PERM–ALT1): Any user can make reservations for any facility	Add Reservation	All users	None	All facilities
(ADD_RES_PERM–ALT2): Specific users can make reservations for any facility	Add Reservation	Some user	None	All facilities
(ADD_RES_PERM–ALT3): Specific users can make reservations for specific facilities	Add Reservation	Some user	None	Some facility
(ADD_RES_PERM–ALT4): The system shall allow specific users to make reservations for specific facilities through a specific middleman	Add Reservation	Some user	Some user	Some facility

Fig. 3. Sample Permission-related Requirements

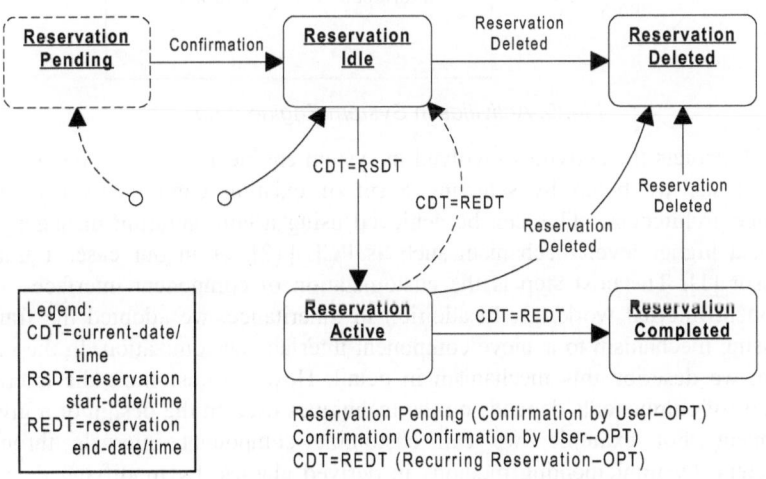

Fig. 4. State Transition Diagram with Variant Requirements

3. System Engineering Process Model

An architecture is defined by a collection of system components and interactions among those components [11]. Unlike an architecture for a specific software system, a reference architecture must be flexible and re-configurable in terms of component structure, component interfaces and component implementation. We engineer a system by customizing a reference architecture, that is by selecting architecture components, adding more components, customizing component interfaces and modifying component implementation to meet requirements of a specific system we wish to build. Object-Oriented frameworks [6], Bassett's frames [1] and table-driven architectures (such as in compiler-compilers) exemplify different approaches to designing and customizing reference architectures. In OO frameworks, we use inheritance to customize abstract classes that form the core of a framework. Frame components, on the other hand, include code intermixed with pre-processing commands such as insert, select or delete. Customization of frames is done by executing pre-processing commands. In our domain engineering projects, we use a combination of the inheritance, frame processing and table-driven methods to represent and customize reference architectures.

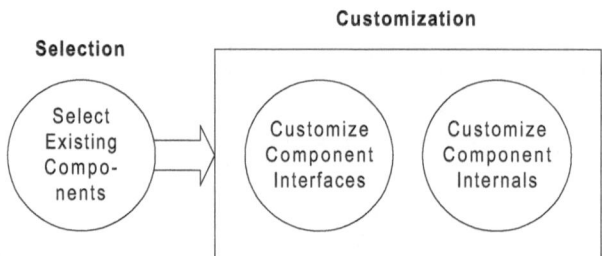

Fig. 5. Activities in System Engineering

Fig. 5 depicts the activities involved in system engineering. Based on specific requirements, we begin by selecting a set of existing components from the reference architecture. This can be achieved using a configuration management system, a higher level mechanism such as PCL [12], or in our case, a frame processor [1]. The next step is the customization of component interfaces and component internal workings. In addition to inheritance, we adopted the frame processing mechanism to achieve component interface customization. In the next section, we describe this mechanism in detail. How we customize the internal workings of components depends on the techniques used in the design of a given component. For example, we can customize component internals through parameters, by implementing methods in derived classes, by modifying data in tables driving generic code, or by pre-processing.

4. Customization of Component Interfaces

In many instances, we must customize architecture component interfaces to reflect specific variant requirements a given system is to satisfy. In the facilities reservation (FR) domain, we are experimenting with frames and Object Management Group's Interface Definition Language (IDL) [10] to achieve this.

Prior to system engineering, we developed a reference architecture model (Fig. 6)for the FR domain. Based on this model, we also developed a system interface specification (Fig. 7) containing interface declarations that are most common among systems in the FR domain that we studied. This system interface specification is written in IDL. For example, our system interface specification contains interface declarations for important data structures for keeping track of facility and reservation data, as well as various operations that will manipulate this data.

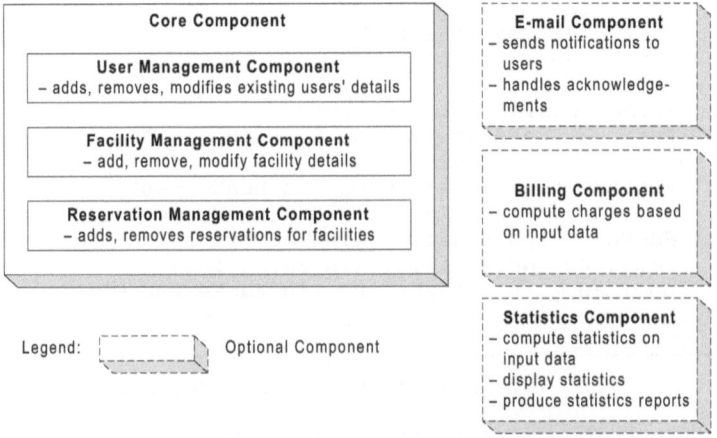

Fig. 6. Reference Architecture Model for FR Domain

We partitioned the system interface specification into a number of generic interface declaration blocks (IDBs). Each generic IDB takes the form of a single frame and contains interface declarations that perform a particular function. Using a frame processor, we configured these generic IDBs based on specific system requirements and mappings that dictate how requirements should translate to interfaces. The result is a set of specialized IDBs that are eventually combined into a single set of interfaces for the system. This set of specialized interfaces specifies a particular range of functionality for an FRS.

As an example of component interface customization, consider the case where an FRS is to allow any user to make reservations for any facility. This is the "(ADD_RES_PERM–ALT2)" requirement in Fig. 3. Sample Permission-related Requirements. To accommodate this requirement, we analyzed the generic IDBs to determine how they should be augmented or modified in order to provide the functionality required by this requirement. Then, we designed a specification frame (SPC) [1] that performs these modifications with the appropriate frame commands. We also annotated parts of the SPC with the requirement name (in C-style comments) to facilitate the traceability of requirements. An excerpt of this SPC is shown in Fig. 8.

```
module FRSModule {
    typedef long FacNo;
    typedef long ResNo;
    struct TimeDateStruct {
        string date;
        string time;
    };
    struct FacStruct {
        FacNo facID;
    };
    typedef sequence<FacStruct> FacSeq;
    struct ResStruct {
        FacNo facID;
        TimeDateStruct start;
        TimeDateStruct end;
    };
    interface FRSInterface {
        ResNo      addReservation(in FacNo facID, in ResStruct
                       resData);
        ResStruct getReservation (in ResNo resID);
        boolean   cancelReservation (in ResNo resID);
        FacNo     addFacility (in FacStruct facData);
        FacStruct getFacility (in FacNo facID);
        boolean   removeFacility (in FacNo facID);
    };
};
```

Fig. 7. Excerpt from System Interface Specification

```
.% Modify the Type Declarations
.COPY FRS_TYPE_DECL.F
. INSERT-AFTER TYPE_DECL
typedef long PermNo; // (ADD_RES_PERM-ALT2)
struct PermStruct { // (ADD_RES_PERM-ALT2)
    PermNo permID;
    UserNo permOwnerID;
};
.END-COPY FRS_TYPE_DECL.F
.% Modify the Interface Declarations
.COPY FRS_INT_DECL.F
. INSERT-AFTER FRS_INTERFACE
PermNo addPermission (in UserNo permOwnerID);
        // (ADD_RES_PERM-ALT2)
PermStruct viewPermission (in PermNo permID);
        // (ADD_RES_PERM-ALT2)
boolean removePermission (in PermNo permID);
        // (ADD_RES_PERM-ALT2)
.END-COPY FRS_INT_DECL.F
```

Fig. 8. Excerpt from SPC for "(ADD_RES_PERM–ALT2)" Requirement

5. Concluding Remarks

In this paper, we have discussed some aspects of handling variant requirements in reference architectures. We argue that variations should be addressed at the architecture level rather than at the code level. It is more intuitive and usually reduces the amount of configuration work that has to be done. It is, however, necessary to give a precise description of variant requirements if we are to address them at the architecture level. We have outlined some novel domain analysis methods and software engineering techniques that make it possible to deal with variations at the design level. These techniques include object-oriented methods, data-driven techniques and frame technology. We have briefly discussed how we have applied these techniques in our domain engineering work in the facility reservation domain.

6. References

[1]   Bassett, P. *Framing Software Reuse - Lessons from Real World*, Yourdon Press, Prentice Hall. 1997.

[2]   Cheong, Y. C. *Domain Engineering for Facilities Reservation Systems.* Honours Year Project Report. National University of Singapore. 1997.

[3]   Floch J. and Gulla, B. *Enabling Reuse with a Configuration Language.* In Proceedings of the Fourth International Conference on Software Reuse, pp.176-185, Orlando, Florida. April 1996.

[4]   Gomma, H., Kerschberg, L., Sugumaran, V., Bosch, C. and Tavakoli, I. *A Prototype Domain Modeling Environment for Reusable Software Architectures.* In Proceedings of the Third International Conference on Software Reuse, pp.74-83, Rio de Janeiro, Brazil. November 1994.

[5]   Jarzabek, S. *Modeling Multiple Domains for Software Reuse.* In Proceedings of the ACM SIGSOFT Symposium on Software Reusability, SSR'97, ACM Press, Boston. May 1997.

[6]   Johnson, R. *Frameworks = (components + patterns).* In Communications of the ACM, vol. 40, no. 10, pp. 39-42. October 1997.

[7]   Karhinen, A., Ran, A. and Tallgren, T. *Configuring Designs for Reuse.* In Proceedings of the 1997 International Conference on Software Engineering, pp.701-710, Boston, MA. May 1997.

[8]   Lam, W. and McDermid, J. A. *A Summary of Domain Analysis Experience By Way of Heuristics.* In Proceedings of the ACM SIGSOFT 1997 Symposium on Software Reusability, pp.54-64, Boston, MA. May 1997.

[9]   Natori, M., Kagaya, A. and Honiden, S. *Reuse of Design Processes Based on Domain Analysis.* In Proceedings of the Fourth International Conference on Software Reuse, pp.31-40, Orlando, Florida. April 1996.

[10] Object Management Group. *The Common Object Request Broker: Architecture and Specification.* Revision 2.1. August 1997.

[11] Shaw, M. and Garlan, D. *Software architecture: perspectives on an emerging discipline.* Prentice-Hall Inc., New Jersey. 1996.

[12] Sommerville, I. and Dean, G. *PCL: a language for modelling evolving system architectures.* Software Engineering Journal, pp.111-121. March 1996.

[13] Tracz, W. *DSSA: Pedagogical Example.* ACM Software Engineering Notes, pp.49-62. July 1995.

Architecture-Centric Software Development Based on Extended Design Spaces[*]

Lothar Baum[1], Lars Geyer[1], Georg Molter[1],
Steffen Rothkugel[2], Peter Sturm[2]

[1]System Software Research Group, University of Kaiserslautern
D-67653 Kaiserslautern, Germany
{lbaum,geyer,molter}@informatik.uni-kl.de

[2]System Software and Distributed Systems, University of Trier
D-54286 Trier, Germany
{sroth,sturm}@informatik.uni-trier.de

Abstract: The realization of software projects can be significantly eased by extending the focus of reuse to architectural aspects instead of concentrating on separate software elements. Yet in any case, operational techniques are required to support the retrieval and selection of reusable items. To this end, we extend on the concept of design spaces which allows to describe the relevant properties of software elements in a semi-formal way. Moreover, we show how the concept of extended design spaces can be deployed in tools supporting component- and framework-based software development.

1 Introduction

The reuse of software elements promises to yield the highest benefit when applied in the context of a specific application domain. There are several reasons for this observation. Usually, the domains are well understood by domain experts; i.e., there exists profound knowledge and experience concerning the development of applications. The experts agree on commonly accepted base abstractions upon which applications can be built, and there is only limited variation of products and processes to be applied.

One important item for reuse is the set of proven system architectures for applications of a certain domain. This is completely along the lines of the current trend towards reusing higher level abstractions rather than just recycling code. Most notably, by deploying a proven system architecture during realization of a new application, some of the most crucial structural design decisions can be reused. But because reusing one single architecture for each application may be as unfavorable as building each application from scratch anew, there must be a way to support the selection of an appropriate architecture for a specific application. As a prerequisite, a technique for classifying system architectures is required. For this purpose, the concept of *design spaces*, as presented by Lane in [11][12], is a promising approach. Design spaces provide a semi-formal technique for both expressing architectural issues and assessing the requirements of the application under development. They moreover allow to leverage domain-specific knowledge, i.e., experiences made during the realization of earlier software projects, by providing design rules for subsequent projects.

---

*This research was supported by the Deutsche Forschungsgemeinschaft as part of the Special Research Project 501.

Frank v. d. Linden (Ed.): ARES '98, LNCS 1429, pp. 197-204, 1998.

In this paper, we present our approaches for architecture-centric software development based on the reuse of software components and frameworks. In order to construct tools for actively supporting reuse of these elements, we propose extensions to the original concept of design spaces. This technique promises to provide a contribution to reducing the overall development effort and increasing the quality of new applications.

After a description of the two approaches to architecture-centric software development, the paper continues with an introduction of the original design space technique. In the subsequent section, we propose an extension to the concept of design spaces. Thereafter, the deployment of extended design spaces in the context of both component- and framework-based development approaches is discussed. The paper concludes with a report on the current status as well as further work in this area.

2 Architectural Reuse with Components and Frameworks

A significant part of the overall potential of software reuse lies in reusing abstract architectures in addition to separately viewed software artefacts. In this respect, we currently investigate two different approaches.

The first one is based on reusing *software components*, i.e., software artefacts ranging from small classes to bigger modules that were designed for reusability. Supporting reusability implies components to have delimited functionality, a well-designed "general purpose" interface, and a clear and precise description of their purpose and properties [5][8]. Conventional approaches to component-based reuse often assume the existence of implicit component models [2][14] like objects communicating by message passing. In our approach, however, we see individual components as related to a specific architecture, i.e., associated with structural properties or constraints. For example, components often cannot be freely combined, but have dependencies suggesting a certain architecture and precluding certain other combinations. In order to provide sufficient flexibility for their deployment in a broad range of applications, we concentrate on generic components that comprise variants of the same functionality. A tool-supported instantiation process then allows to tailor the components to the specific application's needs.

In our second approach, the items of reuse are *frameworks*, i.e., semi-complete solutions based on a specific architecture for the given application domain [4][10]. Frameworks implement default behaviour common to all solutions in the domain, while leaving gaps for application-specific functionality. Applying a framework during the realization of a software project thus means adapting the existing code and adding missing functionality, thereby instantiating the framework's architecture.

For both approaches, a comprehensive and precise description of the properties of the reusable items is required that comprises e.g. their interface, their purpose, and the hooks that are to be (re-)implemented. Essential to this description is a representation of architectural aspects—implicitly by dependencies between components or explicitly as implemented by a framework. A well-known technique to describe architectural issues is the concept of *design patterns* [6]. Design patterns describe solutions to general or domain-specific problems as a set of objects together with their interconnections. However, rules for applying such patterns are stated informally, thus making tool support difficult or impossible. Furthermore, only that part of an overall architecture actually following agreed-upon patterns can be described. *Architecture description languages*, e.g. [3][7][13], provide a more general technique to capture structural aspects of software systems. However, they provide no methodical guidelines for deploying the described architectures in specific software projects.

Being able to represent architectural aspects is a prerequisite for any technique for capturing design rules. Consequently, it is also a prerequisite for any method to find a proper system architecture for a given set of requirements [15]. In that respect we were looking for a technique to describe design rules in a way that can be exploited by tools to support the overall design process. This question is closely related to the problem of selecting the appropriate items from a pool of reusable artefacts. To this end, a precise description of their semantics is required—a general problem of reuse which is currently often "solved" by informal text. More formal approaches can only be found in some well-understood and rather limited areas. As an example, the OMG currently investigates several proposals for formally capturing business semantics [9] for the new Business Object Facility (BOF).

None of the presented techniques can in our opinion give a comprehensive solution to the problems of requirements specification, description of semantics and architecture, and capturing of design rules. The concept of design spaces appears to be a pragmatic and promising approach to address these problems collectively.

3 The Concept of Design Spaces

The development of a system belonging to a given application domain always takes place in a plethora of design choices. In the case of a multimedia server, e.g., one design choice concerns the handling of data streaming requests if transmission resources are short[1]. Possible alternatives are denial of the request, delivering with reduced but guaranteed quality, best effort transmission, or degradation of all current streams. The entirety of such design choices along with the possible alternatives make up the domain's multidimensional *design space* [1][11][12]. The *dimensions* of a design space are related to single design choices, each describing possible variations in one system characteristic. Each dimension enumerates possible alternatives, called *categories*. For example, the design alternatives introduced before are categories in the dimension of handling requests in case of resource shortage.

Some of the dimensions—as in the example above—address the observable behaviour or the functionality of the system, i.e. *what* the system does, and at what performance. The sub-space spanned by these dimensions is therefore called the *functional design space*. Most of the dimensions in the functional design space directly correspond to application requirements. The remaining dimensions cope with the system's structure, i.e. *how* the system achieves its tasks. This sub-space is called the *structural design*

---

[1] The examples in the following discussions will be oriented at multimedia server functionality, one of our domains of interest.

space. It represents the architectural choices and decisions to be made during system design. For example, the decision whether to choose a monolithic or a distributed implementation for an application, the communication paradigm used in a distributed system, or the strategy used for scheduling processes are dimensions in a structural design space.

In most cases, the dimensions are not independent. As an example, giving guarantees about the quality of data transmission requires real-time scheduling capabilities of the multimedia server resp. the underlying operating system. Such dependencies can be expressed by weighted *correlations* between two or more categories of different dimensions (cf. figure 1). Correlations describe how design alternatives will fit together in one system. Correlations of positive weight mean that the categories form a good match, whereas negative correlations imply that the categories cannot or should not be used in conjunction.

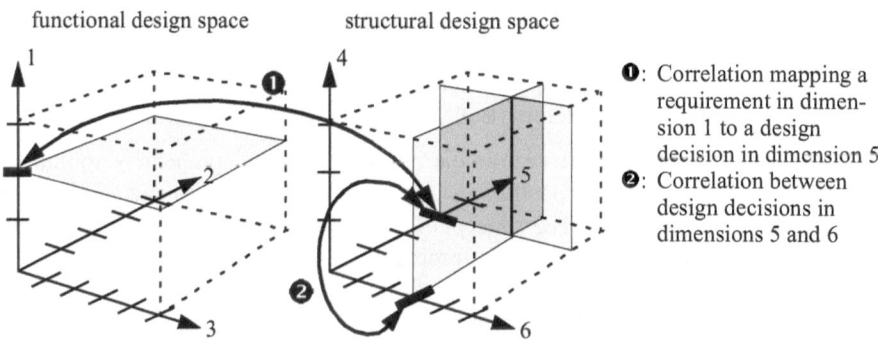

Fig. 1: Functional and structural design space

Correlations between categories in the functional design space and categories in the structural design space can be used for mapping functional requirements to structural design aspects. In that sense, they can be interpreted as *design rules* helping the "journeyman designer" [12] to choose adequate designs for a given set of requirements. One possibility to derive such design rules is to compare system implementations according to their design space classification. If e.g. successful system implementations for similar functional requirements appear in clusters of the structural design space, this might be a hint that the deployed architectural alternatives are advantageous in the given context.

Correlations within the structural design space represent *design consistency constraints*. They provide a facility to prevent bad design decisions by explicitly describing the advantages and disadvantages of different structural combinations. Such constraints can be derived from existing system architectures as well.

4 Extended Design Spaces

In order to effectively deploy the concept of design spaces in architecture-centric software development processes, we propose some extensions to make the approach more precise and manageable. A major problem is that the semantics of correlations are not clearly defined. Moreover, there is no way of structuring design space descriptions, which makes them complex and hard to understand. In order to overcome these problems, we refined some of the key elements of the design space concept and introduced new types of dependencies between dimensions.

As a basis for providing a more precise semantical definition of the key elements, a *typing scheme* for the design space dimensions is introduced. *Simple types* are enumerations of discrete alternatives as already introduced in the original concept, or continuous datatypes like Integer or Float. The simple types can be used to define *compound datatypes* like sets and intervals. These compound types facilitate the definition of correlations and their processing in tools. They moreover allow the characterization of reusable, generic software artefacts whose exact properties—e.g. concerning their timing behaviour—are not fixed but will be determined only during the implementation of applications using them. Existing applications, however, can be characterized by at most one category from each dimension.

In addition to correlations representing design rules and design consistency constraints, the extended design space concept also allows *correlations between dimensions in the functional design space.* They represent interdependencies between requirements (e.g., trade-offs between contradictory goals) that can be used to denote consistency constraints for the requirements specification.

The concept of extended design spaces moreover comprises a *refined definition of the notion of correlation* itself, as shown in figure 2: Correlations are relationships between categories from different dimensions of the design space. Each side of a correlation may be a boolean expression over the values of specific dimensions, e.g. "category A of dimension 1 or category B of dimension 1 and category C of dimension 2". In this way, arbitrarily complex correlations can be described.

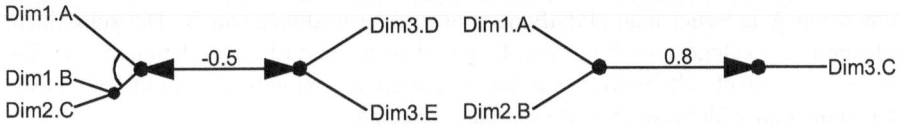

Fig. 2: Examples of correlations

There are two qualitatively different kinds of correlations. *Strong correlations* express either complete incompatibility or strict dependence of categories. *Weak correlations,* on the other side, describe the fact that the combined selection of some categories is advantageous or disadvantageous, i.e., these properties can often respectively only rarely be observed together in systems of the given application domain. For weak correlations, we propose a quantification on a scale ranging from -1 to +1. A value of +1 indicates that the respective categories can favorably be used together, while a value of -1 expresses that the categories should not be combined in one system. Zero-correlations—which can be omitted—indicate that the categories are independent of each other.

Correlations may either be *symmetrical* or *asymmetrical*. The latter kind of correlations describes relationships of the type "if the characterized system has property A, then it should also have property B". Symmetrical correlations, on the other side, describe a kind of equivalence: The existence of a symmetrical correlation of 1.0 between two categories A and B expresses that it is highly probable that a system has either both properties or none of them.

The remaining extensions to the concept of design spaces are intended to provide means for better structuring the design space description. One of these extensions permits the defininition of *groups* of design space dimensions referring to some distinct part of the overall system functionality, e.g. fault tolerance or scalability aspects. This is primarily intended to make the design space more manageable. It allows to emphasize that certain classification criteria are closely related, and thus facilitates understanding of the design space by the application developers.

Another structural extension allows to explicitly state that certain dimensions are only applicable to a subset of all systems belonging to the respective domain. To this end, a concept of *hierarchical dependencies* is introduced. Such a dependency expresses that if a system has certain properties—modelled by a specific category of the higher-order dimension—then it cannot be sensibly characterized according to the dependent dimension. As an example, consider a dimension describing the variety of communications mechanisms that can be used in the implementation of distributed systems. An application can only sensibly be classified according to this dimension if it is indeed implemented as a distributed system—which may be modelled by a specific category of a structural design space dimension. In this way, it is possible to tailor the taxonomy used for classifying systems to the characteristics of the application domain.

One more augmentation is the possibility to define an *order* on the design space dimensions, indicating in which sequence they should be applied. This allows the domain experts to record their experience that classifying an application according to dimension A is easier than classifying it according to dimension B. The subsequent selection of a category in dimension B may then be eased by correlations narrowing the set of available alternatives, e.g. because some design choices should not be used in conjunction with those properties already selected.

5 Using Extended Design Spaces for Architecture-Centric Software Development

The development of applications in a specific domain can be significantly eased by applying the reuse techniques introduced above. On the one side, the deployment of software components allows to reuse distinct parts of the application's overall functionality. On the other side, architectural reuse comprises design decisions, structural building blocks like design patterns, or complete system architectures, which in our approach are made available in the form of highly-specialized frameworks.

The concept of extended design spaces enables semi-formal specifications of both a certain application's requirements and the properties of reusable items. This is a suitable starting point for addressing the problem of retrieving and selecting appropriate reusable artefacts for a given task, one of the most crucial issues for all reuse techniques. It is complicated by the fact that the properties of reusable items like components or entire frameworks are not precisely known before their instantiation or deployment in an actual implementation. The introduction of composite types like sets provides a solution to this issue, thus allowing tools to retrieve a set of possibly adequate items which can then be presented to the developer. Moreover, at this stage, the correlations between dimensions in the functional design space can be evaluated to ensure that the selection of reusable items is based on a consistent set of requirements.

In more detail, reusable components may be retrieved by comparing the design space classification of the application's requirements to the characterizations of available components. Similarly, in the case of reusable frameworks, the structural recommendations obtained from evaluating the correlations indicating design rules can be matched against the characterizations of the available frameworks. In this way, the selection of reusable artefacts can be performed rather seamlessly and to a large degree based on the requirements specification—i.e., in an early stage of the software project. This is especially important in architecture-centric development processes, as the various development steps can then be driven by and towards the abstractions identified by the system architecture. Moreover, the concept of extended design spaces combines the facility for selecting reusable items with constructive support for the implementation of new functionality, if no reusable items for a specific purpose can be found. In that case, the structural recommendations gained by evaluating the correlations facilitate the implementation of the missing functionality, because the difficult transition from requirements to design decisions was—at least partly—anticipated.

To effectively deploy the concept of design spaces in architecture-centric software development processes, tools are required that offer support beyond simple presentation of the design space for the respective application domain. The construction of such tools is facilitated by the description and structuring techniques introduced above. By using them, domain experts can provide customized development processes capturing their experience about how software should be realized in the specific application domain.

6 Current and Further Work

In order to validate the concept of extended design spaces, we are currently working on classifying a set of systems from the building automation domain according to an extended design space for this application area. Then, the hints obtained from the correlations between the design space dimensions are compared to the characteristics of the existing systems. Mismatches are indications for inadequacies or mistakes in the design space description. Either some correlations are actually wrong and need to be corrected, or the design space omits to consider certain relevant characteristics of the scrutinized systems that have to be investigated in more detail. This approach can be further generalized to a methodology for iterating and refining design spaces. In this way, experiences from past software projects can be reused during realization of new applications.

In order to deploy the concept of design spaces for actively supporting reuse-based software development, appropriate tools for classifying systems and capturing requirements have to be made available. The implementation of such a tool is currently in progress in our group. The next step will then be to integrate design spaces in an operational way into our architecture-driven development approach. It is our long-term goal in this field to devise a process model for reuse-based software development centered around the concept of extended design spaces.

7 Acknowledgements

The authors wish to gratefully acknowledge Stefan Albus and Sascha Bötzel for their contributions and hints concerning the concept of extended design spaces.

8 References

[1] Aalst, J.W.; Carey, T.T.; McKerlie, D.L.: *Design Space Analysis as Training Wheels in a Framework for Learning User Interface Design*, Proc. of ACM/ SIGCHI Conference on Human Factors in Computing Systems CHI'95, 1995

[2] Adler, R.M.: *Emerging Standards for Component Software*, IEEE Computer, March 1995

[3] Allen, R.; Garlan, D.: *Formalizing Architectural Connection*, Proc. 16th. Int'l Conf. on Software Engineering, IEEE Computer Soc. Press, Los Alamitos, Calif., 1994

[4] Codenie, W. et. al.: *From Custom Applications to Domain-Specific Frameworks*, Communications of the ACM, Vol. 40, No. 10, Oct. 1997

[5] Dellarocas, C.N.: *A Coordination Perspective on Software Architecture: Towards a Design Handbook for Integrating Software Components*, Ph.D. Thesis, Massachusetts Institute of Technology, Feb. 1996

[6] Gamma, E. et. al.: *Design Pattern: Elements of Reusable Object-Oriented Design*, Addison-Wesley, Reading, Mass., 1994

[7] Garlan, D.; Monroe, R.T.; Wile, D.: *ACME: An Architecture Description and Interchange Language*, Tech. Report, Carnegie Mellon Univ., Pittsburgh, 1996

[8] Goguen, J.A.: *Reusing and Interconnecting Software Components*, IEEE Computer, Feb. 1986

[9] Heiderich, J.: *Representation of Business Semantics in an OMG Business Object Facility*, in: König, H.; Geihs, K.; Preuß, T. (eds.): *Distributed Applications and Interoperable Systems*, Chapman & Hall, 1997

[10] Johnson, R.E.: *Frameworks = (Components + Patterns)*, Communications of the ACM, Vol. 40, No. 10, Oct. 1997

[11] Lane, T.G.: *Guidance for User-Interface Architectures*, in: Garlan, D.; Shaw, M.: *Software Architecture—Perspectives on an Emerging Discipline*, Prentice Hall, New Jersey, 1996

[12] Lane, T.G.: *Studying Software Architecture Through Design Spaces and Rules*, Tech. Report CMU/SEI-90-TR-18, Carnegie Mellon Univ., 1990

[13] Luckham, D.C. et al: *Specification and Analysis of System Architecture using Rapide*, IEEE Trans. on Software Engineering, Apr. 1995

[14] Object Management Group: *CORBA Component Imperatives*, OMG Report ORBOS/97-05-25, 1997

[15] Prieto-Diaz, R.: *Classifying Software for Reusability*, IEEE Software, Jan. 1987

Architecting for Domain Variability

Jacques Meekel[1], Thomas B. Horton[2], Charlie Mellone[3]

[1]Motorola, Inc., Corporate Software Research & Development
Boynton Beach, FL
[2]Motorola, Inc., Integrated Software Products
Boynton Beach, FL
[3]Dept. of Computer Science and Engineering, Florida Atlantic University
Boca Raton, FL

Abstract: This paper addresses how domain analysis served to help create reusable architectures and components in the development of a real-time embedded system. The resulting product is Motorola's FLEX[TM] Kernel, a set of components to support development of portable wireless communication devices. The paper discusses this experience in terms of discovering and developing reusable frameworks for this domain. Our approach to incorporating tailorability into these components is described and compared with a recently published approach.
Keywords: Reuse, domain analysis, frameworks, architecture, tailorability.

1. Introduction

Many companies have looked towards software reuse as a way of reducing product cycle time, allowing industry to deliver new products to market as quickly as possible. In this paper we describe a Motorola project that used a domain-specific engineering approach to develop a software platform for a family of one-way and two-way pager products. An earlier paper [1] described this project and provided details on how domain analysis was used to discover and develop reusable frameworks. This paper puts an emphasis on the type of variability found in this domain, and describes the design strategies used to support this variability.

The product developed by this project, the FLEX[TM] Kernel (http://www.mot.com/MIMS/MSPG/ISP/products/flexkrnl), provides software components that can be used to quickly bring new wireless communications devices based on the FLEX[TM] Protocol (such as pagers) to market. The components and subsystems that make up this product use a set of well-defined APIs that allow developers to create a custom operating system that manages I/O devices, message data, and other system resources in a portable wireless device. A developer can use FLEX[TM] Kernel components to build a product without having to deal with the full complexities of the FLEX[TM] Protocol for wireless communication. The components support varying levels of functionality, thus making FLEX[TM] Kernel a scalable approach for the

Frank v. d. Linden (Ed.): ARES '98, LNCS 1429, pp. 205-213, 1998.

design and implementation of devices that span a wide range of levels in a tiered-family of products.

As described in [1], the project succeeded in effectively mapping domain model representations to design-level components in a way that produced frameworks that can be used to support product development in this domain.

In addition, the project addressed the necessity of supporting *tailorability* to allow the FLEX™ Kernel architecture and components to be easily adapted to meet the requirements of new products. Our problem domain lends itself to an analysis of tailorability requirements that is similar to the approach recently described by Demeyer et. al. [2] However, a somewhat different solution to these issues was required due to constraints on how reusable components can be implemented for embedded systems such as a pagers.

Before describing how this experience has led to these insights about framework development and tailorability, the paper discusses the project and the domain analysis methods used.

2. The Project and Its Goals

As noted earlier, the goal was to produce a software architecture and a set of components to allow new products to be brought to market more quickly. Code in these portable wireless communications devices is written in the C language and not C++, due to constraints in the embedded system's microprocessor power and the software development environment. However, an object-oriented approach to domain analysis was used. The project's goals include targets to strictly limit any increase in either code size or efficiency in the reusable components produced. This is because considerable cost-savings can be realized when as little memory as possible is used, and because these products must achieve highly optimized real-time performance to be successful.

An OO approach to domain engineering turned out to be very useful despite the fact that an OO implementation would not be carried out. Part of this success might be due to our definition of a component as a large-grain system building block which embodies a unique subset of system features and behaviors. (It is larger than functional procedures or object classes.) This definition, adapted from [3], considers a component as a unit of configuration and deployment in the sense that a component should be independently configured, packaged, and distributed for reuse without the consideration of other components. A subsystem is a component which consists of other components.

An OO implementation would have many advantages, one being a choice of several approaches for supporting tailorability. In their paper "Design Guidelines for 'Tailorable' Frameworks" [2], Demeyer et. al. describe an approach to this problem in the domain of so-called "open systems", which have important requirements in three areas: interoperability, distribution, and extensibility. Their solution for supporting tailorability begins with the recognition of *axes of variability* in the requirements of a target system, followed by the development of particular object-oriented design components that address each axis of variability. Our project demonstrates that the concept of axes of variability is consistent with a domain analysis approach in understanding how a framework must be made tailorable, but our non-OO implementation for embedded systems requires different solutions to create a design that is readily adaptable.

3. Domain Analysis

The success of a domain-engineering approach depends on identifying the components required for future product family applications. This identification has been achieved by analyzing and classifying the key common features and their variations across current and future Motorola products in this domain as well as competitor products. This process, adapted from [4], is illustrated in Figure 1.

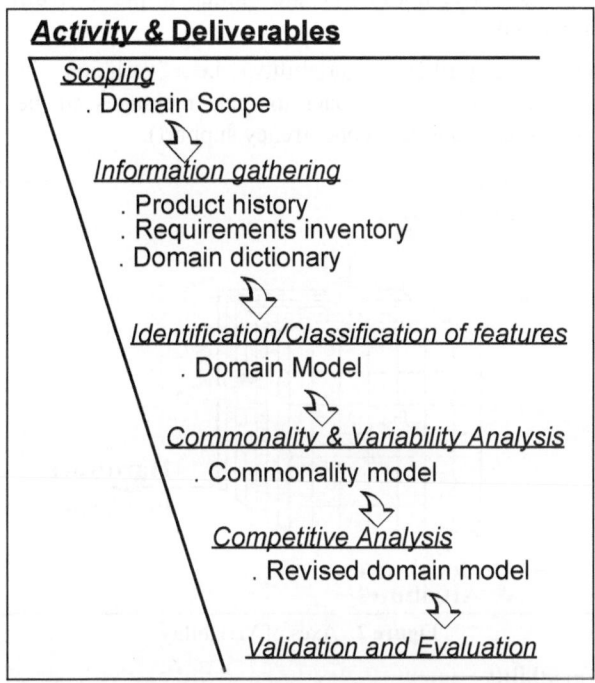

Figure 1. Domain Analysis Process

The OMT (Object Modeling Technique [5]) notation was used to describe the domain model. Object models were developed from existing documentation of product requirements and reviewed by domain experts. Analysis led to development of subsystem views of the object models, based on requirements-oriented aggregation of functionality. Scenarios played a crucial role in validating these models; they were created and analyzed for a number of existing products and used to describe interactions between the external actors and the devices.

Section 4 addresses in details the commonality and variability analysis while Section 5 describe the strategies used to support the variability.

4. Commonality & Variability Analysis

Demeyer et. al. [2] suggest in their approach the recognition of *axes of variability* in the requirements of a target system. Variability in the domain we analyzed appears to focus along three categories or axes, as represented in figure 2:

- feature variability, i.e., variation in the definition and implementation of a specific feature, or additional features provided for higher-tier product (e.g., variation in checking the duplication of messages, or providing a choice of pleasing alerts in addition to a standard alert);

- hardware platform variability, i.e., variation in the type of microcontroller (8-bit vs. 16-bit, CISC vs. RISC), memory (internal RAM, external RAM, FLASH), and devices (e.g., segmented, dot-matrix and bitmap displays of different size) that need to be supported;

- performances and attributes variability, i.e., variation in the required performances (e.g., number of back-to-back messages to be received) and attributes (e.g., failure handling, concurrency support).

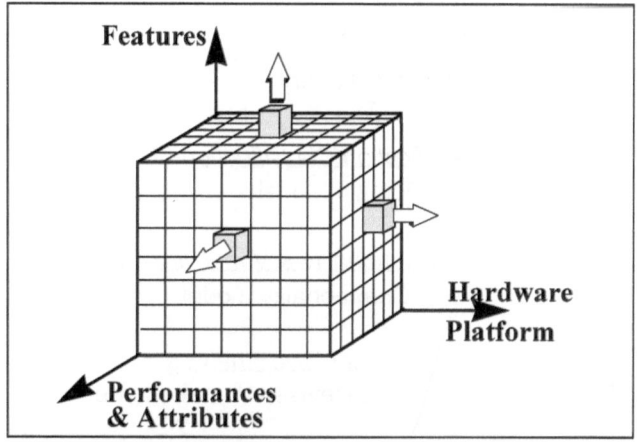

Figure 2. Axes of Variability

4.1 Feature Variability

To analyze and describe commonalities and variations in the feature set, we introduced variations to the OMT modeling notations. This allowed us to annotate the object model to represent commonalities and variations in classes and relationships as well as operations and attributes. Some of these variations were simply "typographic" in nature; for example, as illustrated in figure 3, a common attribute or operation is shown in bold italics. This type of notation is very similar to the one described by Davis [6]. In addition, higher-tier products in the domain with additional functionality were modeled by adding optional classes that encapsulated these additional features.

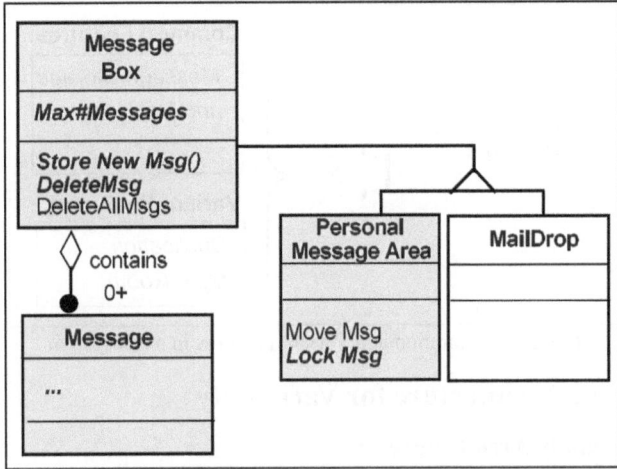

Figure 3. Notation for commonalities and variations

Finally, to create the commonality model we examined a number of existing and future products; this usually led to identifying a small set of changes to our early models that were required by that product's variation in requirements. In this sense, the commonality and variability analysis leads to an additional dimension of our view of the domain models (Figure 4).

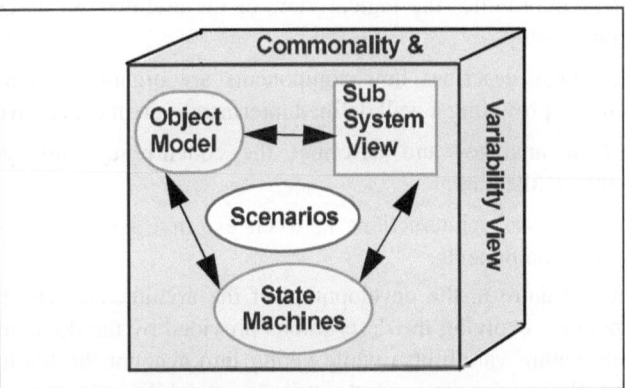

Figure 4. Views of domain models

Analyzing feature commonalities and variations led to important conclusions regarding both how we understood requirements for products in this domain and how we moved into the design of reusable software components.

We learned that product requirements in this domain are better classified according to the type of service provided rather than the "traditional" market segmentation that had been defined and used by marketing, and followed by engineering groups. Such services ranged from basic or fundamental services common to all products in the domain to advanced or high-end services provided by fewer products. Figure 5 shows our view of one subsystem in terms of the relative number of basic features compared to features that vary.

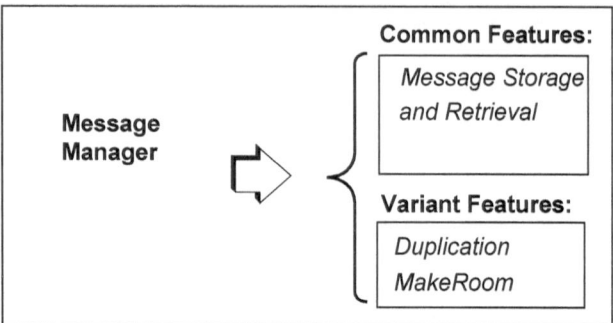

Figure 5. Common and Variant Features in a Subsystem

5. Deriving an Architecture for Variability

5.1 Product Family Architecture

The goal of the project was to define an architecture for a family of products, i.e., a high-level partitioning of software into components, the specification of those components and their interactions, and a set of guidelines explaining how these components can be applied to applications within the domain.

Reusing Kruchten's definition of architecture [7], our architecture is described using four different views:

- the *Object View* provides the logical view of the architecture describing objects and their relationships;

- the *Layered View* describes how components are organized in a hierarchy of layers, each one providing a well defined interface to the layers above it;

- the *Task View* analyzes and describes the concurrency and synchronization aspects of the architecture;

- the *Scenarios* describe interactions between external actors (e.g., the end user) and the system components.

As shown in Figure 6, the development of the architecture was carried out by using and sometimes evolving the descriptions provided by the domain model (more specifically the feature variability) while taking into account the hardware platform variability and the performance and attribute variability. More details on this transition are provided in [1].

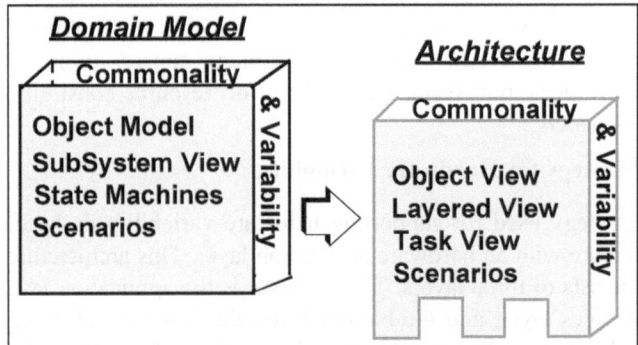

Figure 6. From Domain Model to Architecture

5.2 Design Strategy for Feature Variability

The design strategy that was used to support feature variability is based on the concept of a framework. Figure 7 below shows how, using what was learned in the domain analysis, a component is organized. The set of common features are features that are provided by all products using the component. Custom features are features that will require to be changed to respond to existing and future variations. At the application layer, these variations are directly related to user feature variations identified during the domain analysis.

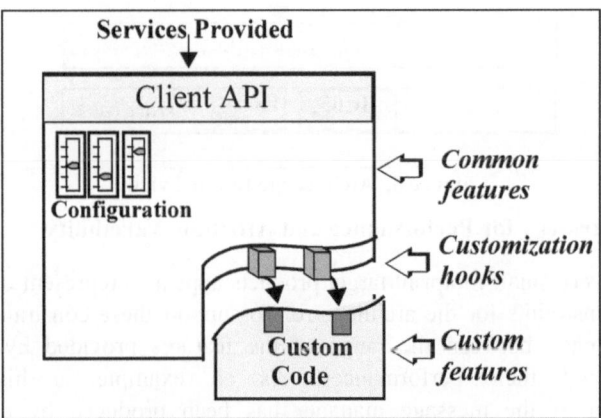

Figure 7. Component organization

At the hardware abstraction layer (see 5.3.), these variations are mostly related to the range of hardware configurations that need to be supported.

Each component provides a consistent client API notwithstanding the multiple variations that can be derived, and a predefined set of hooks for customization. This set of hooks defines a customization API that relates directly to the points of variations represented in Figure 2.

Although not implemented using an object oriented language, the organization of these components is indeed similar to the concept of framework as defined by Taligent[8] and Lewis [9].

The guidelines proposed by Demeyer et. all [2] for "tailorable" frameworks recommend extending the original design with "axis objects", objects dedicated to encapsulate variations on each axis. If this strategy appears more systematic and more flexible, it does not seem well suited for resource-constrained embedded systems such as pagers.

5.3 Design Strategy for Hardware Variability

The primary strategy used for supporting hardware variability is the definition of a layered architecture with an hardware abstraction layer. This architecture, represented in Figure 8, consists of three layers. The top layer is the application layer, the middle layer is the services layer, and the bottom layer, the hardware abstraction layer. By encapsulating hardware device dependencies and implementing device specific drivers, this layer shields the other layers from most of the variations in hardware platforms.

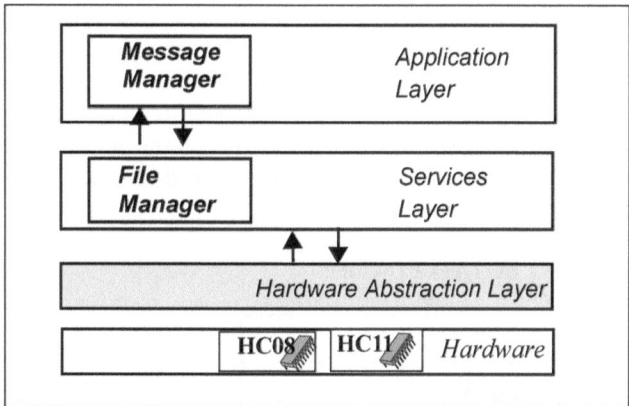

Figure 8. Architecture Layered view

5.4 Design Strategy for Performance and Attribute Variability

The low-end, very small footprint target products appear to represent one of the most challenging constraints for the architecture. To support these constraints, a trade-off had to been made between the range of the features provided by some critical components and their performances. As an example, a highly efficient implementation of the message manager has been produced by constraining at compilation time the number of folders and the number of messages within each folder.

6. Conclusion

Developing a product family architecture requires not only identifying the commonalities across the domain, but also understanding the variability. The commonality analysis provides the capability to determine the core components and their common features. The variability analysis captures the measure of tailorability required from the architecture. As such the axes of variability identify the projected stress points of a domain architecture.

To support those degrees of variability, specific design strategies need to be developed, as the guidelines proposed by Demeyer et. al [2] in the context of open systems. In the wireless embedded domain targeted by FLEX^{TM} Kernel the axes of variability found and some of the strategies selected differ from Demeyer. However, we used a similar overall approach that has shown to be beneficial: analyze the domain to identify the variability axes, and define specific design solutions to support each axis.

References

[1] J. Meekel, T. Horton, C. Mellone, S. Dalvi, R. France, "From Domain Architecture to Architecture Frameworks", ACM Symposium on Software Reusability, Boston, May 1997.

[2] S. Demeyer, T. Meijler, O. Nierstrasz, P. Steyaert, "Design Guidelines for Tailorable Frameworks", Comm. ACM , October 1997, pp 60-64.

[3] W. Kozaczynski, J. Ning, "Component-Based Software Engineering", Panel Introduction, IEEE Fourth International Conference on Software Reuse, April 1996.

[4] G. Arango, "Domain analysis methods" in Software Reusability edited by W. Shafer, R. Prieto-Diaz and M. Matsumoto, Ellis Horwood Ltd., 1994, Chapter 2.

[5] J. Rumbaugh & all, Object-Oriented Modeling and Design, Prentice Hall, 1991.

[6] M. Davis, "Adaptable, Reusable Code", ACM Symposium on Software Reusability, Seattle, April 1995.

[7] P. Kruchten, "The 4+1 View Model of Architecture", IEEE Software, Nov 1995.

[8] Taligent, "Building Object-Oriented Frameworks", White Paper, Taligent Inc., 1994.

[9] T. Lewis, Object Oriented Application Frameworks Manning Publications, 1995.

Commonality Analysis: A Systematic Process for Defining Families

David M. Weiss

Lucent Technologies Bell Laboratories, 1000 E.Warrenville Rd.
Naperville, IL 60566
weiss@bell-labs.com

Abstract. The success of family-oriented software development processes depends on how well software engineers can predict the family members that will be needed. Commonality analysis is an analytical technique for deciding what the members of a family should be. It is in use at Lucent Technologies as part of a domain engineering process known as family-oriented abstraction, specification, and translation (FAST). Lucent software developers have performed commonality analyses on more than 20 families; results have been sufficiently encouraging that the analysis process is rapidly undergoing institutionalization.

1. Introduction

The success of family-oriented software development processes depends on how well software engineers can predict the family members that will be needed. This problem is hard because the idea of a family, although well-known, is not well formalized, there are no rules that enable engineers to identify families easily, prediction of expected variations in family members is difficult, and there is usually no time allocated in the development process for conducting an analysis of the family. Nonetheless, the payoff for doing so can be quite high; its result is of critical importance to the product family architects and potentially reduces drastically the time and effort needed for design and for production of family members.

This paper describes an analytical technique, known as commonality analysis, for deciding what the members of a family should be. This technique is in use at Lucent Technologies as part of a domain engineering process known as family-oriented abstraction, specification, and translation (FAST). In this paper we will use the terms domain and family synonymously. The goal of the FAST process is to develop facilities for rapidly generating members of a family; it is a variation on the Synthesis process described in [2]. Performing a commonality analysis is an early step in the FAST process.

Frank v. d. Linden (Ed.): ARES '98, LNCS 1429, pp. 214-222, 1998.
© Springer-Verlag Berlin Heidelberg 1998

1.1   Developing Families

Techniques for building families were documented in the software engineering literature starting in the 1970s (see, e.g., ([1], [4], [5], [6], [7], [8]). These techniques often centered on constructing an architecture that would accommodate expected changes in the software, but most said little about how to decide what the members of a family should be.' When the expected changes are just those that correspond to predictions about what family members one will need, we will call such an architecture a family architecture.

Regardless of how one plans to create and maintain a family architecture, one must have confidence that there is a family worth building.   Performing a commonality analysis is a systematic way of gaining such confidence and of deciding what the scope of the family is, i.e., what the potential family members are. It reduces the risk of building systems that are inappropriate for the market and provides guidance to architects of the systems, helping them to create a design that reduces the cost and time to create new family members.

1.2   An Example: The Host At Sea Buoy Family

To illustrate the ideas presented here, this paper uses as an example the Host At Sea (HAS) Buoy family. The HAS Buoy example was invented to typify the problems encountered by designers of real-time systems and first appeared in [10]. Briefly, HAS Buoys float at sea and collect data about their environment and broadcast the data at regular intervals. The HAS buoys form a family, since they have common requirements concerning their functionality, but they may be configured with different sensors in different numbers, with different radio and navigational gear, with different computer systems of different capabilities, and with a variety of other equipment.

2. Defining Families

The work cited previously on design of families suggests that the key issues in family design are identifying and making useful the abstractions that are common to all family members, and structuring the design to accommodate changes. Input to the architect(s) for the family should then consist of either the abstractions themselves or the information needed to identify them, and also the expected changes. Commonality analysis is based in part on the idea that there are two primary sources of abstractions:

- the terminology used to describe the family, and
- assumptions that are true for all family members.

To identify the scope of the family the analysis must also include predictions of how family members will vary. Every commonality analysis used in the FAST process focuses on these three elements: terminology, commonalities, and

---

' For example, one technique focused on constructing a set of information hiding modules, each independently adaptable to independently occurring changes ([7]).

variabilities. Hereafter, for convenience, commonality analysis will refer both to the artifact produced by the analysis and the process of performing the analysis.

2.1   Terminology

Most software development methodologies now suggest that developers equip themselves with a dictionary of standard terms. These terms serve to make communications among developers easier and more precise and are often a fruitful source of abstractions. For just these reasons a dictionary of terms is a part of a commonality analysis document.

2.2   Commonalities

Identifying common aspects of the family is a central, and the eponymous, part of the analysis. Accordingly, a commonality analysis contains a list of assumptions that are true for all family members. Such assumptions are called commonalities. Commonalities are requirements that hold for all family members and are another fruitful source of abstractions. As an example, the HAS family of buoys is likely to have as a commonality the assumption that all members of the family must monitor air temperature, wind speed, and precipitation.

2.3   Variabilities

Whereas commonalities define what's always true of family members, variabilities define how family members may vary. Variabilities define the scope of the family by predicting what decisions about family members are likely to change over the lifetime of the family. A commonality analysis contains a list of variabilities and the range of values for each variability. These ranges of values act as parameterizations of the variabilities, and are known as parameters of variation.

Fixing a value for a parameter of variation specifies a subset of the family. As an example, variabilities for the HAS family may include the required precisions of measurement of the monitored environmental conditions. The parameters of variation corresponding to these variabilities specify the ranges of values for the precision. The range for the parameter of variation for precision of temperature measurement might be .1 to 10 degrees. Fixing a value for this parameter, such as 1 degree, then specifies a subfamily all of whose members require that precision. Note that in this example the parameter of variation has a numerical value, but in many instances the set of values will be non-numeric, and could include such possibilities as choices among algorithms, choices of functions to be used in a computation, or choices among an enumerated type or Boolean.

In addition to specifying the range of values for each variability, the analysis also specifies the time at which the value is fixed, i.e., the binding time for the decision represented by the variability. Some typical binding times are run time, system (family member) build time, and system (family member) specification time.

3. FAST Commonality Analysis

Standardizing and institutionalizing an approach such as commonality analysis requires that we be able to describe both the artifact to be produced, i.e., the commonality analysis document, and the process by which it is produced.

3.1 Contents of a Commonality Analysis

Table 1 shows the organization of a FAST commonality analysis document. In addition, a list of tasks left to do to complete the analysis is often maintained as part of the document while it is being created.

To aid in the analysis of the family and to improve the readability of the document, commonalities (and variabilities) are organized into sublists that deal with separate concerns. For example, a commonality analysis for the weather buoys might have a section of commonalities (and variabilities) that deals with the sensors that are part of the buoy, another section that deals with the reports produced by the buoy, and others that deal with other concerns relevant to the family. Note that such a structure is specific to the family.

During the course of any analysis technique used in systems development issues arise that are difficult to resolve and that have a strong effect on the result. Such issues, along with the alternatives considered for their resolution, are included in a separate section of the document. This practice helps keep the analysts from going in circles, and provides insight for later users into the reasons for the decisions made by the analysts. Such insight is particularly useful for reviewers of the analysis, for developers of a language used to specify family members, for creators of the design for the family, and for engineers new to the family.

An issue for buoy analysts might be whether or not buoys could be equipped with active sensors, such as sonar, that might be used for purposes other than weather reporting. Such a feature might widen the market for buoys, but might impose design and operational constraints that would make it unrealistic to include such buoys in the same family as floating weather stations.

Commonality analyses focus on requirements for the family, but often uncover useful design and implementation information during the analysis, which is often documented in one or more appendices so that it need not be rediscovered.

3.2 The Commonality Analysis Process

FAST commonality analyses are performed in a series of meetings of domain experts, facilitated by a moderator. Meetings are usually held at regular intervals, but their duration and frequency may vary widely. The analysis team produces the document during the meetings as a group, by consensus, guided by the moderator. One group member, the recorder, has the responsibility to record the group's decisions in the commonality analysis document during the meetings, using the standard structure of a commonality analysis as shown in Table 1.

Typically, each participant, except the moderator, is expert in one or more aspects of the family. The moderator is expert in the FAST process, can recognize well-formed, clear, and precise definitions, commonalities, variabilities, parameters of variation, and useful issues, and knows how to guide the discussion to produce them. The moderator is also frequently the recorder. As the recorder edits the document it is continuously displayed for all participants during each meeting. Each participant receives a copy of it, either electronically or in hard copy, at the end of each session.

Section	Purpose
1. Introduction	Describes the purpose of performing the analysis and the expected use. Typically, the purpose is to analyze or define the requirements for a particular family and to provide the basis for capabilities such as • a way of specifying family members • a way of generating some or all of the code and documentation for family members • an environment for composing family members from a set of components that are designed for use in many family members
2. Overview	Briefly describes the family and its relationship(s) to other families.
3. Dictionary of Terms	Provides a standard set of key technical terms used in discussions about and descriptions of the family.
4. Commonalities	Provides a structured list of assumptions that are true for all members of the family.
5. Variabilities	Provides a structured list of assumptions about how family members may vary.
6. Parameters of Variation	Quantifies the variabilities, specifying the range of values and the decision time for each.
7. Issues	Provides a record of the alternatives considered for key issues that arose in analyzing the family.
8. Appendices	Includes various information useful to reviewers, designers, language designers, tool builders for the family, and other potential users of the analysis.

Table 1 Organization of a Commonality Analysis Document

3.3 Stages of the Analysis

The commonality analysis process is organized into several stages, as follows.
• Prepare: The moderator ensures that all resources needed for the initial sessions are in place.
• Plan: The moderator and domain experts meet to agree on the purpose and scope of the analysis and to review briefly the expected activities and results of the commonality analysis process.

- Analyze: The moderator and domain experts meet to analyze the family and characterize its members up to the point of producing parameters of variation, i.e., they produce all sections of the document except section 6.
- Quantify: The moderator and domain experts meet to define the parameters of variation for the family, section 6. of the document, and prepare the document for review.
- Review: Reviewers external to the team that produced the analysis conduct a review of it, possibly using techniques such as an described in [9].

Figure 1 shows the stages of the analysis, the activities that proceed in each stage, and the ordering among the stages, indicating concurrency and iteration both among activities within a stage of the analysis and between stages. For example, defining terms, identifying commonalities, and identifying variabilities may proceed concurrently; they are all iterative with identifying and resolving issues.

Although the duration for completing a commonality analysis varies depending on the mode in which the group works, the total effort is approximately the same, i.e., about 24 staff weeks. The result of this effort is usually a document of 25-50 pages, excluding appendices.

4. Results

The author is personally familiar with 17 different commonality analyses that have been tried at Lucent, and one analysis outside Lucent [3]. In addition, there are perhaps another 10-15 cases within Lucent where the author is aware that an analysis is in progress. Of the 17, 10 have been completed, one was never finished, and six are in progress.

Although some groups consider the analysis to be just an early step in their application of the FAST process, nearly all have come to view it as a worthwhile endeavor in itself. Their analyses have been and are being used for the following purposes.

- Continuation of the FAST process, i.e., to design a domain specific language and then to generate the code and documentation for family members from specifications in the language. Teams usually estimate during the process that they will get an improvement between 2:1 and 3:1 in productivity gains from using this approach. Early data from development tends to validate these estimates.
- Basis for a family architecture. Some groups create an object oriented design for their family. Variabilities, for example, are viewed as decisions to be encapsulated within classes or information hiding modules [8].
- As reference documentation. The analysis is viewed as a repository of critical information about the family that has hitherto never been documented, and that many project members have never previously known or understood.
- Basis for reengineering a family. Some projects use the analysis as a way to start reorganizing and redesigning an existing set of code into a unified domain.

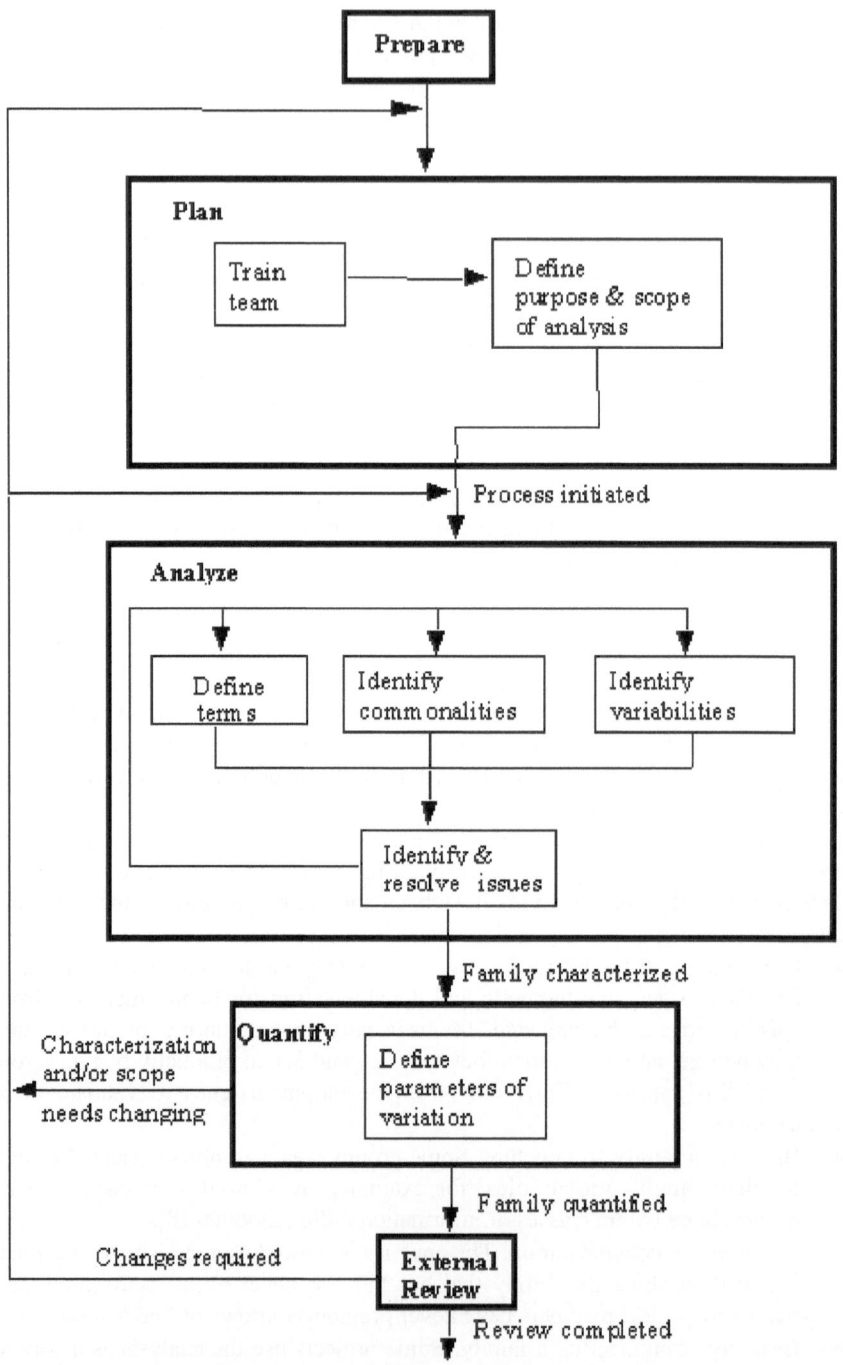

Figure 1 Commonality Analysis Process

- As a training aid. The commonality analysis is used to train new project members.
- As a plan for evolution of the family. The commonality analysis is used as a description of the products (and/or services) that are expected to be offered to customers in the future.

It is difficult to offer quantitative evidence that performing a commonality analysis alone leads directly to improvements in understanding a family, in design and code for a family, and in other aspects of software development for a family. Informal surveys of developers who have performed such analyses indicate that they believe they have gotten value from the analysis. This effect may just be a result of giving them time during their development interval to think about issues they do not ordinarily have time to consider. The commonality analysis process structures this time and the artifact that results from it in a way that clearly focuses the developers on issues of changeability. Other techniques may work equally well.

The commonality analysis process (and FAST) started as an experimental process at Lucent in 1992 and is still evolving. It is now being institutionalized via a set of training courses and support groups. In most cases, projects decide to try the process because they need to find ways to satisfy the demands of a growing set of varied customers at lower cost with shorter development intervals, i.e., they are seeking a competitive advantage.

5. Acknowledgements

Thanks to the many Lucent software developers and their managers who have been willing to try the commonality analysis process. Thanks also to those who accepted the challenge of becoming moderators and thereby showed that people other than the inventor of the process could moderate a commonality analysis. Eric Sumner played a key role in finding the first few groups of developers at Lucent who were willing to try a commonality analysis. The experiences of moderators such as Mark Ardis, David Cuka, Neil Harrison, Lalita Jagadeesan, Robert Lied, and Peter Mataga all contributed to the evolution of the process. David Cuka has been particularly instrumental in suggesting improvements to the process. Robert Chi Tau Lai and Mark Ardis made many useful suggestions for improving this paper.

6. References

[1]   Britton, K. H., Parker, R.A., Parnas, D.L.; A Procedure For Designing Abstract Interfaces for Device Interface Modules, Proc. 5th Int. Conf. Software Eng., 1981

[2]   Campbell, Grady H. Jr., Faulk, Stuart R., Weiss, David M.; Introduction To Synthesis, INTRO_SYNTHESIS_PROCESS-90019-N, 1990, Software Productivity Consortium, Herndon, VA

[3] Campbell, G.,O'Connor, J., Mansour, C., Turner-Harris, J.; Reuse in Command and Control Systems, IEEE Software, September, 1994

[4] Dijkstra, E. W., Notes on Structured Programming. Structured Programming, O.J. Dahl, E.W. Dijkstra, C.A.R. Hoare, eds., Academic Press, London, 1972

[5] Parnas, D.L., On the Design and Development of Program Families, IEEE Transactions on Software Engineering, SE-2:1-9, March 1976

[6] Parnas, D.L., Designing Software For Ease Of Extension and Contraction, Proc. 3rd Int. Conf. Soft. Eng., May 1978

[7] Parnas, D.L., Clements, P.C.; A Rational Design Process: How and Why to Fake It, IEEE Transactions on Software Engineering, SE-12, No. 2, February 1986

[8] Parnas, D.L., Clements, P.C., Weiss, D.M.; The Modular Structure Of Complex Systems, IEEE Transactions on Software Engineering, SE-11., pp. 259-266, March 1985

[9] Parnas, D.L., Weiss, D.M.; Active Design Reviews: Principles and Practices, Proc. 8th Int. Conf. Soft. Eng., London, August 1985

[10] Software Engineering Principles, Course Notebook, Naval Research Laboratory, 1980

Structuring Design Decisions for Evolution

Anssi Karhinen, Juha Kuusela

Nokia Research Center, P. O. Box 45
FIN-00211 Helsinki, Finland
anssi.karhinen@research.nokia.com
juha.kuusela@research.nokia.com

Abstract. Software system has to face many changes during its life cycle. Some of these changes can be anticipated some come as surprises. Software systems can be designed to be flexible in terms of anticipated changes. Flexibility is achieved by structuring the system utilizing abstraction, indirection, late binding or some other variance mechanism. Surprising changes are still a problem. Partially this problem can be alleviated by proper management of design knowledge. We propose a mechanism to organize design decision so that this organization can be used to analyze change requests and determine their impact on system architecture. We demonstrate this using an industrial example.

1. Introduction

The life span of an industrial software system can be decades. During this time it has to be adapted to changing requirements. Some of these changes can be anticipated while others come as surprises.

There usually exists many different options on how to react to a change request. For example if the request is a new functional feature to the system, it might be possible to make a straight forward implementation for it and attach it to the system or the new feature could be added by adding a parametrization to an existing feature. The different options have different tradeoffs in terms of required amount of work and impact on system structure or architecture.

Modifications to the software systems tend to be mainly additive. Addition seems to be the best option in short time scale: addition of a new feature takes less work than restructuring and retesting existing parts. Continuous addition, however, leads to a situation where it is hard to control the impact of changes to the system architecture and the architecture slowly degrades. The degradation of system architecture and constant addition of new features lead to uncontrolled growth of the system and the organization that is maintaining it.

Frank v. d. Linden (Ed.): ARES '98, LNCS 1429, pp. 223-234, 1998.

The decisions on how to react to change requests are often made relying only on local information of the single change request and other non-architectural information like the amount of available resources and delivery schedule. Analytical information on change requests and its relation to the system as a whole is missing. The requests are not classified, nor are the impacts of different options on how to react to the requests. System evolution is not taken into account.

In order to improve the situation designers making the change need to be more informed. They need to know the rationale behind the structures of the design. This rationale allows them to base their decisions on global information of the system structure. They will be able to utilize existing flexibility in the design when the change had been anticipated and they can understand the consequences of different modification alternatives when the change is a surprise.

Lot of design knowledge is accumulated over the product life cycle. An efficient mechanism is needed to support change management based on the accumulated design knowledge. We propose the Design Decision Trees (DDT) [2] as a mechanism to organize and access this body of knowledge. Design decision tree can be used to map the change requests to the existing design. This makes it possible to classify different options and to react to them and analyze their architectural implications.

2. Variance in Large Software Systems

Many large software systems are maintained as a group of coexisting variants, called software product family [4]. The members of a software product family share most of the requirements but each variant also has its own unique set of requirements.

The main problem in maintaining a software product family is how to continue to share effort and reuse design and implementation while providing more and more variation of features and capabilities in the family members.

To get a more detailed picture of this problem we have to take a closer look on how and why the family members vary.

2.1   Classification of Variance

Variance in software systems can be classified to be either predictable or unpredictable. In predictable variance we have a domain model of variance and the reasons for it. For example in telecommunication standards there exist an international standard for the communication protocol between telephone exchanges. In addition there exists a finite number of national variants of that protocol. Now if we are designing the software for a telephone exchange we can analyze the variance in the requirements for protocol software as complete information for the variants is available. Predictable variance can be anticipated [5].

In many cases however the variance in requirements cannot be analyzed or known in advance. For example if our software system is using third party components the vendor of those can change the components arbitrarily without communicating he reasons behind the changes. In such case if we need to continue to support the old component also we must generate variants of our system without a model for the variance.

2.2   Options for Managing Variance

There are at least four different approaches to achieving sharing and reuse in families of software products: implementation configuration, customization, modularization and design configuration [6].

Families of products that achieve variation by implementation configuration have one design for all products. The design is usually simple because variance is completely managed by implementation, and the design disregards differences between products. Implementation configuration does not require a model of variance for predicting future requirements. Variation is considered to be unpredictable. In order to achieve sharing and reuse between different products, program text manipulation through conditional compilation and source code configuration management is used. As the number of products in the family grows, managing variation through configuration on the implementation level becomes very complex.

Managing family variance by customization means that all variants are supported by one "universal" product that may be customized by the maker or by the customer to behave as any specific variant. Hence customization enables one to change product capabilities, supported features, and modes of operation. All possible components must be present in the design and implementation of the product. The active set of components is selected by customization procedures.

The remaining two approaches do not rely on a single design for all the products in the family. They differ in the kind of variation they accommodate.

In modularization, variation is localized to structural elements of the design and variants are produced by selecting appropriate set of components. The shared part of the design (the family architecture) is a framework that is further extended by selecting existing and specifying new components, and establishing relationships between them. Both the choice of the components and their relations may change from product to product.

Designing and developing a family architecture and generic components that may be shared by different products in a family is a complex task. Furthermore, such product implementations often require more runtime resources than simpler implementations of variant products.

In design configuration [6], variability in the product is addressed on the design level and each product in the family has a different design. The management of different designs relies on tool support to manage dependencies between the products in the family.

If the variability in the application domain is ad hoc, customization and modularization do not effectively achieve sharing and reuse. On the other hand, implementation configuration does not use design as a tool for managing complexity and thus leads to overly complex implementations.

3. Variance, System Structure and Design Decisions

Inherently software is very flexible. Unfortunately the larger a system gets the more inflexible it becomes. Existing system structure constrains evolution. When you make a change you have to
- conform to the interfaces of those modules you communicate with,
- use the data representations of those interfaces,
- use the data representation of all data stores,
- base your execution architecture on the existing operating system and its scheduling principles,
- use only the time slot allocated to you,
- conform to the fault tolerance mechanisms,
- respond to all other housekeeping request,
- and use only accepted development process and supported programming languages and tools.

You should be able to make the addition without breaking any undocumented expectations other modules have about logical dependencies or timing properties of the system.

All these restrictions are created during design. Design decisions constrain the design more than anything else and consume the inherent flexibility of software systems. This is not a surprise as the purpose of design decisions is to remove uncertainty and define the system structure. However the order in which decisions are made is very important. Early decisions should be based on non varying aspects of the system and they should be made so that those parts that are expected to vary can have alternative designs.

4. Design Decision Tree

A software designer faced with the task of translating the requirements into an implementation must first of all recognize what are the essential problems that must be addressed by the design including the needs to test and later modify the program as requirements change. This task of identifying and understanding the problems must precede the search for the solution.

A software design pattern combines a description of an essential problem recurring in a particular context and an experience-proven solution to it. Patterns serve as perceptual filters that help to understand the requirements in terms of the designs they imply and offer a consistent set of effective solutions to these problems. By ordering design patterns into a decision tree (DDT) they can be incrementally specified. In such a structure changes to designs triggered by new requirements are considered under the constraints imposed by earlier design decisions. To avoid replication when representing variations and alternatives DDT structures architectural knowledge hierarchically into finegrain elements, decisions.

A natural organization of a DDT is from the more general design decisions to the more specific. This way a DDT allows incremental specialization of context, requirements and constraints along with the corresponding specialization of the design. Branching helps to explore the alternative designs and their differentiating qualities in the context of the problem requirements and the preceding design decisions.

At any level independent decisions may be ordered based on the tightness of constraints they impose on the design space. Decisions that introduce fewer constraints should be taken first as they less likely to be reversed. Known variance can be taken into account as additional requirements. Since decisions are tied to the system structure, design decision tree allows a close control of the variance supported by the system structure, without making the structure overly generic and thus expensive and inefficient.

DDT's do not grow very large. Each DDT typically shows the reasoning behind one essential design decision, the alternatives considered and the consequences. It also shows what are the later decisions that were affected by this decision. As a group DDT forest shows all the important decisions.

DDT offers a simple mechanism that supports tracing design decisions to requirements and exploring the alternative solutions. This supports management of unexpected variance. In a design decision tree it is often possible to point out the first decision that should be reversed once a requirement has changed. Based on the place of the decision in the tree it is possible to estimate cost of the change. Most of the time earlier decisions are more expensive to reverse than late.

5. Controlled Evolution by Using DDT

Design decision trees can be used to analyze change requests and determine different options to deal with them. The decision trees provide a way to argue about different tactics and to accumulate knowledge about the evolution of the system.

A change request can be analyzed in the context of the requirement space. A change request usually means that new requirements are set for the system or existing requirements are modified. DDT can be used to analyze the impact of new requirements to the requirement space and to investigate the changes different implementation strategies cause to the system structure.

Design decision tree also to protects the system structure by communicating design rationale. Some systems are constructed to be flexible and gracefully evolving. However the structure of the system and the knowledge behind its design is seldom communicated. They stay implicit and may be only recognized by experienced software designers examining the structure of software in the products. Long lived systems are shaped over time by many developers that do not share the knowledge and understanding of the problems addressed by the design of the software. Without support system erodes.

6. An Example: A Boot Loader for Distributed System

Our example is a boot loading and initialization system for a distributed software system. A boot loader system is a critical component in telecommunication and networking systems and it contains many sources for variation. We cover the design decisions mainly at general level although our example was derived from a real system, a telephone exchange.

Different subscribers are attached to telephone exchange through subscriber access equipment. This equipment is typically located outside the actual exchange site. The distance from the exchange to the access device can be many kilometers.

Subscribers have different requirements for their connections. For example common telephone subscribers require an analog connection that can understand either pulse based or tone based signaling for dialing. Subscriber that operates a wide area data network might need a fast digital connection to the exchange. To satisfy the needs of different subscribers there exist different kinds of access devices. They are connected to the exchange through different lines, depending on the type of the exchange. The topology of the connection network is a star with the exchange in the middle and the subscriber access nodes at the points of the star.

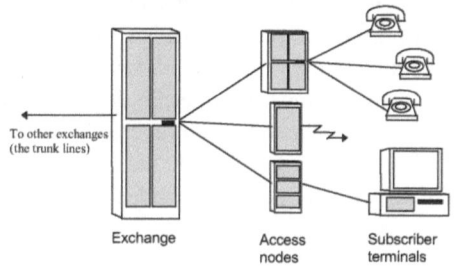

The access devices contain software that implements the different services offered by them. This software is subject to

Figure 1: Access network of an exchange

change as new services are some times added to access nodes and bugs in the software must be fixed. The initialization procedure of a software package may change when the software is updated. The updates are not necessarily made simultaneously to all similar access nodes thus similar devices with different initialization requirements may coexist in the system.

There can be hundreds of access devices connected to a single exchange and the physical location of them can be hard to get to. For these reasons their software must be managed in a centralized fashion from the exchange. The exchange operator must be able to download new software packages to the access nodes and initialize them.

At the startup of the network the software in the access devices must be loaded and initialized according to certain constraints. For example the order in which the devices are initialized can be important as the initialization may take considerably long.

The boot loader system is responsible for the loading the software into access nodes and for the initialization of them.

6.1   DDT for Boot Loader

In this chapter a DDT for a boot loader in a distributed software system is presented. Design options for a general distributed boot loader system are considered but the DDT covers only the decision path that leads to a boot system that is suitable for a telephone exchange system described above.

Special attention is paid to the potential variance in the system as the ability of a design to absorb change is largely determined by the ability of the system to accommodate variance. In practice this means making decisions that are likely subjects to variance as late as possible.

In situations where variance is already present in the application domain a modular design approach to manage the variance can be used. The variance can be localized into certain components of the system. For example the different interfaces of access node initialization hardware may be localized in a hardware driver module that offers similar set of abstract initialization services regardless of the node type.

In the DDT notation each node represents a taken design decision. It is guarded by entry criteria that is placed over the arc leading to the node. The entry criteria is the most general constraint that the decision must fulfil in order for it to be taken. Often the entry criteria is used to represent desired system level properties like "fast performance" or "robust operation".

Inside a decision node are three fields. The first field is the actual design decision that is being made. Second field contains the constraints which must be fulfilled by the context where the decision is considered. Third field contains the implications of the decision.

Whenever a real design process takes place the design decisions are always ordered. Each decision that is taken restricts the set of possible further decisions. This means in practice that some decision that has been made early in the process might make it impossible to later make a decision crucial to achieving some system level criteria.

In a DDT all subsequent decisions are made in the context introduced by earlier decisions so an invalidation of an early decision may cause invalidation of most decisions below it.

We studied the boot loading system of a real telephone exchange and identified the key design decisions that must have been made while constructing the system. The system also reflects the order in which the decisions have been made. The ordering of design decisions allows us to asses the evolution characteristics of the design.

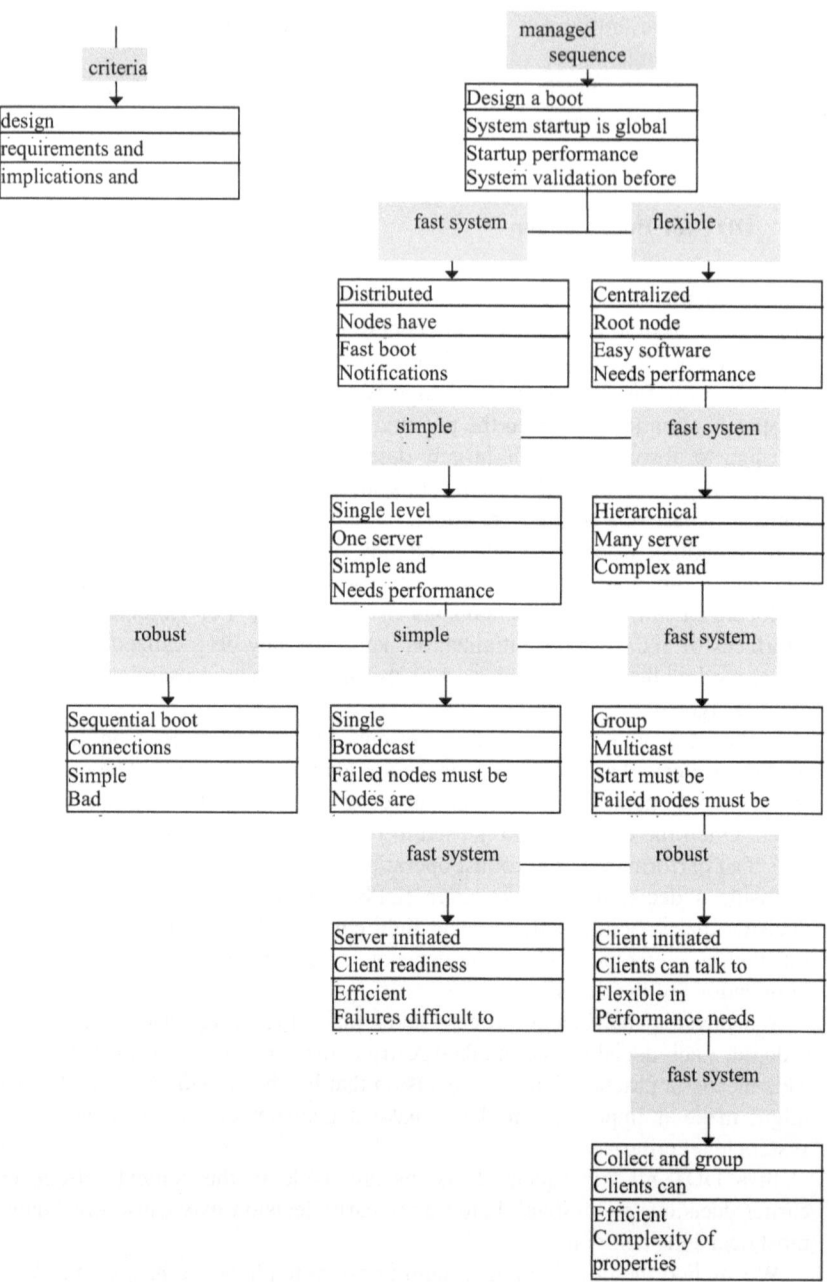

Figure 2: DDT for a boot system

In the first node of the example DDT a decision to design a booting system is made. This may sound trivial but not every system needs a separate start up system. Parts of the system may be started and shut down autonomously for example.

Second decision is the topology of the boot system. We considered three possibilities: completely distributed system, centralized system and a hierarchical system. There were many factors and tradeoffs for each solution. The example system that we studied was centralized.

A distributed booting system where the nodes boot autonomously is least sensitive to the capacity of the communication network. On the other hand it requires that nodes have permanent local memory since the software to be loaded is not fetched over the network but loaded locally.

Local memory in the nodes is not needed in a centralized booting system. On the other hand a centrally controlled system does not exclude the use of local memory. In this respect the central system is more flexible.

A centralized system can be seen as a special case for hierarchical scheme where the boot control nodes for a hierarchy and the leave nodes in this tree each serve a partition of the nodes to be booted. A hierarchical system would have some performance benefits by enabling parallel exception handling and by interleaving the services of different nodes. Also if the physical topology of the network was hierarchical it would be a natural choice, however our system is single level because there is only one node capable of acting as a server.

If the nodes were homogenous the boot system node could use simple broadcast to send the same software simultaneously to all nodes. In our example system the software for nodes can be different.

On the next level in the DDT is investigated whether the underlying network supports multicasting of messages. If multicasting is supported, like in the example case, the boot loader node can serve nodes in parallel. Otherwise the nodes must be serviced sequentially.

There are two options for the initiation of the communication in the boot protocol. The central boot control node can initiate communication after an appropriate period that is needed for the nodes to power-up or the nodes can request the central boot server to supply the loading and initialization sequence. The latter option is chosen in our case as the power-up times of the nodes have substantial variation and this scheme automatically adapts to this.

Next a buffering scheme of the requests in the boot server is considered. The main requirement for the buffering is the ability to combine similar requests into pools that are then serviced using multicast mechanism. As the access devices in our example are independent of each other we decided to allow arbitrary reordering of request pools.

6.2   Sources of Variance in the Boot Loader

The boot loader in our telephone exchange contains many sources for predictable variance.

The nodes in the system have different load and initialization procedures. They contain a bootstrap loader in ROM and there exist different variants of this software. The bootstrap loader must be used to load the actual boot client and initialization program into the node. Also the behavior of the different access nodes varies in the error situations. Some of the latest models contain an elaborated selfdiagnostic software that can report errors in an itemized fashion while the oldest models just silently die.

It is also possible that in the future the access nodes could support writeable permanent memories (FLASH memory).

The number of nodes can vary from few nodes to few hundred nodes at the present. The maximum size of the system is likely to grow in the future. Also the number of different devices keeps growing.

The communication channels from the boot loader node to the access nodes uses the same technology (PCM) in the current exchanges. However, the speed of the channels may vary from 16 Kbs to 64 Kbs. In the future radical changes in the technology and the speed of the links can be expected.

Topology of the communication network is a star with the boot load controller node in the middle. Although there is no variation in the topology right now it is possible that it can change.

6.3   Analyzing Change Requests

The DDT can now be used to analyze the impact of different change requests for our system. In the analysis only the decisions that were actually made are taken into account. Alternative decisions are removed from the DDT. This makes the topology of the DDT a genuine tree.

First the decision nodes that are effected by the new requirements in the change request are located. Next the effected nodes that are not in a subtree spanned by another effected decision node are selected. These nodes are the closest ones of the effected nodes to the root of the tree.

Next we analyze the effect of the new requirements on the selected decisions. If a decision is invalidated all the decisions in its subtree are also possibly invalidated or they are rendered meaningless. It is clear that the closer to the leaves the impacted decisions are located in the tree the smaller the effect on the design is going to be.

Invalidation of a decision node doesn't necessarily result in invalidation of all subsequent decisions. It is also possible that the effected decision node can be simply removed. This happens when the decision issue of the node is rendered meaningless. For example if the system hardware is changed some architectural options might become impossible.

A change request can also result in new nodes to be added to the DDT. In these cases the decisions below the new node must be analyzed in the context of the new decision. It is possible that parts of the tree will be invalidated in this case.

6.4   Examples of change request analysis

Let's first analyze a case where the timing requirements of the access devices are changed. A new line of access equipment is introduced that has a limit for the time that it can wait for the boot server to service the request. The limit is hardcoded into the ROM in the devices and it cannot be altered.

Our design currently allows the boot server to collect requests into buffers and serve the grouped requests in arbitrary order. This leads to unpredictable variance in the response time of the boot server.

Now we can locate the design decisions that are affected by the new requirements from our decision tree. It turns out that the design decision that allows the reordering of requests is actually the last one in our tree. We can immediately see that the impact of the change request on the architecture of the system is not going to be very big.

By adding a new design decision at the bottom of the DDT the system can be adapted to take the timing requirements of nodes into account. This decision refines the decision to allow collection and grouping of requests.

In the second example we get a change request where the capabilities of the access equipment are increased and our system is required to take advantage of those. A mass storage module is attached to each node. The storage device is large enough to contain all software that is to be loaded in each access device.

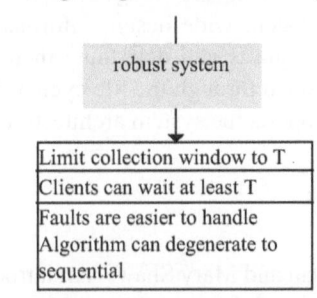

Figure 3: additional DDT for a change in timing requirements

We can locate the decision that is affected by the new requirements to the root of our DDT. The impact of this change request is going to be very big on the system architecture. The new requirements together with the constant growth in the number of access nodes in typical exchange configurations lead us to consider a distributed architecture justified. We decide to aim to maximize performance and the scalability of the system in the future.

We can now analyze the decisions below this node in the new context. It is easy to see that all of the decisions made in these nodes are rendered meaningless in the new context of distributed boot system. A new design decision path must be built starting from the "Distributed boot system" node.

We can argue that the decision of whether the nodes have permanent writable storage has been made too early in our example design. If we could have made it in a later stage the impact of the addition of mass storage to the access nodes wouldn't be so big. Such system could for example facilitate both autonomously booting nodes and centrally controlled nodes.

7. Conclusions

Software system has to face many changes during its lifecycle. Some of these changes can be anticipated some come as surprises. Software systems can be designed to be flexible in terms of anticipated changes. Flexibility is achieved by structuring the system utilizing abstraction, indirection, late binding or some other variance mechanism.

Often designers are not able to utilize existing structures while responding to a change. They make the decisions on how to react to change requests relying only on local information of the single change request. Change request is not analyzed in terms of the overall design. Requests are not classified, nor are the impacts of different options on how to react to the requests. As a result the overall system structure deteriorates.

We propose a mechanism to oppose this development by making the design knowledge explicit. This knowledge is organize into a design decision tree. Such a tree contains system wide design information in a form that can be used to analyze change requests and determine their impact on system structure. Since the tree is maintained through the life cycle it is the evolving back bone of design knowledge. It supports the system architecture and prevents its deterioration.

8. References

[1]   David Garlan and Mary Shaw, "An introduction to software architecture", in Advances in Software En-gineering and Knowledge Engineering, V. Ambriola and G. Tortora, Eds. New York, World Scientific, 1993, vol. 2 ACM Press 95.

[2]   Alexander Ran and Juha Kuusela, "Design Decision Trees", in Proceedings of the Eight International Workshop on Software Specification and Design, March 1996, IEEE Computer Society Press.

[3]   Meyer, B., Reusability: The Case for Object-Oriented Design, IEEE Software, March (1987)

[4]   Parnas, D., On the Design and Development of Program Families, IEEE Transactions on Software Engineering, vol.SE-2, no.1, pp.1-9 (1976)

[5]   Prieto-Diaz, R. Domain Analysis for Reusability, Proceedings of COMPSAC'87 (1987)

[6]   Karhinen, A. Ran, A. Tallgren, T. Configurable Designs, To appear in the proceedings of ICSE'97 (1997)

Structural Views, Structural Evolution, and Product Families

William L. Scherlis *

School of Computer Science, Carnegie Mellon University, Pittsburgh, PA 15213

1 Introduction

Product families are united by common abstractions. When common abstractions can be directly translated into common implementation design elements and software components, reengineering and reuse are facilitated. But direct translation is often limited, however, by exigencies of performance, packaging, and product evolution. The result is an introduction of code-level sacrifices in commonality in which abstraction boundaries are reconfigured, inter-component communication patterns are tangled, and components are specialized and tailored. The consequences of these code-level sacrifices in commonality can be significant, since work is shifted from leveraged common design elements to a diversity of product-specific realizations. While this diversity may offer specific advantages in performance or packaging, it also can negate the potential leverage of reengineering and reuse at the product-line level.

In this position paper, we consider an approach to product-line reengineering that may mitigate some of these difficulties. The approach is based on a combination of design management, program analysis, program annotation, manual restructuring steps, and tool-assisted semantics-based program manipulation techniques. A premise is the folkloric observation that design decisions, while conceptually localized at the outset, translate (as a result of optimization and evolution) into components and code fragments that may be widely diffused in an actual system implementation. The concept of design patterns, for example, is an acknowledgement that the realization of a single design concept may involve multiple interrelated program elements. While patterns are useful design abstractions, however, even their structure may be diffused as code is tailored and specialized.

* This material is based upon work supported by the National Science Foundation under Grant No. CCR-9504339 and by the Defense Advanced Research Projects Agency and Rome Laboratory, Air Force Materiel Command, USAF, under agreement number F30602-97-2-0241. The U.S. Government is authorized to reproduce and distribute reprints for Governmental purposes notwithstanding any copyright annotation thereon. The views and conclusions contained herein are those of the authors and should not be interpreted as necessarily representing the official policies or endorsements, either expressed or implied, of the Defense Advanced Research Projects Agency, Rome Laboratory, the National Science Foundation, or the U.S. Government. Author email: scherlis@cs.cmu.edu.

Frank v. d. Linden (Ed.): ARES '98, LNCS 1429, pp. 235-240, 1998.

In the absence of design information, revision of a design decision at code level is thus complicated by the need to reverse-engineer the code into a model that reunites the diverse elements into the lost common abstraction. Abstraction recovery is a familiar challenge in reengineering (and now especially familiar in the form of the "Year 2000" problem). When extensive optimization has been performed, whether by designer, programmer, compiler, or program manipulation system (e.g., with partial evaluation), this problem becomes very hard. We focus in this position paper on a problem that is less challenging, more tractable in the long term, and perhaps more valuable too, in which design information (either recovered or retained) is assumed to be available. Specifically, we consider a combination of program analysis, annotation, and manipulation techniques as a means to support code-level product-line evolution, even when individual products need to sacrifice conformity to a common set of abstractions and structural constraints.

Structural locality and views. When a software engineer alters a program, he or she needs to aggregate conceptually all parts of the program that bear on the change being made. Powerful abstraction mechanisms provide ways to organize program text so these conceptual "localities" are often also syntactic localities, enabling both programmers and their tools to focus attention within a local scope and avoid expensive or infeasible global analyses. This facilitates evolutionary change, understandability, and composability, and is a motivator for increasingly powerful abstraction mechanisms.

Different tasks require different organizing views, however, and there are many cases where a single perspective, as embodied in a particular organization of code, is not adequate. For example, in object-oriented programs there are many notions "relatedness" among code fragments in which conceptual localities are diffused in the actual code base. This suggests the concept of a "structural view" of code, components, or system. Here is a simple example: In single-inheritance object-oriented languages such as Java and Ada95, given a single method name, distinct organizational perspectives arise when looking at that name with respect to class hierarchy, package structure, and overloadings. In this case, the pertinent views can all be readily extracted from a body of code with minimal analysis.

The idea of a structural view is to bring together pertinent structural elements as needed to facilitate a particular analysis, capture of design information, or evolutionary change. At an early stage of design, a specification-derived abstraction may be embodied in a single software component (or architectural element). As design proceeds and design trade-offs are addressed, this convenient relationship will be undermined in various ways.

Examples of structural sacrifice. Many kinds of change could be made that involve alterations to structure, and most of these are familiar at the level of routine coding. A component could be inlined and specialized in multiple places. The component could be replicated, with each copy specialized to serve particular subsets of uses. A component could be combined with other components and specialized. Portions of a component may have common features with portions of other components, motivating their being extracted into new separate subsidiary components. Case analysis could be used to facilitate specialization of a fragment of code. (This "trick" from partial evaluation is frequently used explicitly by programmers to achieve analogous optimizations at the function or class levels, or even on class hierarchies.)

Consider a case where a design decision is made to copy a particular mutable data structure whenever there is a possibility of an alias being introduced. This decision can translate into a large number of distinct operations placed in diverse code locations, along with an invariant, often not explicitly expressed in design or code, that a programmer maintains informally. An analogous case at larger scale is the insertion of data structure maintenance operations (such as rebuilding a database index or balancing a search tree) at strategic points in a system. When in each local context these operations are integrated and optimized on the basis of particular properties of that context, changes in the abstraction become increasingly difficult to implement. There is an directly analogous situation among the diverse elements of a product line.

In each of these cases, given only the resulting program text, recovery of the original design structure can be difficult or intractable. Thus, while a product line may be founded on common abstractions, the realizations of these abstractions in the individual members of the product line may not be related in any obvious way.

2   Approach

Under these circumstances, how can we make evolutionary changes to a common abstraction in a product line? We consider four ideas related to the particular aspect of structural change: (1) systematic techniques to carry out structural change, (2) maintenance of design records to avoid information loss, (3) mixing informal and formal steps in structural evolution, (4) simultaneous multiple views.

1. Systematic techniques for structural change. Program analysis, annotation, and manipulation techniques for carrying out structural changes in software are being investigated by a number of researchers. Techniques include code migration across abstraction boundaries, class hierarchy reorganization, systematic representation change, specialization of types and classes, coalescing of abstractions (to introduce "back channels"), and the like. Many of these techniques are usable even in the absence of specifications of functionality or architecture, and can offer specific correctness guarantees.

Program refinement techniques may also be applicable. But while there is an obvious relation between support for evolution and for refinement, these concepts should not be equated. The techniques listed above, for example, do not necessarily refine code, they merely reorganize it. There may not be meaningful directionality in the change, in the sense of program refinement. (Note, however, that without explicit attention to design record, program transformations tend to lose information: Return to a previous state in a derivation may require global analysis, even when the steps from that state all involved only local changes.)

What happens to software architecture as code is restructured? We argue that software architecture is itself an idealization, since optimizations can disturb boundaries. Indeed, structural architecture may itself be only a (particular) structural view of code and components, and structural changes to code may not affect the architecture, but only the account of its relationship (as a view) with the actual code. This motivates an aggressive approach to record keeping through the development and evolution process.

2. Role of design record. Judging by reverse engineering costs, a large amount of information is lost in the programming process. It has been estimated that the DoD spends almost as much reverse engineering older systems (i.e., recovering lost or unexpressed information) as it spends developing new systems. Information can include functional and architectural specification elements, formal and informal expressions of design rationale, test cases, configuration information, and so on. Information is lost for three reasons. First, it was expressed at an earlier point, but the information was not appropriately associated or linked within a system design record and so cannot be readily located. Second, the information is present, but the system has evolved and so the correctness of the information can no longer be confirmed. Third, the information was never explicitly captured because the cost of doing so (expressing and capturing it) is too great.

When structural changes are made using formal techniques, tools can gather information, including suitable anchors in various versions of code and specification, that constitutes a record of action. This can link a code fragment back to its original context, as well as linking an initial common abstraction to its various manifestations distributed in multiple versions of detailed design and program text. It also enables a "replay" approach to revisiting early design decisions (as was proposed by several groups more than a decade ago). Design record is obviously primarily a matter of fine-grained bookkeeping. The challenge is to reduce expression costs so capture can be done even in early prototyping efforts.

There are alternatives to replay that often may be more appropriate. The premise of replay is that the best way to revise a decision is to *return* to the point where it is most explicitly manifest, make the change, and revisit subsequent decisions. In many cases, however, the abstractions were never clearly evident, either because of design tradeoffs or because they were tacit even in the specification. That is, there is nothing to return to in the replay model. An alternative approach is to use structural analysis and manipulation techniques to create new organizing views of a body of code that brings the abstractions into sharper focus.

Structural manipulations also have value for reuse. Designers of shared program components wrestle with how to balance performance and generality—whether to sacrifice performance and use overly general standard components, or to handcraft many specialized instances, with consequent risks and costs. Many commercial applications achieve high performance through extensive code replication and specialization. Conventionalized domains with established components could be made more broadly useful if structure manipulation tools could facilitate both the tuning of interfaces and the specialization of components.

3. Manual and hybrid techniques. It is an obvious point, but when mechanical techniques cannot be used manual methods must be used to make structural changes, or to make assertions or claims about specification or code. (Perhaps ironically, acceptance of the use of manual and informal techniques could make systematic and formal techniques more readily adoptable by practicing software engineers, because of the need to address the difficulty of incrementally assimilating the systematic techniques into practice.) When manual techniques are used, however, design record maintenance can be more difficult. One possible approach is to maintain a formal binding of annotations to code (and links among code fragments) even when the annotations themselves are informal and textual. The potential is that abstractions can be reengineered even when they have been dispersed through informal steps, because the design management system provides dependency/impact analysis and a comprehensive catalog of possible places to look.

4. Use of multiple views. Creation of a new structural view of a component or system can involve extensive analysis, annotation, and manipulation effort. Often the manipulations involve primarily rearrangement of abstraction boundaries, and the underlying computation is essentially the same. In these cases, the new view can coexist with other views as alternative perspectives on a system, bringing together different elements depending on which abstractions pertain to a particular evolutionary step. Of course, when computationally significant changes are made, they may invalidate a view (for example, because they exploit a code juxtaposition evident only in other views). The point, however, is that the range of kinds of structural views required for program evolution is rich, and can conceivably include views of a system organized around specific specification elements.

3   Conclusion

Status. In the Fluid/ACT project at Carnegie Mellon University, a tool prototype (under development for the past year) will enable exploration of many of these ideas. The tool will support annotation, analysis, and manipulation of Java programs. Restructuring manipulations can be carried out to create multiple structural views. It maintains a flexible intermediate representation with fine-grained versioning to provide design-record support. The tool is interactive, carrying out analyses and manipulations under programmer guidance and providing visualization support. (See the referenced papers for details concerning Fluid/ACT approaches to program structural manipulation and to annotations and analysis.)

Summary. Structural manipulation facilitates reorganization and tailoring of software component interconnection designs. An initial structural design is a significant commitment in usual software practice. It has long-term consequences, but it is rarely correct at the outset and even more rarely suffices for the lifetime of an evolving product line. Even in conventionalized domains and product lines, where there is general agreement on pertinent abstractions and associated software representations, the key abstractions may nonetheless need to evolve in small ways. Barriers to management of structure often inhibit architectural and API evolution, due to high cost and risk. In systems that involve mobile code and dynamic runtime reconfiguration, management through structural views may have particular value in relating behavioral constraint and structural commitment.

4 Bibliography

[Batory93] D. Batory, V. Singhal, M. Sirkin, and J. Thomas, Scalable software libraries. ACM SIGSOFT Symposium on foundations of software engineering, 1993.

[Bowdidge94] R.W.Bowdidge and W.G. Griswold, Automated Support for Encapsulating Abstract Data Types. ACM SIGSOFT Symposium Foundations of Software Engineering, 1994.

[Chan98] Edwin Chan, John Boyland, and William Scherlis, Promises: Limited Specifications for Analysis and Manipulation. International Conference on Software Engineering 1998, to appear.

[Draves97] Scott Draves, Automatic Program Specialization for Interactive Media. CMU School of Computer Science Technical Report, 1997.

[Griswold93] W. G. Griswold and D. Notkin, Automated assistance for program restructuring. ACM TOSEM 2:3, 1993.

[Guttag93] John V. Guttag and James J. Horning, et al., Larch: Languages and Tools for Formal Specification, Springer-Verlag, 1993.

[Johnson88] Ralph Johnson and Brian Foote, Designing reusable classes. Journal of Object-Oriented Programming, June/July 1988.

[Kiczales96] Gragor Kiczales, Beyond the Black Box: Open Implementation, IEEE Software, January 1996.

[Morgan90] Carroll Morgan and P.H.B. Gardiner, Data refinement by calculation. Acta Informatica 27 (1990).

[Morgenthaler95] J.D. Morgenthaler and W.G. Griswold, Program analysis for practical program restructuring. ICSE-17 Workshop on Program Transformation for Software Evolution, 1995.

[Muller94] Hausi Müller, Kenny Wong, and Scott R. Tilley, Understanding software systems using reverse engineering technology, Colloquium on Object Orientation in Databases and Software Engineering: 62nd ACFAS, Quebec, 1994.

[Opdyke92] William Opdyke, Refactoring Object-Oriented Frameworks. PhD Thesis, University of Illinois, 1992.

[Scherlis96] W. Scherlis, Small-scale structural reengineering. ACM SIGSOFT Second International Workshop on Software Architecture, 1996.

[Scherlis98] W. Scherlis, Systematic Change of Data Representation: Program Manipulations and a Case Study. European Symposium on Programming. Springer, 1998.

Product Family and Reuse in Separate Market Driven Profit Centers

Jeroen Brouwer, Ad Jurriens, Henk van Kessel, Alef Schippers

Philips Electronics, QJ1335, P.O. Box 10.000,
5680 DA Best, The Netherlands
alef@best.ms.philips.com

1. Introduction

This paper addresses the issues with respect to product definition and product development, for an organization where several business-lines with their own bottom-line responsibility want to use a product-family approach.

2. Problem Definition

When an organization decides to use a product-family approach for more efficiency, several issues come up.

In our case we currently have several application product groups, which each address a certain separate segment of the market. Also there are product groups which build common components. All groups have their own financial bottom-line responsibility.

Each application product group defines, develops, produces, maintains and sells systems to the market, with its own system architecture.

From the past, there is a distrust whether the common component groups react quickly enough on issues which pop up in the market.

One year ago the organization decided that the next generation of systems could only be developed if the product groups would cooperate. This mainly because of:
- development cost reduction,
- material & labor cost reduction and
- additional common functional requirements.

This lead to a single platform development project, which will also create the first complete systems to be delivered to the market.

Frank v. d. Linden (Ed.): ARES '98, LNCS 1429, pp. 241-248, 1998.
© Springer-Verlag Berlin Heidelberg 1998

The issue now is that future systems have to be developed in such a way that:

- Time to market can be short,
- The architecture is not polluted,
- Problems from the field are adequately solved,
- The right priorities are set (long term versus short term),
- Development resources are used efficiently and effectively,
- Available (external) assets are used as much as possible
- Ideas, Specifications, Designs and Implementations are reused consistently.
- There is no single starvation (the biggest profit maker gets all it asks, while the smaller ones never get a thing),

The assumption is that the (application oriented) product groups can keep their bottom-line responsibility.

3. Scope

When thinking about an organization which is able to enforce reuse, a number of issues come to mind, which should be accounted for. These are:

- which business model is used
- which processes should be in place
- which organization is needed to support the business model and the processes
- how to handle configuration management
- etc.

This paper only describes the second bullet.

It is assumed that the current business model will not change drastically, so the application groups will be profit centers which define, develop, produce, maintain and sell systems to the market. It is still open whether component groups should be regarded profit or cost centers.

The results of all these groups are consolidated at a so called "general business" level.

4. Processes for Reuse

The following model describes information flows and processes needed to develop systems wanted by a Market in an efficient way.

The architecture of the systems is such, that there is a big common part (called the platform) and certain (smaller) parts which follow the market dynamics easily. The platform can be created and maintained by one development activity, while there are several development activities close to the market and application, which will create and maintain elements specific for that market and application (Product_Specific).

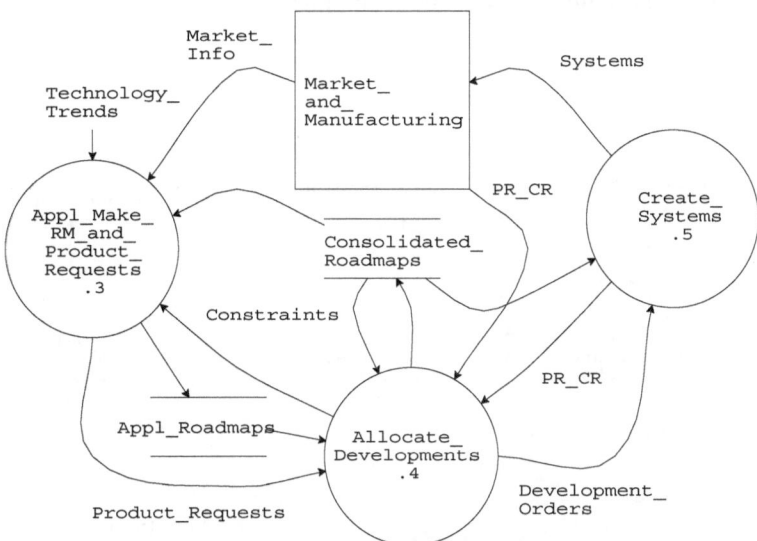

Market_Info and Technology_Trends are translated into Roadmaps and Product_Requests (created per market and application area).

The product requests include feature lists, priorities and expected revenues, so a good, business driven decision can be made.

The Appl_Roadmaps are matched onto the available technology and resources in the complete organization, to get Consolidated Roadmaps at general business level.

Based on the consolidated roadmaps and product requests, a decision is taken whether a feature is to be created as product specific or as platform extension. These decisions are taken at general business level, keeping the following issues in mind:

- prevent future inefficiencies
- prevent pollution of the architecture
- available and needed capacity with the required skills
- estimates of costs and revenues
- market priorities

Two kind of decisions are needed
1. Long term decisions, handling the contents of yearly releases of the platform. Typically these are requests for a new product development
2. Short term decisions, handling more specific requests. Typically these are requests from ongoing product development or Problem Reports and Change Requests.

Based on the decisions development orders are issued to create the systems and the platform.

4.1   Making Roadmaps and Product Requests

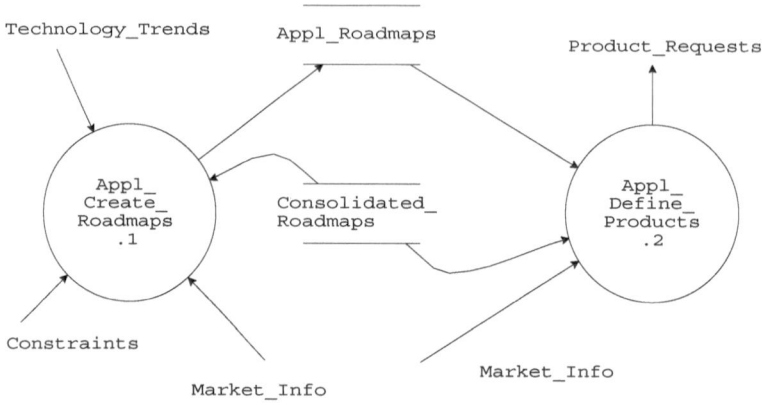

Making Roadmaps and Define Product Requests is part of the Business Process Planning (BPP). The Application (or Appl_) is added in the model to show that it has to be done for each Application area separately. The BPP is a process that precedes the Product Creation Process (PCP). The BPP consists of Strategy determination (Marketing planning, Technology planning, and Policy definition) and Planning (Product line planning, Business planning, Programming).

Roadmaps are made for each application area separately. The main inputs are Market Info (such as competitors product info, new or improved application functionality, etc.), and Technology Trends (such as new operating systems, new user interface world standard, other technological inventions that must be inserted in the products). The current consolidated roadmaps at general business level are used as an input also. This must be seen as the basis where to built upon.

The Products are Defined for each application area separately. It generates product requests, based on the application roadmap and market info. The priority of various (technology and market driven) product enhancements is determined. The product requests are input to Allocate Developments.

4.2   Allocate Developments

Based on Application Roadmaps and Product Requests, the Consolidated Roadmaps at general business level are made, and is decided which developments are started. Furthermore these developments have to be allocated.

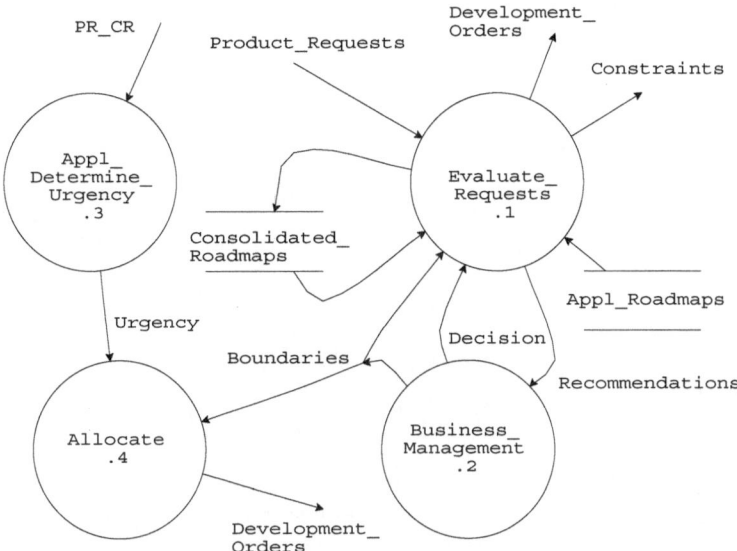

The long term decisions (right part of the picture) are taken on general business level. All requests in the form of product requests or applicational or technological roadmaps are held against the already committed consolidated roadmaps.

Based on issues like market priority, available and required skills, costs, revenues, etc., Development Orders are issued, provided they are within the Boundaries set by Business Management. If these boundaries should be exceeded, then a recommendation (with several scenarios) is presented to business management, who then takes a decision.

For short term decisions (like PR_CR on existing products), the application area decides on the urgency (left part of the picture). Then at general business level, the change is allocated, within the boundaries set by business management.

4.3   Create Systems

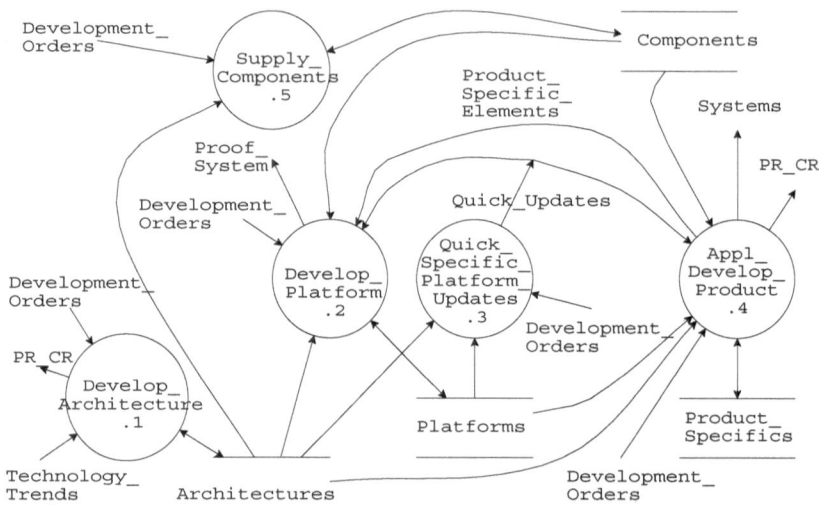

The Create Systems process takes care that the Systems are being developed in accordance to the consolidated product portfolio and resulting Development Orders.

The key issue that is addressed in this way, is the top down planning of platform development and reuse, which is a necessary requirement for profitable reuse.

Development orders can be of various types covering one or more phases like Concept & Feasibility study, project definition phase etc.

The development orders can be orders to develop new releases of the platform, development of new systems and taking care of Change Request and Problem Reports that come from the field and the manufacturing environment.

Also, mainly based on longer term market trends and technology trends, development orders to change the architecture (that is the base of the platform) can be issued.

As a concept that is used to verify the usefulness of the developed platform, the project contents will be made such that the platform performance and functionality is proven by a system that will be delivered to the market place.

Within the create systems process a number of main processes can be seen that make it possible to create the desired systems. Criteria used for the process definition are clear process objectives and scope. Each process has its own time cycle.

Develop Architecture

An important issue in the new way of working with a product family based on a common set of assets is the control of the Architecture, being the basis of the product family concept.

The architecture can be seen as a set of concepts that are the basic rules that need to be met fully throughout the family (e.g. Keep User Interface and Application clearly separated) together with a global framework.

Essential characteristic of the architecture is the fact that it is independent of the specific technology that can be used to implement the architecture; a communication channel for instance can be implemented by a LAN connection or an RS232 interface depending on required speed and price requirements.

The Develop Architecture process takes care that the architecture is maintained over the years based on the long term technology and market requirements. This to assure that the architecture asset (=money invested) is and stays being used in an optimal way.

The orders that are input to the process can vary from an order to study the impact of certain trends for the architecture, to an order to adapt the architecture to accommodate new necessary requirements, e.g. due to other application area's that are to be covered (change of application domain).

Develop Platform

The platform development process takes care of the creation of the required parts of the platform based on the architecture.

Furthermore it is concerned with, again, the external technology- and market trends that influence the technical implementation of the platform.

The deliverables of the platform development consist of a set of hardware building blocks and software building blocks (executables) that can be integrated to a complete system that is sold.

The platform becomes available in releases with fixed intervals (e.g. once a year). To support e.g. bug fixes in the platform that are needed platform wide (e.g. because of a safety issue) also versions of a specific release can be created.

The desired situation is that only platform releases are delivered and that versions of the certain releases are minimized.

The development orders can both concern new functionality or incorporation of system features/functionality that needs to become part of the platform and are not yet part of the platform.

Quick Specific Platform Update

This process is only active in an exceptional situation, where it is required to have a Specific Update of the Platform, to support a specific product release or fix a bug, that cannot wait until the new platform release becomes available. This platform update is product specific and temporary and will only exist until the next platform release is available.

NOTE: Although the model enables to do quick platform updates, we strongly advise not to use it. The possibility is included, because experience learned us that these action will be taken. It is better to be prepared then and manage it.

Application Develop Product

This process (which exists per application area) takes care that the necessary parts of the system for a specific application area are developed. It also takes care of the integration of the systems using the platform deliverables, other components and own build components (Product_Specifics).

Building the total system can range from packaging and configuring a number of platform parts, to the building and integration of application specific parts, platform parts and other components.

The control and maintenance of the product specific components is also performed in this process, resulting in system releases and versions that are delivered to the market place.

Supply Components

This process concerns the orders to create and maintain or buy those Components (subsystems) that are not part of the platform, but have a generic use. The current architecture is the base for the component design and interfaces.

ERW'97 Session Report: Reuse Adoption Experiences Across a Large Corporation

Sergio Bandinelli

ESI – European Software Institute
Parque Tecnológico #204 Zamudio, Bizkaia, Spain
Sergio.Bandinelli@esi.es

Abstract. This paper briefly reports on the ERW'97 (European Reuse Workshop '97) by providing an overview of its sessions. The session regarding the adoption of reuse practices across a large organisation is presented in more depth. In this session, experiences and lessons learned in the ROADS project (Reuse Oriented Approach for Domain based Software) were presented and discussed. The ROADS project consisted of the realisation of four pilot experiments of reuse adoption in four different Business Units at Thomson-CSF and put domain architecture issues in the context of the overall reuse processes.

1. Introduction

The European Reuse Workshop (ERW '97) was held in the Royal Windsor Hotel (Brussels, Belgium) on 26th and 27th November 1997. It was the first of a series of workshops with the aim of sharing and promoting reuse adoption initiatives across Europe and world-wide. ERW gathered together almost 60 applied researchers, industrial software practitioners and managers involved in software process improvement and in the adoption of reuse practices.

This paper reports on some of the reuse experiences presented in the workshop. We first describe the workshop organisation and provide an overview of all the sessions. This paper, however, does not address all of the workshop sessions, but focuses the attention on one specific session regarding the application of reuse across a large organisation

This session consisted of the presentation of a series of reuse experiments carried out in Thomson-CSF within the project ROADS (a Process Improvement Experiment project partially funded by the European Commission). The project was carried out in collaboration with the European Software Institute (ESI) and Prosperity Heights Software (PHS). The author took active part in the project and thus the session report is enriched with first hand information collected during the execution of the project.

The rest of the paper is structured as follows. Section 2 provides an overview of all the ERW'97 sessions. Section 3 introduces the ROADS project, the

Frank v. d. Linden (Ed.): ARES '98, LNCS 1429, pp. 249-256, 1998.

assessment and improvement experiences.   Finally, Section 4 concludes by deriving some useful lessons from the project.

2. The European Reuse Workshop (ERW'97)

At ESI (European Software Institute) we observed that there is an increasing interest in Europe in understanding and applying reuse practices and that much work was already being carried out in this field. A measure of this is the number of initiatives funded by the Commission under the ESSI programme and the interest demonstrated by ESI members in reuse technology. For this reason ESI decided to organise a European Reuse Workshop to review the state of the art and practice and to foster the interchange of reuse experiences among software practitioners.

The workshop had an excellent representation from the European industry (more than 60% of the participants), complemented with high quality representation from the academia. A significant number of European countries were represented, including Austria, Belgium, Finland, France, Germany, Italy, Spain, Sweden and UK and there was also participants from overseas (Canada and USA).

The workshop theme, "Process and architectural issues in reuse adoption" captured two key aspects of software reuse today: on the technical side, the architectures as a main reusable asset across projects and on the organisational side, the processes needed to consolidate reuse practices in a developing organisation.

Most of the workshop time was dedicated to discussion-oriented experience sessions. Each of these sessions gathered a set of position papers addressing related issues. There were six experience sessions structured as follows:

- Experience session 1: Reuse in the context of process improvement: models and current practices, chaired by Mike Mannion, Napier University.
- Experience session 2: Development for reuse: from software components to domain analysis and product family architectures, chaired by Magnus Nilsson, Ericsson.
- Experience session 3: Reuse co-ordination and experiences in a large corporation, chaired by Jean-Marc Morel, Bull S.A.
- Experience session 4: Reuse in the Information Systems domain, chaired by Bob Smith, ESI.
- Experience session 5: Reuse projects in SMEs and large companies, chaired by Jean-Marc De Baud, Fraunhofer IESE.
- Experience session 6: Reuse beyond the software development cycle: non-technical factors in reuse adoption, chaired by Sergio Bandinelli, ESI.

In addition to this, the workshop included two keynote presentations and a final panel session.

Mehdi Jazayeri, Professor of Computer Science and Head of the Distributed Systems Group at the Technical University of Vienna, gave the first keynote presentation. The title "The promises and the premises: a critical look at software reuse" anticipated a controversial presentation. Mehdi Jazayeri argued that nowadays the emphasis on reuse is misguided, that is, reuse distracts from the real goals, promises more than can be delivered and is based on wrong premises. Finally he pointed out that reuse is not always the right thing to do. It must always be the result of a good engineering judgement and practice.

Paul Bassett, Senior Vice President of Research in CAP-Netron Inc. and author of the book "Framing Software Reuse: Lessons From the Real World", gave the second keynote presentation entitled "Ushering in the Era of Software Manufacturing". Paul Bassett defined reuse as the process of adapting generalised components to various contexts of use. In other words, he stated that "reuse" is considered at construction time, while "use" is a run time concept. Paul Bassett then presented frame technology as a way of doing adaptive reuse. The reusable frames contain commands and variables, which define the execution and construction behaviour of the frame. The frame commands guide the assemblage of the frame into source modules as in a manufacturing process. He finally presented remarkable results from projects using frame technology. This included a time-to-market reduction of 70% and a project cost reduction of 80%.

The panel session addressed a number of issues that were raised during the workshop. It was chaired by John Favaro (Intecs Sistemi) and the panelists included Colin Tully (CTA), Grady Campbell (PHS), Alexander Ran (Nokia Research Center) and Paul Bassett (CAP-Netron Inc.).

3. Reuse across a Large Corporation

Experience session 3 reported on the experience gathered in the reuse adoption experiments of ROADS project (Reuse Oriented Approach for Domain based Software). These pilot experiments were performed during 1996 and 1997 in four different Business Units of Thomson-CSF, with the collaboration of the European Software Institute (ESI) and Prosperity Heights Software (PHS). The project is partially funded by the EC as a PIE (Process Improvement Experience) under the ESSI programme.

Each of the experiences addressed a distinct domain and was motivated by different business objectives:

- The first experiment is carried out in SDS (Systèmes de Dètection de Surface) in the domain of Air Traffic Control (ATC) and has the main objective of improving time-to-market.
- The second experiment is performed at DSM (Division Systèmes de Missiles) in the domain of control and command of short range air defence systems. The most important aspect in this domain is reliability and thus the business driver here is to improve the reliability of systems.
- The third experiment is done at Thomson Training & Simulation (TT&S) Unit in the domain of training simulators. The business goal here is to obtain significant reduction of costs.
- The fourth experiment is carried out at SYSECA in the domain of Traffic Management (planning of traffic). The objective is to improve the flexibility and robustness of applications.

The methodological approach followed was common to all of the experiments and co-ordinated at the corporate level. The approach consisted in an adaptation of the reuse adoption process described in [SPC93a]. (See Figure 1).

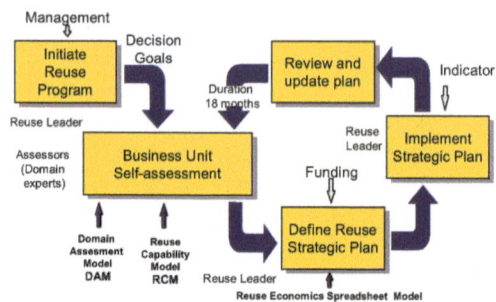

Figure 1
Reuse Adoption Process (Adapted from [SPC93a])

The initiation of the reuse programme at Thomson-CSF has its roots in process improvement. Thomson-CSF started a corporate process improvement programme in 1992 using the CMM model [SEI95] as a basis. As part of this programme, several Thomson Business Units have undertaken improvement actions to reach levels 2 and 3 of the CMM. Since the CMM does not explicitly address reuse issues, this action was complemented with the creation of a specific SIG (Special Interest Group) on reuse in 1994 and a reuse leader was appointed at the corporate level. The ROADS project was carried out in this organisational context.

The first step in the ROADS experiments consisted in the assessment of the current situation. This included a domain assessment and a reuse capability assessment in each of the business units, preceded by a training action to present the overall approach to the staff involved in the project.

The planning and implementation of the reuse actions was performed in an incremental manner. Each of the increments consisted in developing an action plan and going through the domain engineering activities as defined in the Reuse-Driven Software Processes (RSP) [SPC93b]. The documents produced during the increment were reviewed at the end of the increment and the feedback was used to plan the subsequent increment. The duration of each increment was quite short (typically around 3 months) to ensure a fast feedback loop.

3.1 Assessment Experiences

Two types of assessment were conducted at the beginning of the ROADS experiments: a reuse capability assessment to characterise the state of practice as far as reuse is concerned and a domain assessment, to measure the reuse potential of the domain. The main objective of the assessments was to guide the planning of reuse adoption by helping to identify the priorities for each Business Unit.

The assessment teams included persons belonging to the unit being assessed (i.e., self-assessments) plus a facilitator with the role of introducing the assessment model and manage the meeting. The assessment team size ranged from three to eight individuals. The typical duration of each of the assessments was one day.

The reuse capability assessments used the Reuse Capability Model (RCM) [SPC93a]. This model consists of a set of goals grouped in four reuse capability levels: Opportunistic, Integrated, Leveraged and Anticipating. The assessment process rates the extent to which the organisation meets each of these goals.

The domain assessments examine the domains from a business perspective to provide an indication of the potential for profitability in applying reuse. The assessment model used, called Domain Assessment Model (DAM) [SPC93a] consists of five factors, namely market potential for products, existing domain assets, commonalities and variabilities between systems in the domain, domain stability and maturity and domain standards. Each of the factors is rated in a 1 to 5 scale and the results are plotted in a Kiviat diagram to appreciate the relative strength of each of them.

3.2 Improvement Planning and Implementation

At writing time, five increments have already been performed in each of the ROADS experiments. The incremental nature of the adoption process makes it possible to start obtaining results very early in the reuse adoption process. This is fundamental to keep the process on the right track and to demonstrate (to management and to the practitioners working in application projects) the benefits of the approach by providing tangible results and benefits.

The typical plan for an increment includes the following items:

- *Domain definition*, including a glossary and domain communalities and variabilities.
- *Decision model*, a formalisation of the variabilities of the domain including the range of variability.
- *Product family engineering*, development of configurable and adaptable work-products of all kinds (including requirements documents, domain architectures design, code test, project plans, contracts, etc.)
- *Process engineering*, discussion on the changes to be introduced in the current application development process
- *Domain strategy and planing* of the subsequent increment.

Generally speaking, all the experiments completed successfully the domain definition and most of the decision model (at least for some significant sub-domain). Regarding product family engineering, each of the experiments concentrated the efforts in those work-products that could maximise the return on investment. This depends, among other factors, on the nature of the domain and on the stage of development of application projects. Finally, process engineering was the activity that most stretched people's ability, since it required to identify the changes in the current practice to incorporate reuse.

To illustrate the kind of problems faced in the project, we provide a couple of examples regarding two of the four experiments: one corresponds to the experiment in the domain of Air Traffic Control (ATC) and the other to the one in the domain of training simulators.

Air Traffic Control domain

The Air Traffic Control group has a line that develops small systems for control centres in airports. These systems have been delivered world-wide to more than 15 Civil Aviation Authorities of various countries, including Denmark, Mexico, Bulgaria, various ex-SSSR republics, etc.).

Since 1992 the international competition has become stronger. This motivated an investment in architecture and the establishment of an incremental and modular development approach. In other words, a "baseline" product is incrementally enriched with new functionality, as required by clients. The additional functionality represents a small part of the code since most of it is reused from previous applications (see Figure 2).

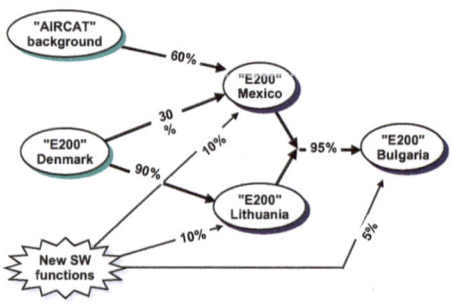

Figure 2
Evolution of the system and reuse rates

This advanced situation regarding reuse in this Business Unit was reflected in the results of the reuse capability assessment, which showed that several of the Leveraged level goals were meet to a great extend. Not surprisingly, the first benefits obtained from the ROADS project in this domain were not in the reuse in coding phase, but on other phases of the development process. For example:

- the decision model was started to be used in the Bid-NoBid phase (to decide whether a contract is within the boundaries of the domain),
- the baseline product was better defined and some documents, such software specification and
- software development plan, were standardised to allow for automatic generation.

Training Simulators domain

We have concentrated the attention on the driver trainer domain. The reuse capability assessment showed that the organisation achieves most of the

Opportunistic level goals and some of the Integrated level ones. This organisation has been recently assessed at level 3 of the CMM and the domain assessment showed that there is good reuse potential. However, the reuse practices are unplanned and based on code cut&paste.

Figure 3 shows that the effort associated with the different application projects in the domain tends to decrease as the number of projects increases. However, a new functional definition of the domain creates a break, making the subsequent project (the first after the break) much more expensive.

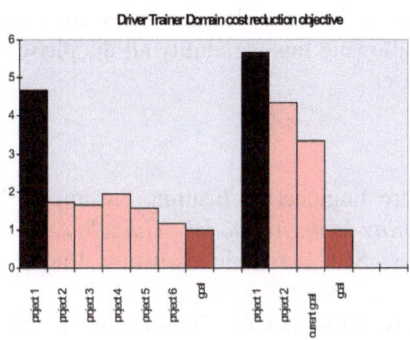

Figure 3
Cost of project application in domain trainer domain

In this context, the ROADS project served to document the existing application projects (according to commonalities and variabilities). This had al least two tangible benefits. On one side, it provided the basis for better anticipating the impact of functional breaks. On the other side, it served as a tool to create awareness about the current existing functional capabilities in the domain. This latter issue is especially useful among commercial/business staff to reduce costs when negotiating new applications with customers.

4. Conclusions and Lessons Learned

There are a few lessons that can be derived from the experience accumulated so far in the project. These lessons are general enough to be useful for other similar experiences.

A first observation is that the participation of domain experts in all the activities is essential for the success of the experiments. However, domain experts tend to be overloaded and it may be difficult to involve them in the key activities.

Regarding assessment experience it is important to point out that there is not necessarily a direct relationship between process maturity (e.g., in terms of CMM levels) and reuse capability. The latter depends on other factors such as the experience the organisation has in a domain, the level of standardisation in the domain, etc. We can conclude that

- The assessments served as a means for reaching a common understanding within each of the units to determine the strengths of the organisation and the priorities for improvement.
- It was unclear which improvement actions would address the unaccomplished goals, making it difficult to plan improvements and assess progress.

The experiments showed that the architecture plays a central role in determining the existence of a product-line in a given domain. For example, without a fixed agreed architecture it would be impossible to do incremental developments in the air traffic control domain. However, the same variations and flexibility that is necessary for a domain architecture are required for all other work-products. By allowing this variability all the phases of system development can benefit from reuse.

5. References

[SEI95]   Software Engineering Institute - Carnegie Mellon University, *The Capability Maturity Model - Guidelines for Improving the Software Process*, SEI Series in Software Engineering, Addison-Wesley, 1995.

[SPC93a]   Software Productivity Consortium, *Reuse Adoption Guidebook*, SPC-92051-CMC, November 1993.

[SPC93b]   Software Productivity Consortium, *Reuse-driven Software Processes*, November 1993.

Author Index

Alonso, A.	161	Kozlowski, W.E.	6
Ananda, A.L.	188	Kramer, J.	49, 106
		Kuusela, J.	4, 223
Balzer, R.	158		
Bandinelli, S.	249	Layes, M.	32
Baum, L.	197	Linden, F.J. van der	1, 66, 170
Bechtold, R.T.	143	Lyskawa, H.	6
Beckman, H.	89		
Bellay, B.	89, 115	Meekel, J.	205
Bergey, J.	123	Mellone, C.	205
Brouwer, J.	241	Mendonça, N.C.	106
		Molter, G.	197
Clements, P.C.	1, 140		
Crane, S.	57	Niemelä, E.	14
Cysewski, G.	6		
		Obbink, H.	1
DeBaud, J.-M.	87, 132	Ogris, M.	89
Dolan, T.	172	Oliveira, W.L. de	148
Dueñas, J.C.	148	Ommering, R. van	76
Eixelsberger, W.	89	Perry, D.E.	49, 51
		Perunka, H.	14
Gall, H.	89, 115	Piechowka, M.	6
García-Valls, M.	161	Pryce, N.	57
Ganz, C.	32	Puente, J.A. de la	140, 148, 161
Geyer, L.	197		
Girard, J.-F.	132	Rösel, A.	39
Gromadzki, T.	6	Rothkugel, S.	197
Hamer, P. van de	66	Saunders, A.	66
Horton, T.B.	205	Scherlis, W.L.	4, 235
Huber, B.	24	Schippers, A.	241
		Sligte, H. te	66
Jarzabek, S.	188	Smith, D.	123
Jazayeri, M.	87	Sturm, P.	197
Jurriens, A.	241	Szejko, S.	6
Kalan, M.	89	Tilley, S.	123
Karhinen, A.	223	Trausmuth, G.	97
Kessel, H. van	241		
Knor, R.	97	Vahamaki, O.	6
Kolb, P.	24		
Korpipää, T.	14	Weiderman, N.	123

Weidl, J.   97   Wortmann, J.C.   172
Weiss, D.M.   170, 214
Weterings, R.   172   Yu C. C.   189